*Learning to Learn
from Experience*

EDWARD CELL

Learning to Learn from Experience

State University of New York Press
ALBANY

To Margie

Published by
State University of New York Press, Albany

© 1984 State University of New York

Printed in the United States of America

For information, address State University of New York Press, State University
Plaza, Albany, N.Y. 12246

Library of Congress Cataloging in Publication Data

Cell, Edward.
  Learning to learn from experience.

  Includes bibliographical references.
    1. Learning, Psychololgy of. 2. Experience.
  3. Developmental psychology. I. Title.
  BF318.C44 1984   153.1'5   83-9283
  ISBN 0-87395-832-2
  ISBN 0-87395-833-0 (pbk.)

10 9 8 7 6 5 4 3 2 1

Contents

Preface

This book grew out of my work on a committee concerned with an experiential education program at Sangamon State University. More than anything else, our energy was absorbed by the task of integrating experiential and academic learning. Underlying this aim, however, was another, more difficult problem: How can we determine and create the conditions under which useful learning from experience takes place? After all, we often don't learn from experience and even when we do our learning may be dysfunctional.

The more I thought about this problem the more convinced I became that the most important goal of a program such as ours would be not that students would learn effectively from the learning situation in which we helped them locate, but that they would improve their ability to learn from experience. The outcome was an experimental course on learning to learn from experience, and the creation of this book.

Because our success in living depends on our ability to learn from our experience, the subject has importance for all of us and many have taken the course out of general interest. This book, then, is written for the general reader as well as for those involved in a program of experiential learning. For the latter, a few words about the view which underlies these materials of the nature of experiential learning and its relation to learning of the academic sort may be of interest.

I take significant learning to involve a *change* in the learner. It is a change in behavior, in interpretation, in autonomy or in creativity. Ordinarily we take in information, organize it, make whatever response, if any, seems advisable, and monitor the results in those comfortable and familiar ways that have become our second nature, our habit. How well we do this may be important but the immediate information does not produce learning. We respond to it as we have learned to in the past. It, in turn, leaves us unchanged in our ability to act, understand, and evaluate in the future. Education worthy of the name must lead to a different tomorrow.

What, then, of experiential versus academic sources of personal change? Morris Keeton and Pamela Tate define experiential learning as:

> learning *in which the learner is directly in touch with the realities being studied*. It is contrasted with learning in which the learner only reads about, hears about, talks about, or writes about these realities but never comes in contact with them as part of the learning process.[1]

We may push farther with John Wild's distinction between primary thinking and secondary reflection. As we are transacting with our world our minds are continually at work interpreting these transactions and the situations in which we enact them. This is primary thinking. It is the spontaneous and usually habitual activity that forms the background of our actions and reactions. We are vaguely aware of some parts of it and not at all aware of others. Much of it, that is, takes place subconsciously. Then at times we disengage ourselves from our involvements to think about some of them more carefully and systematically. This is secondary reflection.

Primary thinking is often laced with bias, prejudice, superstition, fanaticism, provincialism, exaggeration and the like. Through secondary reflection we may challenge and work toward overcoming these distortions. If we learn to carry the results with us and to apply them deliberately as we renew our transactions with our world, we gradually transform our primary thinking. Through this process secondary reflection becomes the foundation of human freedom—a life rooted in one's own reason, experience and judgment.

It may also happen that in our primary thinking we sow the seeds of greater clarity, of enrichment, or of alternatives in our ways of seeing and understanding. Secondary reflection helps to bring these beginnings to fruition and to clear the way for further beginnings.

There is no sharp dividing line between primary thinking and secondary reflection, and we often move back and forth between the two. In academic learning, the focus is on secondary reflection but the learning process commonly involves us with instructors and students and so activates our primary thinking. Our courses aim to provide us with perspectives, conceptual tools, and conceptual skills that enlarge our ability to reflect creatively and realistically, yet we may also be deeply influenced, say, by the sensitivity, integrity and rigor—or lack of these things—with which others pursue insight and truth.

Similarly, although in experiential learning the emphasis is on active, direct engagement with our world, we often intersperse our activities with moments of reflection.

In academic learning we grasp and evaluate concepts and interpretations by relating them to our own experience. We may do this directly or we may do it indirectly in the sense of using our own experience to understand the examples by which an idea is explained. If our experience relative to a course or discipline is limited, the academic process may be aided by gaining new experience in the area. Such enrichment of the academic process is one justification for making experiential learning part of an academic program.

Another justification is to increase the effect of academic learning on our experience. Studies show that formal education usually brings about only small changes in attitude and behavior. Perhaps small changes in large numbers of people add up to something important. But if an experiential component to our academic programs significantly increases the transfer of learning from the classroom to the job or some other area of daily life, it adds markedly to the worth of formal education.

As I have already maintained, though, the greatest justification of an experiential component in formal education seems to me to lie not in the content of what is learned from those experiences but in what is learned about the *process* of learning from any experience. An age of rapid change puts a special premium on the ability to learn continually from our transactions. In what follows the basic aim is to help the reader to learn to learn from experience, and so to enlarge his or her autonomy.

This emphasis on developing autonomous learners brings into focus the special importance that the liberal arts and experiential learning have for one another. As Ronald Fry and David Kolb so aptly put it:

> Increasing numbers of critics view education in the liberal arts as irrelevant to preparation for life and career.
>
> These challenges seem particularly frustrating and ironic to those of us who are committed to liberal arts education. We have seen in our own experiences and those of our associates that the basic competencies that can be acquired from liberal arts education are the most relevant for life in our rapidly changing world. . . . We see around us a world controlled by

technological, scientific, and professional elites struggling with problems that exceed the boundaries of their specialties, searching for the very perspectives, ethical principles and understanding of the human condition that we seek to develop in our students. . . .

What is needed is an educational approach that integrates personal experience and practical application with perceptive appreciation and understanding concepts, and in so doing requires the development of all these competencies.[2]

Ormond Smythe singles out moral and political education as the area "where experiential learning may make its most profound contribution to the liberal arts."[3] Moral education has been neglected, he argues, at least in part because it carries with it the twin pitfalls of indoctrination on the one side, and a fruitless bull session on the other. Experiential learning provides a way of avoiding these problems. "A student who must live with the actual consequences of acts has a discipline that no bull session can provide and that no program of indoctrination can test and develop."[4]

In these and other ways, a strong case is being made for the importance of the liberal arts and experiential learning to one another. Yet we in the liberal arts have tended to be less responsive than have other educators to the experiential. Vocational education has been hands on from the start, professional education has its internships, science its labs. But in the humanities we tend only to read about, hear about, talk about and write about those realities so central to being human that we are concerned with.

In Chapters 1, 5, 6, and 7, this book seeks to explore some of the areas of learning, such as emotional development, self-identity, understanding others, learning to be autonomous in an organization, and the overall project of becoming a person, in which the interface between the liberal arts and experience is especially significant. These chapters build on the foundation of theory presented in Chapters 2, 3, and 4 and are supplemented by the practical considerations in Chapters 8, 9, and 10 in which the basic aim has been to help students learn more effectively from their experience in general.

Let's look at content and organization in a bit more detail. First of all, the overall aim of this book is to help us to see more clearly what experiential learning involves and how it is tested, to understand better under what conditions we learn something that is functional for us and under what conditions we either fail to learn or learn something dysfunctional, and to explore ways in which learning may expand

and strengthen our personal freedom—our capacity to be self-directing. By "functional learning" is meant the kind of learning that either contributes to our autonomy or enrichment, or is at least compatible with them while serving some other valuable aim.

Chapter 1 begins by describing the process of creating and maintaining our existence as a person in terms of learning to make a significant difference in each of our life situations and learning to cope with powerlessness. Learning to make a significant difference is seen as involving the first two kinds of experiential learning discussed in Chapter 2 and coping with powerlessness as based on the third and fourth kinds. The thesis is presented that dysfunctional learning stems especially from obstacles, both internal and external, that we encounter in our efforts to be an effective, significant person. These obstacles are seen frequently to result in the learning of behavior that is defensive or destructive and in the acquisition of beliefs that are introjected from others rather than derived from our own experience and judgment. This thesis about dysfunctional learning is applied in Chapters 5, 6, and 7. A correlative thesis is also presented: that we can be helped to learn more functional interpretations of our experience by adopting three general ideas or rules by which to guide this process.

In the second half of Chapter 1, the thesis is presented that what Carl Rogers calls our organismic experience is a trustworthy source of functional learning when three conditions are met. These are described by Rogers as engaging in a relationship in which the individual "is prized as a separate person, in which the experiencing going on within him is empathically understood and valued, and in which he is given the freedom to experience his own feelings and those of others without being threatened in doing so."[5] The correlative thesis is also presented, that the major cause of learning dysfunctional interpretations is, as Rogers states, that

> *In an attempt to gain or hold love, approval, esteem, the individual relinquishes the locus of evaluation which was his in infancy, and places it in others.* He learns to have a basic distrust for his own experiencing as a guide to his behavior.[6]

These theses are given an especially full application in Chapter 7. The remainder of Chapter 1 outlines a view of human nature and of our development as persons, under conditions of early dependency and of certain social pressures, that underlie these theses concerning functional and disfunctional learning.

In Chapter 2, experiential learning is viewed and discussed as a change in behavior, in interpretation, in autonomy, or in creativity, or in any combination of these. Except for change in behavior, each kind of learning is seen as a change in our ability to do the sort of learning immediately preceeding it. Human freedom or autonomy is equated with an ability to change our interpretations and to act in light of that change. The kind of learning this book seeks to facilitate is identified as change in autonomy—a change in our ability to change our interpretations. Chapter 2 concludes with practical considerations in light of its model of learning, considerations which may help us in selecting and effectively utilizing a learning situation.

Some readers may want to consider reading Chapter 9 directly after Chapter 2. Chapter 9 discusses forty-one learning skills that are used in experiential learning and provides a questionnaire by which readers can construct a profile of their learning skills, indicating which are stronger and which are less well developed. Consideration is given to the question of which skills are especially important to the kinds of learning discussed in Chapter 2 and which to emotional development, understanding other persons, and functioning in large organizations—the subjects of Chapters 5 through 7.

Chapter 3 expands the discussion of the second kind of experiential learning, namely, the fact and value beliefs by which we give a meaningful interpretation to our various life-situations. The complex system of beliefs that we learn is looked at as analogous to a map by which we anticipate the future and explain the present.

Chapter 4 discuses both ways in which we learn dysfunctional interpretations and also motivations we have to resist testing their truth. Special attention is given to our tendency to manipulate experience to fit our interpretations rather than using it to test whether they are functional. Conditions which help us truly to test our beliefs are also considered.

Chapters 5 through 7 utilize the theoretical considerations of the first four chapters to elucidate the learning we do, first in our emotional lives generally, and then specifically in our more intimate personal interactions and our organizational lives.

Chapter 5 analyzes our emotions to show that they are not simply feelings but a complex combination of feelings, interpretations, and actions. The interpretations and actions are developed by the first two kinds of learning described in Chapter 2. The specific form this learning takes in the case of the emotions and the conditions under which it then becomes functional or dysfunctional are examined.

Chapter 6 looks at how we learn not just to know *about* another in an impersonal way but to know her in a personal way, and how such learning becomes functional or dysfunctional. This discussion is based on the analysis in Chapter 3 in which belief and knowledge were displayed as the means by which we anticipate the future and understand the present. The difference between impersonal and personal knowledge is explained in terms of the difference in the *kind* of anticipation each involves. This chapter also explores what it means to grasp the unique identity of the other, and the sources of dysfunctional doubt about whether we really know her.

Chapter 7 examines conditions, typical of large organizations in our country today, under which we learn to respond in ways that undermine our autonomy. The theses of Carl Rogers about functional and dysfunctional learning, in particular, that were presented in Chapter 1 are applied specifically to this problem.

The final three chapters offer some practical strategies and tools for enhancing our experiential learning.

Chapter 8 considers how our learning may be improved by two radically different ways of undergoing our experience. The first is to bring to our experience questions which direct our attention to new things. The second is to suspend, as far as possible, all the ways in which we direct our attention to this or that aspect of a situation, so that we may experience it afresh.

After Chapter 9, which discusses skills involved in experiential learning, Chapter 10 presents some ways of keeping a journal developed by Ira Progoff. His approach to journal keeping is designed to help us reflect on our experience free of preconceived ideas about its meaning for us.

And now, a word about my selection of personal pronouns. To avoid the clumsiness of saying things like ''he or she,'' and ''her or him,'' I've chosen to use the masculine form in some places and the feminine form in others. I believe the principle I've employed in deciding which to use where will become apparent to the reader, especially in Chapter 6.

Finally, among all those to whom I am indebted in the writing of this book, including the many students whose responses have enriched the two courses in which I have used it, my special thanks go to the following: Sangamon State University for providing time and other resources; Susan Brown, Virginia Davenport, Doris Abernathy, Lisa Robinson and Jackie Wright, for their care and skill in typing; Dennis Camp, Judith Everson, John Palincsar, Terry Peters and Peter Wenz, for their helpful editorial advice or substantive comments; and, above all, my brother Donald and my wife Marjorie, for their personal support and endless hours of discussion.

I

*Effective and Ineffective
Uses of Experience*

CHAPTER ONE

Learning and the Struggle to Be

Sometimes we learn a lot from our experience of ourselves and our transactions with our world. Friends share their hopes and fears, we test ourselves in difficult times, power reveals itself in unsuspected places. At other times we seem to learn little or nothing at all. We follow routine, talk with echoes of ourselves, cling to comfortable beliefs. As my colleague Bob Zeller put it, "Sometimes someone will say they've had twenty-five years of experience at something when the truth is they've had one year of experience repeated twenty-four times." Even when we do learn, the result may be anything but helpful. We may learn to narrow our vision, to fear what we need not fear, to explain away unwelcome facts.

Our abilities to learn from our experience are important in every part of our lives. They are basic to solving problems, to maintaining and enriching relationships, to succeeding at new projects. Through them we develop new areas of experience, expand our horizons. They determine how much freedom and creativity we can achieve.

If we can see more clearly what learning involves and how it is tested, if we can understand better under what conditions we learn and under what conditions we either fail to learn or learn something dysfunctional, we can open for ourselves some new doors to more effective learning.

In this chapter, I wish to sketch the place of experiential learning in becoming a self—a process we continue throughout our lives. I also wish to present the thesis that dysfunctional learning principally stems from obstacles we encounter in our struggle to be a significant person. These obstacles often result in the learning of behavior and beliefs that are defensive or destructive or taken over from others rather than derived from our own experience. To be sure, defensive behavior or adherence to introjected beliefs may be the best means we have managed to learn of coping with difficult situations and, in this sense, may be regarded as functional in a limited way. But I am using the term "functional" to mean the kind of learning that either contributes to our autonomy or enrichment, or is at least compatible with them while serving some other valuable aim.

I think that most of us in Western culture think of being a self primarily in terms of making a significant difference in the many situations of our lives. To do this we need to learn to make sense of these situations and to act effectively in them. We need to see in them something that matters to us, something we want to do and are able to do. When we give a situation a meaningful interpretation and act effectively in light of that interpretation, I believe we get the sense "This is who I am, this is what it means to be me in this situation." Meaningful interpretation and effective action are the goals of the two basic kinds of experiential learning that we shall examine in Chapter 2 as situation learning and response learning. The ultimate goal of experiential learning, then, is power. For now, we shall think of this as the power to make a significant difference. Later we shall expand our analysis to include power of another sort.

Unlike the unfolding of acorns into oaks, there is nothing automatic about becoming a person. Our existence as persons is something we must create and maintain; sometimes this is an adventure and a joy but very often it is a struggle in the face of obstacles and threats.

We are more able to make a significant difference in some situations than in others. The sense of self, of having an identity, of being of worth waxes and wanes. At times we feel confident, alive, vital; at other times unsure, lifeless, dull.

Just around the corner may be that circumstance which renders us powerless, unable to find a purpose, to make a difference, to be a person. Organizing our lives around a productive career, we are thrown out of work. Devoting ourselves to raising our family, we find the nest suddenly empty. Investing ourselves in a cause, we betray it. Finding lifelong support, understanding and enjoyment with a circle of close friends, we lose them one by one. Living intimately, richly with another, she dies.

The momentum of past successes in being a person may carry us for a time in the face of our trauma, providing us with a semblance of being someone despite our emptiness in the present. But if our sense of self is shaky to begin with, if the trauma of the present is deep enough, if the cumulative effect of intermittent failures in our power becomes massive, we may be plunged into depression, even despair, living without the promise of a future, bereft of a sense of self.

Much dysfunctional learning grows out of the need to avoid powerlessness. I believe it is when power is not achieved in constructive ways that we often turn to its destructive forms, so that at least we make some sort of difference. We may even resort to violence if it seems to be our only alternative to depression or despair.

Another way to put this is that much dysfunctional learning is a defense against anxiety, for anxiety is an emotional response to an apparent threat to the self that we have not learned how to overcome. Many thinkers in our time, such as the psychotherapist Harry Stack Sullivan or the existential theologian Paul Tillich, have concluded that all of life is basically an attempt to cope with anxiety. Defensive behavior, withdrawal, and violence may be looked at as learned responses to anxiety-creating situations.

The process of becoming a self, then, involves two basic tasks. On the one hand, we must learn behaviors and interpretations that enable us to be a significant person in each of our situations and, through them, in our life situation as a whole. On the other hand, we must learn ways not only to cope with our times of powerlessness but also to come to terms with our ongoing vulnerability to being rendered powerless, to being separated from all that we find meaningful, to having to die. We are the only animals who carry a sense of our vulnerability around with us. We know that our days are numbered, our relationships are fragile, our situations are ambiguous, and all our days are lived against this backdrop of transience and limitation. We turn now to examine both the experiential learning and the obstacles to it that are involved first in being a significant person and then in coping with our inherent vulnerability to becoming powerless.

LEARNING TO BE A SIGNIFICANT PERSON

To be a person is to have the power to make a difference, a difference that *we* find significant, in each of our life situations. This power takes various forms, some personal, some interpersonal, some impersonal, none neatly separated from the others, each susceptible to destructive as well as creative uses.

Personal power is essentially private. It involves others indirectly but is exercised by ourselves alone. We all share distinctively human potentialities for freedom, for creativity, for knowledge of good and evil. These powers are rooted in our self-awareness. Through language, we are able to represent ourselves to ourselves and to explore new possibilities. We may back away from our relationships, examine them, imagine them changed and, in so doing, confront ourselves with a choice. We may struggle with a problem, looking at it first this way and then that, and then still another, until finally we hit upon a creative resolution. We may see ever more deeply into the meaning of being human, and so into the nature of good and evil, as we learn what invalidates and impoverishes our lives, what strengthens and enriches them. We find purpose and fulfillment in the very use of these powers. Our sense of worth becomes less and less tied to having approval from others and more and more grounded in knowing ourselves to be the creators of meaning and value. We shall be examining experiential learning that strengthens freedom and creativity.

Interpersonal power involves others directly in face-to-face relationships. Sometimes when power meets power, each is increased. We cannot play tennis, create dialogue, make love without the other. The greater her power, the greater the potential for our own. There are things we can be with just this person that we could be with no one else. In many instances, we *are* our relationships. Some relationships we merely have, but others are important to our very identity.

At other times when power meets power, each is threatened. At our best, we may find a resolution of this conflict that preserves the strength and integrity of both ourselves and the other. Frequently, though, the power of one or of both is diminished or used in a distorted way. It seems to me, we deeply need to have an effect on each other, and if we cannot do it one way we will do it another. In Chapters 5 and 6 we shall consider two areas of learning that are important aspects of our interpersonal relations.

Impersonal power involves others through the structure of an institution. We give orders and receive them, we promote and are promoted, we make this decision and learn of that one. Our exercise of this power, as well as our coming to have it, involves our personal and interpersonal powers as well, but it may be vastly disproportional to them. We may use this power in radically different ways; sometimes to lead, at other times to manipulate. As effective leaders we engage the powers of others in a way that provides some space for their self-directedness. As manipulators, we use the powers of others in a way that overrides their autonomy.

The rules which structure our institutions will encourage, or perhaps even require, that we lead or that we manipulate, that we participate in decision making or that we follow instructions. The very rules that give us impersonal power also do much to shape it. They may encourage and support our best intentions or they may thwart them, unjust rules frustrating our desire to act justly. Our need to respect ourselves and others may be undercut by structures that are inherently manipulative. We may come to treat others with a considerateness and humaneness that merely masks their ultimate status as means to our organizational ends. We may turn efficiency, expansion, control, or profit into absolute values, sacrificing to them

well-being—our own as well as others'. Power in a large, institution is easily misread, often seductive, always ra-
...d. Learning to gain and to use, to understand and to
..., to cooperate with or stand against impersonal power is an
...eed in our organizational society, an important dimension of
...ral development, but generally neglected, it seems to me, in
...ral training received from church, family and school.

...learning about impersonal or organizational power takes on
...importance when we consider that our use of this power may
... not only persons within the organization but also those out-
... We may participate in decisions that affect the environment,
...cal economy, the wellbeing of consumers. But here, too, it
... our moral training is likely to be weak, focusing on private
face-to-face relationships while neglecting the right and wrong of institutional practices in which profit or power or prestige are complexly
related to other values. We easily become so habituated to life in an
organization that we fail to see many of its deficiencies. For most of
us, I think, there is much of importance yet to be learned or to be
unlearned in our institutional involvements if we can find the right
sort of approach, one that embodies the conditions necessary for
functional learning. We shall examine Samuel Culbert's ideas about
this in Chapter 7.

Whether it be personal, interpersonal, or impersonal, when we
learn to have power, we must struggle against obstacles to the kind of
learning that is genuinely freeing and enriching. First of all, in learning to develop and use our personal powers, we must deal with some
things in ourselves and with influences from our society. On one
side, we need to overcome our desire to be taken care of, our yearning always to be approved of, our wish to retain our childhood
dependencies. Perhaps nothing contributes as strongly to dysfunctional learning as a reluctance to cut the psychological umbilical cord
altogether. In the words of Pogo, ''We have met the enemy and he is
us.'' On the other side, we are faced with those ever-present
pressures to conform, that subtle questioning of our worth, or those
demands that we not think too highly of ourselves. Perhaps most in-
sidious is the bewitching power of those early messages about who
we are and what we are to become, messages that work so effectively
because we rarely so much as glimpse what is happening.

In learning to develop and use interpersonal power we are taught
contradictory things. We are taught to love our neighbor and to compete aggressively or even ruthlessly, to value intimacy and to play
games—messages which, however contradictory, strongly inform our
morality and guide us in the intricacies of our life together. We could
resolve such contradictions by testing each side against the lessons of

our own experiences concerning what is genuinely strenghtening and enriching for ourselves and for those with whom we work and live. But we may fear that we will not be approved of if we do not base our transactions on the expectations and beliefs of others, and what we fear may often be true. The learning which results is dysfunctional, undercutting our ability to judge between values.

In learning to gain and exercise impersonal power in and through our institutions, we absorb rules that are often unspoken and may contradict values and meanings that we have consciously chosen in other aspects of our lives. "What is good for the organization is necessarily good for its members." "The need to make (or maximize) a profit justifies whatever means are necessary." "It is always good to give top priority to the military interests of one's nation." "Everyone who opposes us is either bad or misinformed." "In business matters, women are generally less capable than men." It is difficult to test such rules against our moral and other experience, because we often have little or no awareness of them and yet undergo considerable pressure to conform to them and to rationalize whatever they require of us.

These obstacles to functional learning for each of the kinds of power involved in becoming a person have a great deal in common. In each case pressures to conform and a desire to be approved of may lead us into the dysfunctional kind of learning in which our beliefs are introjected from others rather than being derived from, or at least tested by, our own experience and judgment.

LEARNING TO COPE WITH POWER PROBLEMS

We become persons by learning to have power. But we also need to learn to cope with its limitations, its ambiguities, its loss. Needless to say, this side of being a person produces both functional and dysfunctional learning.

In considering the conditions under which this learning becomes functional, I shall adopt the view of rational-emotive therapy that our success or failure in finding fulfillment as a person is due, more than anything else, to certain general ideas or rules which guide the way we interpret our situations. Dysfunctional interpretations are the result of general ideas that Albert Ellis calls irrational and Aaron Beck, more accurately, I think, terms self-defeating. Among the ideas listed by Ellis, for example, are "the idea that it is a dire necessity for an adult human being to be loved or approved by virtually every significant other person in his community" and "the idea that one should be thoroughly competent, adequate and achieving in all possible respects if one is to consider oneself worthwhile."[1] We shall consider

Aaron Beck's view of rules of this sort in Chapter 3. In the course of our present discussion, I shall present three general ideas that, it seems to me, encourage and sustain functional learning in situations that involve power problems.

Learning becomes dysfunctional when we organize our lives to evade awareness both of our limitations and, behind this, of the threat of powerlessness. We create endless rounds of distractions. We substitute the safety of games for the risks of intimacy. We evade the burden of freedom by embracing pressures to conform. We clothe our nakedness in literary or philosophical illusion. We immerse ourselves in the power of our weapons, our machines, our corporate enterprises. As T.S. Eliot put it, mankind cannot stand very much reality. In learning to live with less self-awareness, we also diminish those distinctively human possibilities for freedom, creativity, caring, and ethical insight which are based on that awareness.

We learn to cope with the threat of powerlessness in a functional way, I believe, by learning to create power for ourselves. Especially, we need to learn to create meaningful interpretations of our life-situations, something we shall examine in the next chapter as transsituation learning and transcendent learning. The key here, it seems to me, is meaning. Friedrich Nietzsche maintained that we can face any situation if we have a sufficient reason. We can deal with any *how* if we have a *why*. Victor Frankl developed a similar view.[2] The will to survive the powerlessness and degradation of the Nazi death camps, he concluded from his own experience, depended on having something important to live for, something deeply meaningful to return to.

In his book *The Courage to Create*,[3] Rollo May concludes that our acts of creation are fundamentally a struggle against death. If we think of "struggle against death" as a struggle against the obstacles to being a unique, significant person and of acts of creation as ultimately acts of self-creation, we have a statement of my thesis. The experience of ourselves as having the power to create power can enter into our interpretations of difficult and threatening situations and into our interpretation of life as a whole in a way that helps us see beyond both our power and our powerlessness. It is by developing autonomy and creativity that we can best learn to cope with the problems of power.

We develop abilities only under the right conditions. However much we may want more empowering activities, more inclusive identities, or more loving relationships, however much our defensive strategies may result in disappointments and contradictions, it is not easy to turn away from living defensively. Learning to have the power to create power for ourselves exacts a price. It asks us to learn to live with insecurity and anxiety, and this requires courage. To become autonomous and creative, in other words, we need to be in touch with sources of courage. These may be activities that we find deeply meaningful, personal relationships that are validating, moments of solitude that convey a sense of oneness and belonging. How to live in ways that generate courage, it seems to me, is, or at least should be, the primary concern of our religions and philosophies of life. Our philosophies are often made to serve our defensiveness, but at their best they foster the conditions vital to meaning and courage. It is to meet these needs that we devote some of our most important learning.

First of all, then, what can we say specifically about learning to cope with the limitations of our power? I have been saying that transsituation learning—learning that increases our autonomy—makes it possible for us to understand life in terms of a power that cuts deeper than powerlessness. Experiences of our power to create power can enter into our interpretations of situations that involve risk and help us to develop the courage of being limited. It seems to me, it is especially useful for our interpretations to include the idea that, *although our power is essentially quite limited, we need for it to be that way*. This is because we become persons most fully in our personal relationships. I believe it is when we are really in touch with another and are in turn touched by her—when we can enter into her point of view and welcome her into ours—that we feel most deeply real as persons. We may say that we *are* our relationships. But in making it possible for us to be a person, the other also limits our power by the sheer reality of her own. And, more than this, the relationship can have its fullest meaning for us only when we limit our own striving for power and security enough to let the other be who she really is.

The basic problem, however, in learning to deal with the limitations of our power may be expressed by the question "How much power do we need?" Considered apart from our project of becoming a person, there is no limit to the amount of power we may desire. When we fail to commit ourselves fully to being the person we have chosen to be, we may fall into a concupiscent desire to extend our power over the entire world, an unquenchable thirst for unlimited fulfillment that reduces everyone and everything to a mere means to this end. Some have sought to conquer every people, others to seduce every man or woman, still others to obtain unlimited knowledge. From Augustine through Luther, to Freud and Goethe, or to such existentialists as Kierkegaard and Nietzsche, our tendency to become concupiscent, whether repressed or openly acknowledged, has been seen as a fundamental problem in becoming a person. In Freud, for example, the incessant striving of the libido produces a desire to do away with ourselves and so to find peace. Similarly, in Nietzsche, the insatiability of our will to power leads to a negation of that will.

We are helped in dealing with the problem of concupiscence or never-satisfied striving, it seems to me, if the interpretations we learn are informed by the distinction between unlimited fulfillment and fulfillment in being a particular person. Basically, this is the distinction between striving to bring everyone and everything into an orbit around our lives, on the one hand, and loving *particular* persons and things, on the other. It is only in giving form to our lives through a choice of particular goals, values and loved ones that we provide a limit to the power we desire. In this way, we can learn that the taste of power is sweet when it is our power to be a truly human person. Power becomes fulfilling for us, I believe, as we learn to love the limits that give form to our humanity and to accept the vulnerabilities that those limits represent.

Secondly, we need to learn to cope with the ambiguities of power. Such ambiguities are really a special form of the limitations of our power. In becoming adult, we fall from innocence, learning that our motives are impure, our feelings ambivalent, our achievements mixed in value. How perfect can we realistically expect ourselves or others or the world to be? How much imperfection can we learn to live with and still love the life we lead? The way we learn to answer these questions will largely determine our ability to cope with the ambiguities both of our power and that of others.

Our learning may become dysfunctional if our experience leaves us overly impressed with the destructive sides of power. We may then try to wash our hands of power in any form, denying any need for it, pretending a kind of innocence no adult can have. We may refuse to see tension in peace, manipulation in submission, contest in brotherhood, strangeness in intimacy. Since simply to live is to exercise power, it seems to me we are left unknowingly seeking it in forms that disguise it. Denying the power we have, we can but exercise it without owning our responsibility. Ignoring conflict, we pursue interests without compromise. Striving for an unambiguously good life, we become self-deceptive and self-righteous. Expecting too much, we eventually may fall into cynical rejection of the whole human scene.

What we learn in situations in which the ambiguities of power stand out will be functional, I believe, only if we can develop the courage of imperfection. We may be helped in this if our interpretation of such situations is guided by the judgment that *our power to create power and our power to love can be of significant worth without being perfect.* Unless we adopt such a judgment, we end up rejecting ourselves and others because no one can meet our unrealistic stand-ards. Perfectionism is a major source of dysfunctional learning.

The third power problem we must learn to deal with is the ongoing threat that we may lose our power to be a person in one or more of our life-situations. Changes may be thrust upon us, sometimes within, sometimes without, for which we can find no response, no means of being a significant person in that place and time. A maiming or disfiguring accident, a surfacing of old irrationalities or compul-sions, a failure in career or intimacy, a growing sense of boredom or disillusion—in these and countless other ways we may come to feel powerless. This feeling, in turn, often becomes associated with our knowledge that we must one day lose our power altogether, and we may then find powerlessness more difficult than ever to cope with.

What we learn in situations in which we feel powerless or sense our power especially threatened is often dysfunctional. We may learn to respond with violence, or with depression or some other form of defensiveness. Or we may learn to feel powerless in situations where in fact we are not, an instance of dysfunctional learning that we shall discuss in Chapter 4 as overgeneralization. Let us briefly consider each of these learning outcomes.

As we noted earlier, if our sense of helplessness strikes us in too sensitive a spot, or comes at too vulnerable a time, or joins forces with too many similar experiences, we may respond with depression. This is often dysfunctional but not always. It may be simply a turning away from attempting to deal creatively with our situation, perhaps clinging to old ways of being rather than exploring changes that might reduce our vulnerability, as is very often possible. Or it may be a constructive way of dealing with our loss, a temporary withdrawal so that we can regain our equilibrium, reorganize our energies. Then, too, it may be a time of confessing to ourselves the inappropriateness of our attitude, the disappointments with a commitment, the ineffec-tiveness of our life style. We may say some goodbyes to clear the way for some new hellos.

Alternatively, as we have said, we may turn to mental or physical violence to avoid depression and the sense of hopelessness it may give way to. Making a difference through sheer force, however empty of personal meaning, may provide an illusion, a semblance, of being someone.

Finally, we may learn to feel powerless when we are not. Earlier failures at mathematics, perhaps owing more to the attitude of the teacher than to ourselves, may convince us we are forever powerless to deal with quantitative problems. Years of helplessness in getting our parents to listen to us may lead us to conclude that we will be similarly ineffective with everyone in authority. Feeling powerless when we are not is what Martin Seligman calls "learned helplessness" in his important study of this phenomenon.[4] Experiments with a variety of animals, including humans, show that when a subject is subjected repeatedly to a painful experience that he is helpless to escape, generally he will then fail to escape a similar experience that others readily learn to avoid. Seligman maintains that learned helplessness not only causes much of the depression that is one of our society's major ills, but not infrequently even results in death.

Under what conditions, then, can our learning in situations of powerlessness or its threat become functional? Martin Seligman argues that self-esteem is the key here. We build confidence in our personal worth and effectiveness through cumulative experiences of having control. This, in turn, Seligman maintains, immunizes us against the crippling consequences that helplessness can have. Subjects, for example, who first learned to escape painful shock and then were subjected to inescapable shock, later were able to escape once again. In effect, prior experiences of power may change the way we interpret an experience of powerlessness. This seems an important condition for functional learning in this area of our lives. But there are distinctions to be made and other factors to consider as well.

First of all, there is the question of *how much* control we need in being a person, and control in what areas. We are frequently helpless in ways that do not disrupt our efforts to be a person. Consider, for example, that we are helpless to control the plane in which we are a passenger, or the other cars that are passing ours, or the weather when we are planning a picnic. Yet, unless the plane is in trouble, or a car is close and out of control, or the weather has become a danger, our helplessness, though objectively true, will not affect our subjective sense of power to be someone. We are helpless in many ways that we simply learn to see as part of being a person rather than as an obstacle to this.

Secondly, there is the related question of what *kind* of control we feel we need. Control that is exploitive of others or that expresses a basically defensive or neurotic stance toward life is likely to diminish rather than increase our courage to deal with our vulnerabilities. The amount of control we seek will depend on how well we have learned to trust others, or nature, or even ourselves. The less we are able to trust, the more control we feel we need and the more vulnerable we are to loss of control. Then, too, when control becomes excessive, we encase life in a rigid clockwork and lose the vitality that is the wellspring of our courage and self-esteem. But if we can trust, if we can sometimes drift with the stream rather than rowing against it, we may find certain moments in which something new breaks in upon us—breaks in beyond all our control—to be times not of threat and recoil but of wonder and delight, a sense of the inexhaustible meaning and power of life.

For example, if we can let the other be who she is, instead of who we want her to be, she may come alive for us in unimagined ways. If, at times, we can give ourselves over to simply receiving, appreciating, understanding the other in terms of her own self-disclosure, we may gain a sense of ourselves beyond our power to transform and control.

It seems to me, then, that we are greatly helped in coping with powerlessness, if our sense of being a self rests on a balance between the power to make a significant difference and the power to be receptive of values from others. Receiving can be as important as making.

Thirdly, there is an important distinction between the self-confidence that rests on *having* functional interpretations and behaviors, and the self-confidence that rests on being able to create *new* interpretations and behaviors. To cope with radical change, with that which eludes our present ways of organizing our experience and of acting effectively, we need the skills and understanding to make the ordering of our lives a growing, changing thing. We need not only the power to be a person but the power to create that power for ourselves. Once again we see the importance of transsituation learning to coping effectively with powerlessness.

We can express this in terms of order and vitality. Our strength of identity, our resiliency, our openness to moments that shake and transcend the ways we have ordered our lives, all derive from our vitality, the orders we create, and our power to create order. To be persons, we must organize our experience and behavior and transform the world around us. Without our cognitive, social, and other orders, we cannot be persons, create meanings, exercise control. Vitality without order is chaotic and meaningless. But if we make too much of any particular order, if we cling to it, if we let it become rigid, we choke off our vitality. Order without vitality is empty, dead. No way of organizing our lives can be fully adequate to our needs, or to all the facets of our being, or to dealing with changes in ourselves and our world. Important conditions for coping with change and with the powerlessness it may create are the existence of the kinds of orders that maintain and enhance our autonomy, our power to create power. A test of our ways of ordering life is the extent to which they make possible the courage and understanding and skill needed to transcend that ordering when necessary.

When we transcend the orders by which we create and maintain ourselves, in effect, we transcend ourselves. In doing this we look at ourselves and our world and can imagine them changed. Such transcendence is ecstatic. We stand outside of the orders that give us being while yet remaining part of them. This may be a dramatic experience or it may be rather "low key." But in such moments, we understand how inescapably responsible we are for the orders by which we live. Our power to transcend ourselves is the heart of our autonomy and creativity.

Fourthly, we must contend with the threat of our ultimate loss of power. Many have reacted with despair to their experience of guilt or loss of meaning. Paul Tillich, for example, discusses our anxiety about guilt in terms of a "despair of having lost our destiny."[5] It seems to me, however, that we do partially achieve our destiny—partially become our best selves—and that to describe partial failure as complete loss is an instance of what we shall discuss in Chapter 4 as catastrophizing. The same can be said about loss of meaning. Be that as it may, it does seem to me that in death all of us face an ultimate loss of our power to be the person we now are.

This is true, I think, even for those who believe in a life beyond this one. Such a life would be comprised, I suppose, of a set of very new situations requiring new interpretations, and this would make us a quite different person. It is largely memory that would connect us to the person we now are.

Death, then, is total separation, a complete loss of power. Many everyday changes also involve separations. We may think of them as deaths of a sort, each requiring its own period of grieving, a period marked in part by such things as listlessness, or irritability, or outright depression. Part of their difficulty for us is the way they betoken our ultimate loss of power. Our success in coping with the threat of death or of lesser separation, I believe, will depend upon the context in which we experience it, the way we interpret our life situation as a whole. As Robert Lifton has concluded from his studies of psychological trauma, we gain power to cope with powerlessness when we have adequately symbolized its threat and related it symbolically to sources of hope, of creative power, of meaning.[6] Insofar as we learn to see life in terms of that which is creative, or healing, or validating, we open up for ourselves the courage that has enabled so many to risk death on behalf of others or to take personal failure in stride when the cause to which they were devoted could nonetheless move ahead. Even concentration camps have been endured without ultimate defeat by those who had a compelling reason. Powerlessness is answered by the courage we find in our deepest meanings and commitments. We may think of this as the courage of transcendence.

We will be helped in coping with this threat of ultimate powerlessness if our interpretation of life is guided by the idea that *the value of what we do and experience is a matter of their quality rather than of how long they last.* In other words, life becomes worthwhile through the quality of the process rather than because of the permanence of our achievements. The brevity of a sunset does not diminish the thrill of its beauty. It is this idea that underlies the effectiveness of symbols of hope, creativity, and meaning in enabling us to cope with the threat of powerlessness.

In summary, we have been saying that to be a person we need the power to make a significant difference and the power to be appreciatively receptive of meanings and values from others. For this, we must learn effective behaviors and meaningful interpretations of our situations. Such learning is often defective because pressures to conform and a desire to be approved of may lead us to take over the beliefs of others rather than basing our beliefs on our own experience and judgment.

In being a person, we must also cope with the limitations and ambiguities of our power and the threat of its loss. For this, we need the power to create power. Our learning, in situations involving power problems, will tend to be dysfunctional insofar as we organize our lives and our thinking to evade awareness both of our limitations and, behind this, of the threat of powerlessness. Conforming to the expectations of others in how we behave and in the way we look at our various situations is often a leading strategy for reducing awareness.

Learning to cope effectively with power problems requires courage: the courage to be limited, the courage of imperfection, and the courage of transcendence. We can learn to learn more functionally by learning to seek out or to create the conditions that make courage possible. At the same time, I have maintained, we will be further helped to learn functionally if we adopt the following general ideas or rules to guide the way we interpret situations:

(1) Although our power is essentially quite limited, we need for it to be that way.

(2) Our power to create and our power to love can be of significant worth without being perfect.

(3) Life becomes worthwhile through the quality of the process rather than the permanence of our achievements.

The process of learning these ideas, of course, culminates in testing them in our own organismic experience.

DYSFUNCTIONAL LEARNING: A HUMANISTIC VIEW

A basic aim of this study is to help us understand better under what conditions our learning becomes functional or dysfunctional. By "functional" I mean the kind of learning that either contributes to our autonomy or enrichment, or is at least compatible with them while serving some other valuable aim. Yet any definition of "functional learning" presupposes, and must be understood in terms of, a view of human nature and of the forces which shape our development as persons. Before getting on with our study, then, we need to consider some main aspects of the view of human nature which underlies it.

I find myself in basic agreement with Carl Rogers's way of looking at human nature and with his concern that we test our views as rigorously as we are able to. He finds substantial evidence, especially in the professional experience of himself and other psychotherapists, that the mind-body unity which he calls our organism is our most trustworthy source of functional learning. "The psychologically mature adult," he contends, "trusts and uses the wisdom of his organism," realizing "that if he can trust all of himself, his feelings and intuitions may be wiser than his mind."[7] We see in such an adult what we see when we observe an infant closely, namely, "that he prefers those experiences which maintain, enhance, or actualize his organism, and rejects those which do not serve this end."[8]

It may sound as though the person being described as psychologically mature is selfish and asocial but this is not so because "deep and helpful relationships with others are experienced as ac-tualizing."[9] According to Rogers:

> when individuals are prized as persons, the values they select
> do not run the full gamut of possibilities. I do not find, in such
> a climate of freedom, that one person comes to value fraud and
> murder and thievery, while another values a life of self-
> sacrifice, and another values only money. Instead there seems
> to be a deep and underlying thread of commonality. I believe
> that when the human being is inwardly free to choose
> whatever he deeply values, he tends to value those objects, ex-
> periences, and goals which make for his own survival, growth
> and development, and for the survival and development of
> others.[10]

Rogers would simply be arguing in a circle here were he simply to define the psychologically mature person as one who in fact values being sensitive to and accepting of others. But his claim is, rather, that persons who are exposed to conditions that he believes are basic to the process of psychotherapy change toward psychological maturity. These conditions are described by Rogers as "a relationship in which [the client] is prized as a separate person, in which the experiencing going on within him is empathetically understood and valued, and in which he is given the freedom to experience his own feelings and those of others without being threatened in doing so."[4] As is abundantly clear from many of his other writings, the third of these conditions, namely, the freedom to experience the feelings of others in a nonthreatening way, requires the therapist to disclose his or her feelings toward the client without being judgmental or rejecting. Rogers refers to this as being real or being congruent; the way the therapist appears matches the way he really feels.[12]

In addition to valuing sensitive and accepting relationships with others, Rogers finds the mature person to value "deep relationships," "being a process," expressing his or her true feelings, being self-directing, and being open to the full range of his own experiences.[13] Such a person also tends to disvalue façades, "oughts," and the fulfilling of expectations held by others.

Far from being essentially asocial, then, there is evidence that we need creative social interaction, for only in this way do we fulfill our need to give and receive love. The possibility that some organismic needs—e.g., for sex or freedom—will threaten the well-being of others is checked, under the right conditions, by organismic needs to give and receive understanding, companionship, affection, and validation. Indeed, healthy interpersonal relations—those characterized by Rogers's three conditions—enhance our freedom and our lives in general as separate persons. To this conviction, I would add that which Erich Fromm defends in his lengthy study of human destructiveness, the conviction that we are by nature aggressive only when we perceive our vital interests threatened, and even then we instinctively prefer to escape from such threat when given the opportunity.[14] In terms of this way of looking at human nature, our need is not to impose controls on our organisms but to create the conditions necessary to their healthy, spontaneous development. Functional learning in the process of being a self is not learning to subject oneself to the right external controls but rather learning to develop freedom and self-directedness.

Seen in this way, our organisms provide the basis for an autonomy which neither accepts uncritically nor attempts to break with the heritage of our culture. To be sure, the voices of collective wisdom that speak to us through our past are scarcely free of authoritarian, self-negating overtones, but through careful listening our organisms will resonate to that which is authentically human. In listening to the stories told by countless human lives, we more richly unfold our own, which (as is true of each) will be a story told only once and yet will be the story of everyone.

Not everyone, of course, has taken such a positive view of our human organism. Under the impact of Freud, for example, we may see ourselves fundamentally as seeking sex, aggression and basic survival needs for food and the like. At this level, we see others simply as means to gratify these instinctive needs. In this view, we are essentially asocial machines driven to reduce ever-recurring biological tensions. We are made social only by the imposition of restrictions on our behavior. The most effective form of this social control is our superego, the internalized voice of authority. This voice of control is repeatedly at war with our yearning for sex and aggression. If this control becomes too powerful and restrictive, therapy is needed to help us achieve a better balance and a modicum of harmony between control and gratification.

We often recognize in such negative portrayals of our human nature a description of much that we see in ourselves and in others. But it is, I believe, a description of what we become insofar as the conditions for genuine growth have been lacking.

There are many, such as Sartre and Skinner, who reject the idea that we have a common human nature in the sense of a tendency, under the right conditions, to prefer basic sorts of values. The belief in such a human nature must be grounded on evidence that (1) under certain growth-promoting conditions, all persons tend to the same sorts of value preferences; (2) the realization of these values is experienced over a long period of time as fulfilling or enhancing; and (3) falure to achieve these values results in a condition of *dis-ease*, expressing itself in such things as psychosomatic illness, loss of enthusiasm for life, antisocial feelings of cruelty, greed, hostility, envy, and the like, or even that loss of all sense of future we know as despair.

If our organismic experience is a trustworthy source of functional learning, why is our learning so often dysfunctional? The major cause is accurately stated by Rogers:

> *In an attempt to gain or hold love, approval, esteem, the individual relinquishes the locus of evaluation which was his in infancy, and places it in others.* He learns to have a basic *dis*trust for his own experiencing as a guide to his behavior.[15]

Our learning is dysfunctinal, then, insofar as we tend to adopt the behavior and beliefs expected of us by others.

As a result, Rogers believes, the following characteristics are typical of most of us: (1) the larger part of our values have been taken over from others and yet we think of them as our own; (2) these values often contradict the unheeded messages of our organismic experience; (3) we are unable to test these values by our experience and so we cling to them in a rigid way; and (4) we have little experience of our own capacity to do our own valuing, and so feel threatened if a change in values seems called for.[16]

A great many psychotherapists, such as Karen Horney, Erich Fromm, Rollo May, and Aaron Beck are in substantial agreement with Rogers about this. According to Albert Ellis, for example, "In existing society our family and other institutions directly and indirectly indoctrinate all of us so that we grow up to believe many superstitious, senseless ideas," and consequently "nothing but a change in the basic ideational or philosophical outlook of modern men and women will significantly reduce their neurotic needs."[17]

Because this way of understanding the source of a large part of our dysfunctional learning is so basic to our study, we shall examine it in some detail before going futher. We shall refer to deriving our beliefs from our own experience as being *centered*, and to taking over the beliefs of others as being *de-centered*.

De-centering ourselves from our own experience starts very early as our parents begin to make known to us their requirements for our behavior. Things we experience as enjoyable we learn are wrong. The reasons relate not to our experience but to the mysterious, frightening, symbolic world of our parents. Here is a world of cleanliness and germs, of acceptable and unacceptable emotions, of good and bad parts of our bodies, of polite and impolite ways of eating and speaking, of right and wrong actions: none of which we understand, because these evaluations correspond very poorly with, or are even unrelated to, what we experience to be rewarding. But we see that these things are important to our parents, and we learn how important their approval is to our need to feel secure, to be held, and the like. Gradually, we identify their approval of us with our personal worth. Bit by bit, we extend this identity to include both approval by certain others and, as our sense grows of the larger society in which we live, an imagined approval by our society.

As we learn the language of our culture and begin to understand the symbolic world of our parents, we internalize their voice—including, especially, the messages of their body language—and now many of our internal communications contradict the messages of our organismic experience. We feel divided, in conflict with ourselves. This is best thought of as a conflict not between mind and body but between socialized self and organism. The organism is not simply a body but a body that thinks and feels and understands. When we think of our bodies apart from our conscious selves, we are dealing with an abstraction. Mind and body are each dimensions of the same organism.

This inner, parental voice, then, combines with the evaluations and expectations communicated to us by other persons to exert strong pressure on us to be a certain way. If we consequently identify ourselves with these things others have told us are good and bad, we will not be receptive to organismic experiences which may contradict them. To take an example from Rogers, perhaps little Janie enjoys pulling her baby brother's hair. She is scolded for this and told she is a naughty girl. Later, she again does the hair pulling, but now she says, "Naughty Jane. Naughty." Gradually, she may come to believe this judgment is based on her own organismic experience, forgetting that she really enjoyed it. If Janie is to learn to trust herself and her own experience, she needs the help of her parents to see that she is not a bad person because she enjoyed doing this or, in other words, that the messages from her organism are not to be discounted because they conveyed this delight. She needs gradually to come to see that her understanding must be enlarged, her judgment refined, and her capacity for enjoyment based on ever more inclusive identifications with others. But such learning is jeopardized by her early experiences of seeing herself a bad girl in the eyes of her parents and others. Our images of self and world, then, may more and more be centered outside of ourselves in the outlook communicated by others, and so may be related less and less to our own experience.

The process of gradually reclaiming ourselves by overcoming decenteredness is complicated by our need to deal with the opposite problem of infantile narcissism. This is a concern for our well-being that excludes any awareness of other persons as important in their own right. It involves an overriding desire to be taken care of. As infants, we see the world only in terms of our own egocentric needs and interests, a focus that serves us well in getting our early needs met. Before long we begin the work of creating ourselves and then a part of our task is to gradually transform our narcissism into a concern for ourselves as social beings—persons who become human only in creative relationships with others.

We create the life-long foundation of our personality, then, in conflict. We are filled with desires and wants; we also try to meet what to us are the often irrational demands of the all-powerful ones. We experience many of these parental expectations as irrational because they often contradict our experience of what tastes good and feels good, and we don't understand why there should be such expectations to begin with.

Our parents have the task of helping us, gradually, to reclaim ourselves. Responsibility for our behavior is to be shifted to us as we gain the necessary experience and powers of good judgment. This is a difficult task and all of us carry through life parts of ourselves that are infantile and decentered. The question for our learning is what roles we let these parts play in our lives, and how much strength we give them.

Our difficulty in becoming centered, autonomous persons, though, is not only rooted in our early condition of dependency. It also arises from characteristics of our society. Experiences in our families, as well as in our churches, schools, organizations and the like, necessarily reflect the dominant trends of our society—or at least of that unit within it which impacts on us most directly. To see more clearly the obstacles to learning to be autonomous, then, we need to look, at least briefly, at the society which not only provides the very possibility of our being persons but also obstructs and distorts it.

Three of the factors that shape society are the striving of individuals to develop and maintain their power to be persons, the production and distribution of goods, and the preservation of our social order. First of all, then, our society is organized in some degree to meet our needs to be significant persons. No society could long exist if it too deeply frustrated the organismic needs of too many of its people. Order cannot be maintained by force alone. A significant degree of voluntary compliance is necessary. Consequently, our social institutions—our families, churches, schools, organizations, and the like—are shaped so that they contribute importantly to our growth as persons.

Secondly, we are powerfully affected by the ways we are related to one another in our economic pursuits. This, of course, is an especially controversial subject but here, too, in the interests of brevity, I shall continue simply to sketch out the point of view underlying my sense of why our learning so often becomes dysfunctional. Typically, I believe, the spirit in which we produce and distribute goods rests on an idea of the sort we are calling dysfunctional, namely, that we are unable to produce enough to go around. The goods and services that make for a rewarding life, we tell ourselves, are unavoidably in short supply. Consequently, we tend to compete against one another in an effort to grab as large a piece of the economic pie as we can, heedless of what we reasonably need. This drive for economic supremacy, it seems to me, is the basic explanation of why we organize the way we work together by using a notion of property under which a few can be regarded as owning the means of production on which we all must depend.[18] To call someone *owner* seems to justify a lopsided distribution of what we work together to produce. But the drive for economic dominance through ownership is made even stronger in being fed not only by an assumption of an unavoidable scarcity of goods and services but also by three other factors: our failure to shape ourselves in a way that adequately limits our desire for power, a too-little satisfied need to feel of worth, and a desire to amass power as a shield against our vulnerability.

Supposing that there is a degree of truth in the view I am presenting, what is the consequence for our learning? Because we *are* our relations, we are deeply shaped by the relations we enter into when we are producing. As breadwinners, we not only spend a large part of our life engaged in these relations, but they have great importance for us. They greatly affect all our other relations. We come to see love and respect also in terms of scarcity, as things to be competed for and somehow to be owned. Success in the organization depends on molding ourselves to the rules of the game and performing in a way that, above all, pleases the boss and others. We come to think of ourselves more in terms of what we have than of what we are; *having* becomes a way of *being*, a token of power and significance. These forces of de-centering are very strong indeed.

A third factor in the shaping of our society that bears significantly on our de-centeredness is the measures taken to preserve our social order. The problem is that our social order embodies a disheartening mixture of that which supports and that which undermines human well-being. Ever present and often ruthless competition for the greatest possible economic success results in grave injustice and injury. However just our society may be in some respects, the rules are stacked against various minorities and the poor generally. The result is a brutalizing economic and spiritual impoverishment of millions side by side with an unparalleled opulence. Women doing the same work as men receive less than three-fifths the pay and often under conditions of sexual harassment. Alongside of these and other aspects of economic injustice must be placed related sources of social discontent that add up to depersonalization and loss of meaning. Antagonism to central features of our social order is deeply embedded in the lives of a great many, less strongly and less consciously present in the lives of most.

A social order that generates deep resistance is not easily maintained. In part, its preservation must depend on force, an ever-recurrent eruption and even systematic use of violence in suppressing discontent. However indispensible, and in many ways well-motivated, our agencies of social regulation are, there are also the governmental violations of privacy and other rights, the widespread police brutality, the moral and spiritual bankruptcy of our penal system that, along with other forms of violent practice, make for a cancerous condition in our life together.

But force alone cannot suffice. If our social order cannot win a large measure of voluntary compliance by the ways in which it does serve our need to be significant persons, then it must weaken our will to resist. Healthy, informed, empowered human beings will not acquiesce in social structures and practices that needlessly injure and degrade. To maintain a social order with such injustice, we must be conditioned to doubt our worth, to see as inevitable the poverty of our power, to accept interpretations that cloud our vision. When great power becomes concentrated in the hands of those who benefit deeply from our present social arrangements, there are uncountable ways in which the system provides rewards for conforming and punishments for resisting. Do we want to hold our jobs, to move up socially, to get a little edge in the games involved? Then here are the attitudes we must take, the behaviors we must learn, the ways of seeing things we must adopt.[19] Again and again the message is given that scarcity is the law of life, that power and a sense of worth are available to some but only at the expense of many others.

Perhaps the dominant factor in sapping our courage to stand against injustice is the erosion of our sense of worth. The more we question our worth the more easily we are controlled. If we are lacking in worth, on what basis can we claim any right to life, liberty and the pursuit of happiness? Just as a major obstacle in therapy is often the client's sense of not deserving a fuller life, so we cannot achieve greater social justice if we cannot confidently claim it as our due. Then, too, if whatever worth we have resides not in ourselves but in gaining approval, we may easily be manipulated as the price for meeting this need.

This approval we seek may be that of the anonymous *they*. We may come to worry deeply about securing and maintaining it. We may buy the products that seem necessary for social success, or at least that guard us from social failure. Again, it may be the approval of teachers, who all too typically reinforce us for meeting their needs for deference and for conforming our minds to their vision of things. The approval we seek may be that of an all-knowing, all-seeing God: our destiny, not only in this world but in a next, may seem to be at stake. Ideas of heaven and hell may come to symbolize our being found as worthy or worthless, and we may struggle long and hard to conform ourselves to a designated way of being saved. Whether from secular or sacred teachings, we may learn to experience a sense of worthlessness in the authoritarian guilt of having failed to meet the demands, fulfill the expectations, gain the approval of someone or something beyond ourselves. Once we take seriously the question of whether we are of worth, we are trapped in this way. For if our worth resided in our own being, as persons capable of creating meaning and value, it wouldn't even make sense to question it. But if our worth does not come from ourselves, then we must look for it elsewhere and seek to meet whatever requirements are imposed. As we turn away from ourselves to seek our worth, our self-confidence is undermined, our will to resist the injustices built into the social game is impaired.

Most damaging of all to our sense of ourselves is the quality of our emotional life. As this has evolved out of the tensions between our striving to develop and maintain our power to be persons; our seduction by the game of economic dominance; the erosion of our self-confidence so that unjust order may prevail unchanged; and other related factors, it is a bewildering mixture of self-validating and self-invalidating scenarios. While such emotions as brotherly (or sisterly) love, humanistic guilt, wonder, and joy enhance our sense of worth and deepen our courage, many more do the opposite. Envy, authoritarian guilt, and resentment are typical of those emotions that, as we shall see, reflect and reinforce feelings of inadequacy and low worth as persons. When we learn such ways of relating, we diminish our power and courage.

Also damaging to ourselves is the passive way we learn to experience our emotions. They are at the heart of our lives as persons, and yet typically we are taught that, in a sense, they don't really belong to us. Rather, they somehow just happen. They simply come over us. They are not, we think, expressions of whom we choose to be. Our only responsibility concerning them is for how we act once we are subjected to them. In a later chapter, we shall challenge this view. For now, it is enough simply to reflect on how essentially passive, how unpowerful, this makes us out to be.

There is something very disturbing about our very need to use the term *worth* in connection with ourselves as persons. *Worth* is a comparative term which has its home in the market place. How much is this house worth? This car? This refrigerator? When we go on to include "this person?" we diminish ourselves. We may sensibly ask about the worth to others of a task we perform or a service we provide. But when we speak of ourselves not as role players or producers but as persons, such a term is surely out of place. The very fact that we need to affirm our worth as persons simply means that much about our life together reduces persons to the level of things in the market. In learning that there is a question about our worth—another of what we are calling dysfunctional ideas—we become more susceptible to external control, less resistant to injustice.

In considering what I see to be characteristics of our society that tend to produce dysfunctional learning, my aim has been not to argue for these convictions but, because I shall be evaluating as well as describing our experiential learning, to enable you better to understand and evaluate my judgments. The personal and social conditions under which we learn are so complex, so ambiguous, so conflicting in their effect on us that no two of us will see them in quite the same way. The same may be said for our nature as persons. Those of you who tend to be conservative may find more salient than I the more constructive aspects of our society and the less creative aspects of our human nature. Doubtless you will feel I have given undue prominence to the problematic side of our life together and to the bent of our nature toward harmony. Others may differ from me in the opposite direction, convinced that I have made too much of the possibilities for a significantly human life within our present social orders and portrayed the problem of outgrowing our early dependence as more basic than it really is. Fortunately, whatever our disagreements, they need not prevent you from using this book to benefit more fully from the lessons of your experience, by improving your ability to meet your goals and to obtain whatever you find desirable.

SUMMARY: FUNCTIONAL AND DYSFUNCTIONAL LEARNING

In this chapter, we have looked at the place of experiential learning in the life-long process of becoming a self and of developing autonomy. Dysfunctional learning has been seen as stemming principally from obstacles we encounter in our struggle to be a significant person. These obstacles, we have maintained, often result in the learning of behavior and beliefs that are defensive, or destructive, or taken over from other persons or from organizations. Dysfunctional ideas or rules that often guide our interpretations of our life situations have been seen as playing a major role in dysfunctional learning. In contrast, we have also indicated three rules that are alleged to support and encourage functional learning. Finally, we have considered Carl Rogers's hypothesis that the major cause of dysfunctional learning is that *"in an attempt to gain love, approval, esteem, the individual relinquishes the locus of evaluation . . . and places it in others."* Support for this belief has been found in examining our early condition of dependency and certain characteristics of our society, especially the drive for economic dominance and strategies by which our particular social order is maintained despite its injustice. In Chapters 5 through 7 we shall look at functional and dysfunctional learning in connection with our emotions, our understanding of others, and our life in organizations.

We have also considered reasons for believing, with Carl Rogers, that, under certain conditions, our organismic experience leads to functional learning, learning that either contributes to our autonomy or enrichment, or is compatible with them while serving some other valuable aim. Under conditions of being in a relationship in which we are prized and understood and which is open and nonjudgmental, learning gives us power, the power to be a significant person through effective action, the power to create meaning through realistic interpretation, the power to cope with threat through ecstatic transcendence. These powers are never all that we would like for them to be, but to love life is to love power despite its ambiguities and limitations, and despite our temptation to abuse it. We may see a characteristic of functional learning in the words of William Blake: ''Energy is eternal delight.''

CHAPTER TWO

The Four Kinds of Experiential Learning

All significant experiential learning is a *change* in the learner—a change in behavior, in interpretation, in autonomy, or in creativity, or a combination of these changes. We shall refer to these kinds of learning as *response learning, situation learning, transsituation learning,* and *transcendent learning,* respectively. Each of these, except for response learning, is a change in our ability to do the kind of learning immediately preceeding it. We begin our examination of this model of experiential learning with a look at the kind of learning that is fundamental to our personal freedom.

A STORY OF LEARNING FROM EXPERIENCE

In the following story, "Sex Education," we see a girl of sixteen learning from an experience in a cornfield. Then, in her middle and late years, we find her learning from difficulties with her son Jake in ways that lead her to see her experience at sixteen rather differently.

"Sex Education"[1]

It was three times—but at intervals of many years—that I heard my Aunt Minnie tell about an experience of her girlhood that had made a never-to-be-forgotten impression on her. The first time she was in her thirties, still young. But she had then been married for ten years, so that to my group of friends, all in the early teens, she seemed quite of another generation.

The day she told us the story, we had been idling on one end of her porch as we made casual plans for a picnic supper in the woods. Darning stockings at the other end, she paid no

attention to us until one of the girls said, "Let's take blankets
and sleep out there. It'd be fun."

"No," Aunt Minnie broke in sharply, "you mustn't do
that."

"Oh, for goodness' sakes, why not!" said one of the
younger girls, rebelliously, "the boys are always doing it. Why
can't we, just once?"

Aunt Minnie laid down her sewing. "Come here, girls," she
said, "I want you should hear something that happened to me
when I was your age."

Her voice had a special quality which, perhaps, young people
of today would not recognize. But we did. We knew from experience that it was the dark voice grownups used when they
were going to say something about sex.

Yet at first what she had to say was like any dull family anec-
dote; she had been ill when she was fifteen; and afterwards
she was run down, thin, with no appetite. Her folks thought a
change of air would do her good, and sent her from Vermont
out to Ohio—or was it Illinois? I don't remember. Anyway, one
of those places where the corn grows high. Her mother's
Cousin Ella lived there, keeping house for her son-in-law.

The son-in-law was the minister of the village church. His
wife had died some years before, leaving him a young widower
with two little girls and a baby boy. He had been a normally
personable man then, but the next summer, on the Fourth of
July when he was trying to set off some fireworks to amuse his
children, an imperfectly manufactured rocket had burst in his
face. The explosion had left one side of his face badly scarred.
Aunt Minnie made us see it, as she still saw it, in horrid detail:
the stiffened, scarlet scar tissue distorting one cheek, the lower
lip turned so far out at one corner that the moist red mucous-
membrane lining always showed, one lower eyelid hanging
loose, and watering.

After the accident, his face had been a long time healing. It
was then that his wife's elderly mother had gone to keep
house and take care of the children. When he was well enough
to be about again, he found his position as pastor of the little
church waiting for him. The farmers and village people in his
congregation, moved by his misfortune, by his faithful service
and by his unblemished character, said they would rather have
Mr. Fairchild, even with his scarred face, than any other
minister. He was a good preacher, Aunt Millie told us, "and
the way he prayed was kind of exciting. I'd never known a

preacher, not to live in the same house with him, before. And when he was in the pulpit, with everybody looking up at him, I felt the way his children did, kind of proud to think we had just eaten breakfast at the same table. I liked to call him 'Cousin Malcolm' before folks. One side of his face was all right, anyhow. You could see from that that he *had* been a good-looking man. In fact, probably one of those ministers that all the women—'' Aunt Minnie paused, drew her lips together, and looked at us uncertainly.

Then she went back to the story as it happened—as it happened that first time I heard her tell it. "I thought he was a saint. Everybody out there did. That was all *they* knew. Of course, it made a person sick to look at that awful scar—the drooling corner of his mouth was the worst. He tried to keep that side of his face turned away from folks. But you always knew it was there. That was what kept him from marrying again, so Cousin Ella said. I heard her say lots of times that he knew no woman would touch any man who looked the way he did, not with a ten-foot pole.

"Well, the change of air did do me good. I got my appetite back, and ate a lot and played outdoors a lot with my cousins. They were younger than I (I had my sixteenth birthday there) but I still liked to play games. I got taller and laid on some weight. Cousin Ella used to say I grew as fast as the corn did. Their house stood at the edge of the village. Beyond it was one of those big cornfields they have out West. At the time when I first got there, the stalks were only up to a person's knee. You could see over their tops. But it grew like lightning, and before long, it was the way thick woods are here, way over your head, the stalks growing so close together it was dark under them.

"Cousin Ella told us youngsters that it was lots worse for getting lost in than woods, because there weren't any landmarks in it. One spot in a cornfield looked just like any other. 'You children keep out of it,' she used to tell us almost every day, '*especially you girls*. It's no place for a decent girl. You could easy get so far from the house nobody could hear you if you hollered. There are plenty of men in this town that wouldn't like anything better than ———' she never said what.

"In spite of what she said, my little cousins and I had figured out that if we went across one corner of the field, it would be a short cut to the village, and sometimes, without letting on to Cousin Ella, we'd go that way. After the corn got really tall, the farmer stopped cultivating, and we soon beat down a path in the loose dirt. The minute you were inside the field it was dark. You felt as if you were miles from anywhere. It sort of scared you. But in no time the path turned and brought you out on the far end of Main Street. Your breath was coming fast, maybe, but that was what made you like to do it.

"One day I missed the turn. Maybe I didn't keep my mind on it. Maybe it had rained and blurred the tramped-down look of the path. I don't know what. All of a sudden, I knew I was lost. And the minute I knew that, I began to run, just as hard as I could run. I couldn't help it, any more than you can help snatching your hand off a hot stove. I didn't know what I was scared of, I didn't even know I *was* running, til my heart was pounding so hard I had to stop.

"The minute I stood still, I could hear Cousin Ella saying, 'There are plenty of men in this town that wouldn't like anything better than ———' I didn't know, not really, what she meant. But I knew she meant something horrible. I opened my mouth to scream. But I put both hands over my mouth to keep the scream in. If I made any noise, one of those men would hear me. I thought I heard one just behind me, and whirled around. And then I thought another one had tiptoed up behind me, the other way, and I spun around so fast I almost fell over. I stuffed my hands hard up against my mouth. And then—I couldn't help it—I ran again—but my legs were shaking so I soon had to stop. There I stood, scared to move for fear of rustling the corn and letting the men know where I was. My hair had come down, all over my face. I kept pushing it back and looking around, quick, to make sure one of the men hadn't found out where I was. Then I thought I saw a man coming towards me, and I ran away from him—and fell down, and burst some of the buttons off my dress, and was sick to my stomach—and thought I heard a man close to me and got up and staggered around, knocking into the corn because I couldn't even see where I was going.

"And then, off to one side, I saw Cousin Malcolm. Not a man. The minister. He was standing still, one hand up to his face, thinking. He hadn't heard me.

"I was so *terrible* glad to see him, instead of one of those men, I ran as fast as I could and just flung myself on him, to make myself feel how safe I was."

Aunt Minnie had become strangely agitated. Her hands were

shaking, her face was crimson. She frightened us. We could not look away from her. As we waited for her to go on, I felt little spasms twitch at the muscles inside my body. "And what do you think that *saint*, that holy minister of the gospel, did to an innocent child who clung to him for safety? The most terrible look came into his eyes—you girls are too young to know what he looked like. But once you're married, you'll find out. He grabbed hold of me—that dreadful face of his was *right on mine*—and began clawing the clothes off my back."

She stopped for a moment, panting. We were too frightened to speak. She went on, "He had torn my dress right down to the waist before I—then I *did* scream—all I could—and pulled away from him so hard I almost fell down, and ran and all of a sudden I came out of the corn, right in the back yard of the Fairchild house. The children were starring at the corn, and Cousin Ella ran out of the kitchen door. They had heard me screaming. Cousin Ella shrieked out, 'What is it? What happened? Did a man scare you?' And I said, 'Yes, yes, yes, a man———I ran———!' And then I fainted away. I must have. The next thing I knew I was on the sofa in the living room and Cousin Ella was slapping my face with a wet towel."

She had to wet her lips with her tongue before she could go on. Her face was gray now. "There! that's the kind of thing girls' folks ought to tell them about—so they'll know what men are like."

She finished her story as if she were dismissing us. We wanted to go away, but we were too horrified to stir. Finally one of the youngest girls asked in a low trembling voice, "Aunt Minnie, did you tell on him?"

"No, I was ashamed to," she said briefly. "They sent me home the next day anyhow. Nobody ever said a word to me about it. And I never did either. Till now."

By what gets printed in some of the modern child-psychology books, you would think that girls to whom such a story had been told would never develop normally. Yet, as far as I can remember what happened to the girls in that group, we all grew up about like anybody. Most of us married, some happily, some not so well. We kept house. We learned—more or less—how to live with our husbands, we had children and struggled to bring them up right—we went forward into life, just as if we had never been warned not to.

Perhaps, young as we were that day, we had already had

enough experience of life so that we were not quite blank paper for Aunt Minnie's frightening story. Whether we thought of it then or not, we couldn't have failed to see that at this very time, Aunt Minnie had been married for ten years or more, comfortably and well married, too. Against what she tried by that story to brand into our minds stood the cheerful home life in that house, the good-natured, kind, hard-working husband, and the children—the three rough-and-tumble, nice little boys, so adored by their parents, and the sweet girl baby who died, of whom they could never speak without tears. It was such actual contact with adult life that probably kept generation after generation of girls from being scared by tales like Aunt Minnie's into a neurotic horror of living.

Of course, since Aunt Minnie was so much older than we, her boys grew up to be adolescents and young men, while our children were still little enough so that our worries over them were nothing more serious than whooping cough and trying to get them to make their own beds. Two of our aunt's three boys followed, without losing their footing, the narrow path which leads across adolescence into normal adult life. But the middle one, Jake, repeatedly fell off into the morass. "Girl trouble," as the succinct family phrase put it. He was one of those boys who have "charm," whatever we mean by that, and was always being snatched at by girls who would be "all wrong" for him to marry. And once, at nineteen, he ran away from home, whether with one of these girls or not we never heard, for through all her ups and downs with this son, Aunt Minnie tried fiercely to protect him from scandal that might cloud his later life.

Her husband had to stay on his job to earn the family living. She was the one who went to find Jake. When it was gossiped around that Jake was in "bad company" his mother drew some money from the family savings-bank account, and silent, white-cheeked, took the train to the city where rumor said he had gone.

Some weeks later he came back with her. With no girl. She had cleared him of that entanglement. As of others, which followed, later. Her troubles seemed over when, at a "suitable" age, he fell in love with a "suitable" girl, married her and took her to live in our shire town, sixteen miles away, where he had a good position. Jake was always bright enough.

Sometimes, idly, people speculated as to what Aunt Minnie had seen that time she went after her runaway son, wondering where her search for him had taken her—very queer places for

Aunt Minnie to be in, we imagined. And how could such an ignorant, homekeeping woman ever have known what to say to an errant willful boy to set him straight?

Well, of course, we reflected, watching her later struggles with Jake's erratic ways, she certainly could not have remained ignorant, after seeing over and over what she probably had; after talking with Jake about the things which, a good many times, must have come up with desperate openness between them.

She kept her own counsel. We never knew anything definite about the facts of those experiences of hers. But one day she told a group of us—all then married women—something which gave us a notion about what she had learned from them.

We were hastily making a layette for a not-especially welcome baby in a poor family. In those days, our town had no such thing as a district-nursing service. Aunt Minnie, a vigorous woman of fifty-five, had come in to help. As we sewed, we talked, of course; and because our daughters were near or in their teens, we were comparing notes about the bewildering responsibility of bringing up girls.

After a while, Aunt Minnie remarked, "Well, I hope you teach your girls some *sense*. From what I read, I know you're great on telling them 'the facts,' facts we never heard of when we were girls. Like as not, some facts I don't know, now. But knowing the facts isn't going to do them any more good than *not* knowing the facts ever did, unless they have some sense taught them, too."

"What do you mean, Aunt Minnie?" one of us asked her uncertainly.

She reflected, threading a needle, "Well, I don't know but what the best way to tell you what I mean is to tell you about something that happened to me, forty years ago. I've never said anything about it before. But I've thought about it a good deal. Maybe———"

She had hardly begun when I recognized the story—her visit to her Cousin Ella's Midwestern home, the widower with his scarred face and saintly reputation and, very vividly, her getting lost in the great cornfield. I knew every word she was going to say—to the very end, I thought.

But no, I did not. Not at all.

She broke off, suddenly, to exclaim with impatience, "Wasn't I the big ninny? But not so big a ninny as that old cousin of mine. I could wring her neck for getting me in such a state. Only she didn't know any better, herself. That was the way they brought young people up in those days, scaring them out of their wits about the awfulness of getting lost, but not telling them a thing about how *not* to get lost. Or how to act, if they did.

"If I had had the sense I was born with, I'd have known that running my legs off in a zigzag was the worst thing I could do. I couldn't have been more than a few feet from the path when I noticed I wasn't on it. My tracks in the loose plow dirt must have been perfectly plain. If I'd h' stood still, and collected my wits, I could have looked down to see which way my footsteps went and just walked back over them to the path and gone on about my business.

"Now I ask you, if I'd been told how to do that, wouldn't it have been a lot better protection for me—if protection was what my aunt thought she wanted to give me————than to scare me so at the idea of being lost and I turned deef-dumb-and-blind when I thought I was?

"And anyhow that patch of corn wasn't as big as she let on. And she knew it wasn't. It was no more than a big field in a farming country. I was a well-grown girl of sixteen, as tall as I am now. If I couldn't have found the path, I could have just walked along one line of cornstalks—*straight*—and I'd have come out somewhere in ten minutes. Fifteen at the most. Maybe not just where I wanted to go. But all right, safe, where decent folks were living."

She paused, as if she had finished. But at the inquiring blankness in our faces, she went on, "Well, now, why isn't teaching girls—and boys, too, for the Lord's sake don't forget they need it as much as the girls—about this man-and-woman business, something like that? If you give them the idea—no matter whether it's *as* you tell them the facts, or as you *don't* tell them the facts, that it is such a terribly scary thing that if they take a step into it, something's likely to happen to them so awful that you're ashamed to tell them what—well, they'll lose their heads and run around like crazy things, first time they take one step away from the path.

"For they'll be trying out the paths, all right. You can't keep them from it. And a good thing, too. How else are they going to find out what it's like? Boys' and girls' going together is a path across one corner of growing up. And when they go together, they're likely to get off the path some. Seems to me, it's up to their folks to bring them up so when they do, they

don't start screaming and running in circles, but stand still,
right where they are, and get their breath and figure out how
to get back.

"And anyhow, you don't tell 'em the truth about sex" (I was
astonished to hear her use the actual word, taboo to women of
her generation) "if they get the idea from you that it's all there
is to living. It's not. If you don't get to where you want to go
in it, well, there's a lot of landscape all around it a person can
have a good time in.

"D'you know, I believe one thing that gives girls and boys
the wrong idea is the way folks *look!* My old cousin's face, I
can see her now, it was as red as a rooster's comb when she
was telling me about men in that cornfield. I believe now she
kind of *liked* to talk about it."

(Oh Aunt Minnie—and yours! I thought.)

Someone asked, "But how *did* you get out, Aunt Minnie?"

She shook her head, laid down her sewing. "More foolish-
ness. That minister my mother's cousin was keeping house
for—her son-in-law—I caught sight of him, down along one of
the aisles of cornstalks, looking down at the ground, thinking,
the way he often did. And I was so glad to see him I rushed
right up to him, and flung my arms around his neck and hugged
him. He hadn't heard me coming. He gave a great start, put
one arm around me and turned his face full towards me—I
suppose for just a second he had forgotten how awful one side
of it was. His expression, his eyes—well, you're all married
women, you know how he looked, the way any able-bodied
man thirty-six or -seven, who'd been married and begotten
children, would look—for a minute anyhow, if a full-blooded
girl of sixteen, who ought to have known better, flung herself
at him without any warning, her hair tumbling down, her
dress half unbuttoned, and hugged him with all her might.

"I was what they called innocent in those days. That is, I
knew just as little about what men are like as my folks could
manage I should. But I was old enough to know all right what
that look meant. And it gave me a start. But of course the real
thing of it was that dreadful scar of his, so close to my
face—that wet corner of his mouth, his eye drawn down with
the red inside of the lower eyelid showing———

"It turned me so sick, I pulled away with all my might, so
fast that I ripped one sleeve nearly loose, and let out a screech
like a wildcat. And ran. Did I run? And in a minute, I was
through the corn and had come out in the back yard of the

house. I hadn't been more than a few feet from it, probably, any of the time. And then I fainted away. Girls were always fainting away; it was the way our corset strings were pulled tight, I suppose, and then—oh, a lot of fuss.

"But anyhow," she finished, picking up her work and going on, setting neat, firm stitches with steady hands, "there's one thing, I never told anybody it was Cousin Malcolm I had met in the cornfield. I told my old cousin that 'a man had scared me.' And nobody said anything more about it to me, not ever. That was the way they did in those days. They thought if they didn't let on about something, maybe it wouldn't have happened. I was sent back to Vermont right away and Cousin Malcolm went on being minister of the church. I've always been," said Aunt Minnie moderately, "kind of proud that I didn't go and ruin a man's life for just one second's slip-up. If you could have called it that. For it *would* have ruined him. You know how hard as stone people are about other folks' letdowns. If I'd have told, not one person in that town would have had any charity. Not one would have tried to understand. One slip, *once*, and they'd have pushed him down in the mud. If I had told, I'd have felt pretty bad about it, later—when I came to have more sense. But I declare, I can't see how I came to have the decency, dumb as I was then, to know that it wouldn't be fair."

It was not long after this talk that Aunt Minnie's elderly husband died, mourned by her, by all of us. She lived alone then. It was peaceful October weather for her, in which she kept a firm roundness of face and figure, as quiet-living, country-women often do, on into their late sixties.

But then Jake, the boy who had had girl trouble, had wife trouble. We heard he had taken to running after a young girl, or was it that she was running after him? It was something serious. For his nice wife left him and came back with the children to live with her mother in our town. Poor Aunt Minnie used to go to see her for long talks which made them both cry. And she went to keep house for Jake, for months at a time.

She grew old, during those years. When finally she (or something) managed to get the marriage mended so that Jake's wife relented and went back to live with him, there was no trace left of her pleasant brisk freshness. She was stooped and slowfooted and shrunken. We, her kinspeople, although we would have given our lives for any one of our own children, wondered whether Jake was worth what it had cost his mother to———well, steady him, or reform him. Or perhaps just understand him. Whatever it took.

She came of a long-lived family and was able to go on keeping house for herself well into her eighties. Of course we and the other neighbors stepped in often to make sure she was all right. Mostly, during those brief calls, the talk turned on nothing more vital than her geraniums. But one midwinter afternoon, sitting with her in front of her cozy stove, I chanced to speak in rather hasty blame of someone who had, I thought, acted badly. To my surprise this brought from her the story about the cornfield which she had evidently quite forgotten telling me, twice before.

This time she told it almost dreamily, swaying to and fro in her rocking chair, her eyes fixed on the long slope of snow outside her window. When she came to the encounter with the minister she said, looking away from the distance and back into my eyes, "I know now that I had been, all along, kind of *interested* in him, the way any girl as old as I was would be, in any youngish man living in the same house with her. And a minister, too. They have to have the gift of gab so much more than most men, women get to thinking they are more alive than men who can't talk so well. I *thought* the reason I threw my arms around him was because I had been so scared. And I certainly had been scared, by my old cousin's horrible talk about the cornfield being full of men waiting to grab girls. But that wasn't all the reason I flung myself at Malcolm Fairchild and hugged him. I know that now. Why in the world shouldn't I have been taught *some* notion of it then? 'Twould do girls good to know that they are just like everybody else—human nature *and* sex, all mixed up together. I didn't have to hug him. I wouldn't have, if he'd been dirty or fat and old, or chewed tobacco."

I stirred in my chair, ready to say, "But it's not so simple as all that to tell girls———" and she hastily answered my unspoken protest. "I know, I know, most of it can't be put into words. There just aren't any words to say something that's so both-ways-at-once all the time as this man-and-woman business. But look here, you know as well as I do that there are lots more ways than in words to teach young folks what you want 'em to know."

The old woman stopped her swaying rocker to peer far back into the past with honest eyes. "What was in my mind back there in the cornfield—partly anyhow—was what had been there all the time I was living in the same house with Cousin Malcolm—that he had long straight legs, and broad shoulders and lots of curly brown hair, and was nice and flat in front, and that one side of his face was good-looking. But most of all, that he and I were really alone, for the first time, without anybody to see us.

"I suppose, if it hadn't been for that dreadful scar, he'd have drawn me up, tight, and—most any man would—kissed me. I know how I must have looked all red and hot and my hair down and my dress torn open. And, used as he was to big cornfields, he probably never dreamed that the reason I looked that way was because I was scared to be by myself in one. He may have thought—you know what he may have thought.

"Well—if his face had been like anybody's—when he looked at me the way he did, the way a man does look at a woman he wants to have, it would have scared me—some. But I'd have cried, maybe. And probably he'd have kissed me again. You know how such things go. I might have come out of the corn-field halfway engaged to marry him. Why not? I was old enough, as people thought then. That would have been nature. That was probably what he thought of, in that first instant.

"But what did I do? I had one look at his poor, horrible face, and started back as though I'd stepped on a snake. And screamed and ran."

"What do you suppose *he* felt, left there in the corn? He must have been sure that I would tell everybody he had attacked me. He probably thought that when he came out and went back to the village he'd already be in disgrace and put out of the pulpit.

"But the worst must have been to find out, so rough, so plain from the way I acted—as if somebody had hit him with an ax—the way he would look to any woman he might try to get close to. That must have been——" she drew a long breath, "well, pretty hard on him."

After a silence, she murmured pityingly, "Poor man!"

A MODEL OF EXPERIENTIAL LEARNING

When we learn we change. We behave differently, respond with new emotions, think in new ways, or become more conscious of our role in shaping our lives. Often these changes occur together; or changes in one of these ways soon leads to changes in one or more of the others.

We can learn more effectively from our experience if we can see more clearly what changes are involved and how we accomplish them. Perhaps we become involved in a new job situation or travel to a new country or enter a new relationship. We're hopeful that we'll do some growing in these experiences but we have only the vaguest idea of what we mean by this. What sorts of changes are involved? What must we do to make such changes? What conditions are necessary? What skills do we need? If we understand these things we're more likely to learn effectively, for we can then help the process along and if things aren't going right we may be able to do something about it.[2]

Getting clear about the changes involved will also help us when we have a more definite learning goal in mind. Perhaps we want to learn to be more assertive in relating to others. But if we have only a vague idea about what to do, say from watching a friend, our progress will probably be slow and disappointing. If we realize at the start that changes in behavior and belief are likely to be necessary we have a far better chance of learning to be more assertive. We very probably need changes in both our behavior and our thinking about our relations with others. Changes in the way we say things and in such body language as eye contact, facial expression, posture, and voice tone and level will give us the means to communicate effectively. But we also need to develop positive beliefs about our right to stand up for ourselves if we are to use these behaviors without inner conflict or subsequent guilt feelings and so make them a part of us.

Learning from our experience involves changing both what we do and how we see things. We begin our discussion of learning from experience, then, by examining these two sorts of change, because seeing more clearly what they are is basic to improving our abilities to learn.

After exploring the processes of change in behavior and change in interpretation of a situation, we will be ready to consider two other sorts of change that are involved in some of our learning. In this sort of learning, we expand our powers to reflect on and change our point of view, and it is just such a development of our powers that is the basic aim of this book.

We are saying, then, that learning involves change and that there are four different levels of change that may take place, either separately or in combination, when we learn. We shall call these different levels *response learning, situation learning, transsituation learning,* and *transcendent learning*. Gregory Bateson has done some helpful work in distingushing levels of learning, and the following discussion will utilize his ideas, although with different terminology and some modification.[3]

Responding

We carry on a stream of transactions with our world. And, when we are not engaging it, we are generally reflecting, dreaming, or wondering about that engagement. Yet most of the time we are not really learning. We are simply responding to a familiar situation in a way we have previously learned. We act out of habit. Someone waves and we automatically wave back. The road bends to the left and, without any thought, we turn the steering wheel a certain amount in that direction as we have done countless times before. True, in each case we take in new information—someone is waving now, the road is bending to the left—but in each case, we treat it as essentially identical with certain information we have received in the past and respond to it in the same way. Nothing is learned. We have not changed. We shall call this *responding* to distinguish it from response learning and the rest.

Behavior of this sort is comparable to that of a thermostat which is set at seventy degrees. The moment it receives information that the room temperature has risen above seventy degrees, it turns on the air conditioner. The moment it finds that the temperature has dropped below sixty-eight degrees, it turns the air conditioner off. It simply repeats again and again what it has "learned" (been programmed) to do in the past.

Response Learning

Consider, next, learning in its most rudimentary form, which we are calling response learning. In this case, we *change* the way we are prepared to respond in a certain situation, either adding a new response to the set of responses we have previously learned or substituting a new response for one we have been using. Instead of continuing our habit of eating dessert, we leave the table to get on the scales and congratulate ourselves on the weight we are losing. While we are inexperienced drivers, the car skids on several occasions and, through trial and error, we gradually learn to turn our front wheels in the direction of the skid.

It is to response learning that behavioristic psychologists have devoted their attention. This learning is comparable to that of a thermostat when its setting is changed from seventy degrees to seventy-two degrees. It "unlearns" the response of turning the air conditioner on when the room temperature rises above seventy degrees and "learns" the new response of turning it on when the temperature rises above seventy-two degrees. It also "unlearns" turning the air conditioner off when the temperature drops below sixty-eight degrees and "learns" turning it off just below the seventy degree mark.

A great deal of response learning proceeds by trial and error. Gradually, we come to perform and to make part of our basic repertoire of responses any act which yields one of the results we are seeking. The result may be something we find rewarding, or it may be the avoidance or removal of something we find punishing. We tell jokes because people laugh at them and we like that. We move into the shade to avoid the excessive heat of the sun. Skinner has termed this, *operant conditioning*.

Other response learning comes about by the respondent conditioning described by Pavlov. He found that by the ringing of a bell whenever meat was presented to a dog, the dog would come to respond to the ringing bell by itself, just as he naturally responds to the sight and smell of the meat; that is, by salivating. Similarly, suppose we imagine being in a certain place and this produces feelings of happiness. If, at the same time, we touch our left upper arm then, a short time later, we will be able to produce these feelings of happiness simply by again touching our left upper arm. By *pairing* the touch with the image, the touch comes to affect us in the same way the image does.

Still other response learning is what we call *rote learning*. In this case, by many repetitions of a sequence—say, of words or movements—each item in the sequence becomes associated with the one next following it and that with the one next following and so on. After we have repeated the alphabet many times, *A* brings to mind the response *B*, which in turn brings *C* and so on. Similarly, after we have practiced a dance step, each step in the sequence comes automatically to elicit the next and that one the next.

It is through response learning that we create ourselves. We *are* what we do. We are not what we dream about being or plan on becoming; wanting to be honest or imagining that we are honest does not make us so. We are honest only if we do honest things. Our dreams and plans have importance only because they may lead us to act differently and so actually to become that dream or idea.

We may also say that we are our relationships. We are not separate, self-contained beings who are what we are quite apart from our transactions. From the beginning, we are relational beings. Born into a nexus of relationships, we gradually create a sense of who we are in terms of those relationships. The qualities we have are the qualities of our involvements with our world. It is by response learning that we form our relationships with others and they with us. By response learning, we make ourselves who we are.

But if we simply say we are our relationships, we leave something out of account—our freedom. We not only *are* our relationships, but we may also transcend them. We may back away from them, evaluate them, imagine them different than they are and, if we like what we imagine, work to change them. Or, since we are our relationships, in transcending them we transcend ourselves, and in changing them we change ourselves. This is the heart of human freedom, an ability to transcend ourselves and, so, to choose ourselves. Freedom, in this sense, has its basis in the second kind of learning, situation learning.

Situation Learning

Situation learning is a *change* in how we interpret a certain kind of situation. We've seen Aunt Minnie twice change her interpretation of her experience in the cornfield. "He looked the way any able-bodied man of thirty-six . . . would look—for a minute anyhow—if a full-blooded girl of sixteen, who ought to have known better, flung herself at him without any warning, her hair tumbling down, her dress half unbuttoned, and hugged him with all her might." And years later: "I know now that I had been, all along, kind of *interested* in him. . . . The worst must have been to find out, so rough, so plain from the way I acted—as if somebody had hit him with an ax—the way he would look to any woman he might try to get close to."

Situation learning is comparable to an alteration in the thermostat by which it also receives information about the degree of humidity in the room and so can be programmed to turn the air conditioner on when a certain degree of humidity is reached. This response was not possible until the thermostat was made able to "interpret" the room situation in terms of humidity.

Our interpretations typically involve two sets of things which, however much we may distinguish them, we do not experience apart from one another. First of all, we place a value on something in the situation. We see some point to being in that situation, something is at stake for us there. We seek to solve a problem, enjoy a friendship, fulfill a routine, maintain our self-esteem. Secondly, we judge how things work in such a situation. If we want to encourage friendship from another, what behavior on our part will do this? If we want to take in a movie, what bus will get us to the theater? When we interpret, then, we provide ourselves with a *why* and a *how*. We find a place for that situation in the ongoing drama which is our life.

Interrelation of Response and Situation Learning

Response learning, in the form of operant conditioning,[4] presupposes situation learning; in other words, it presupposes that we organize our experience in such a way that it has various sorts of meaning for us. Before the experimenter can teach the pigeon to peck a disc or turn in a circle by rewarding the desired behavior, he must first teach the pigeon a meaning of his circumstances. He does this by teaching him that food will appear in an opening in the wall of his box whenever a clicking sound occurs in that opening. This possibility of food, together with his hunger, becomes the basic meaning of being in the box for the pigeon. It is this meaning which determines which movements the pigeon will repeat; namely, those which result in food being presented. In other words, the pigeon will learn those responses which are successful in obtaining food, success having this meaning in this situation. In another situation, success will have a different meaning; for example, the avoidance of shock.

Similarly, before we can develop strategies and tactics in playing chess, we must know the rules, for it is these rules which define the meaning of any situation in the game. A change in the rules would, of course, lead to changes in the moves we make.

The profound effect that our interpretation of a situation has on the responses we learn may be seen in Claudio Naranjo's comment on how one interprets situations involving sexual frustration:

> Sexual frustration in a person who accepts his sexuality is experienced as unfulfilled desire that is not painful and as a sensation of intense vitality. For a person who harbors guilt feelings in connection with sexual desire or interprets lack of fulfillment as rejection, this lack may be properly called frustration, and leads to depression and an unpleasantness *calling for compulsive satisfaction* and a narcotizing restriction in awareness.[5]

We feel compelled to respond by finding a sexual partner if we interpret sexual frustration in one way but not if we interpret it in another. The kind of response we learn will depend on what we are seeking by it and this in turn will depend on what the situation means to us. Responses to feelings of rejection will differ from those to feelings of vitality.

Aunt Minnie, in her home-spun way, also reminds us of this intimate relation between situation learning and response learning:

> Boys' and girls' going together is a path across one corner of growing up. And when they go together, they're likely to get off the path some. Seems to me, it's up to their folks to bring them up so when they do, they don't start screaming and running around in circles, but stand still, right where they are, and get their breath and figure out how to get back.

The intimate interrelation between situation learning and response learning is important to an attempt to do the latter. We add to our basic set of responses for any given type of situation any act which yields some of the results we are seeking in that situation. The set of responses we are prepared to make in the classroom differs from that we are prepared to give at a party, because the way we interpret those situations—the results we are seeking in them—differ. If we want to change our behavior without changing the way we look at things, we must find a new behavior which gives us what we regard as better results than those given by the old behavior.

But notice that if we change the way we look at the situation—change the results we are aiming at—our old behavior may be experienced as much less effective under these new rules of the game, making it much easier to replace it by another. An alcoholic, for example, must do more than simply attempt to stop drinking. He must put a new set of behaviors in the place of his drinking behaviors and, almost certainly, to succeed in this he must also change the way he sees both himself and the many, many situations that are directly related to his drinking behavior.

Our dissatisfaction with something that we do may rest either with the act itself or with its consequences. Negative emotions such as boredom, disappointment, futility, anxiety, guilt, and the like often accompany both actions that are repetitious or merely means to an end or have no meaning for us, and actions in which we are being disingenuous or somehow violating our sense of who we are.

In those cases where our dissatisfaction is with the consequences of an action, the source of this dissatisfaction may be that we are seeking contradictory results, as when we want to act defensively yet also want to be close to others. Or we may learn our behavior largely in terms of its most immediate and direct or obvious consequences while its long range or indirect consequences may cost us dearly, as when we buy a car we can't afford.

Many whose interest is focused in the humanities get rather upset when behaviorist psychologists talk about these and other aspects of response learning. It is easy to turn a deaf ear, for example, when B. F. Skinner talks about our environment controlling our behavior. But what we seem to overlook is that it is *our* environment, the way *we interpret* that situation, so that as we interpret it differently its effect on us changes. If Skinner did not believe that we can do something about how we see our various situations and that this can affect what we do in those situations, it would be pointless for him to write the books that he does. We need not agree with the entire picture that Skinner or other behaviorist psychologists adopt concerning our nature as human beings in order to learn much from them about learning from experience. It may help us to be receptive to what they can teach us if we bear in mind the intimate relation between response learning and situation learning.

We can agree that our behavior is determined by its consequences without losing a sense of freedom. We are free when we are able to change in self-chosen ways, and it is in situation learning that we create alternatives to choose between. Alternative ways of looking at our lives open up the opportunity of learning alternative behaviors. We behave in whatever ways gain us the consequences we most want. What sense would it make for us to do otherwise? This means that our behavior is determined by its outcomes. Let the outcome change, and we will change our behavior. As children, we may have cried or pouted or nagged to get what we wanted. As long as those things worked, we continued to do them. When they didn't work, we tried other ways of acting. Our freedom lies not in our behavior but in our capacity to determine the meanings of our situations, to decide what we want out of them—whether for ourselves or for others. When we change the way we look at things, we change the way we behave.

There is, however, a sense in which our behavior may be free or be unfree. We have the feeling that our behavior belongs to us when it is determined by our desire for meanings and values that we have chosen for ourselves rather than merely taken on in obedience to the expectations of others. We may think of behavior that embodies self-chosen meanings as free and of behavior that is determined by the meaning that others give to our situation—the expectations that they have of us—as unfree.

Earlier we said that we exercise our freedom most fully when we transcend our behaviors and the relationships that bring them into being. We may disengage ourselves from them, evaluate them, imagine them changed and, if we choose to become what we have created in imagination, work to change them. But in relating freedom to situation learning, we need to consider that situation learning takes two forms. First, there is the active reinterpretation[6] of our situation that we make rather spontaneously as we are engaged in it, generally in response to a change in that situation. Often in such cases, this change precipitates a conscious awareness of an interpretation that we have gradually been giving shape to subconsciously. Or we may embrace such an interpretation with very little awareness of what we are doing, acting with only a kind of dumb sense that we are beginning to look at things differently. Second, there is the reflective reinterpretation that we work out when we remove ourselves from the action to see more carefully and critically what has been happening. We need to ask now how this distinction between active and reflective reinterpretation relates to freedom.

The principal difference between the two forms of reinterpretation concerns our ability to correct distortions in our reasoning and narrowness in our attitude. When we are transacting with others, our thinking is often creative but tends to embody our prejudices, our provincialisms, our rationalizations. When we are reflecting on our transactions, we are better positioned to use what discipline and skill we have achieved in overcoming such distortions. But there is no sharp line separating the two; critical habits of mind developed in reflection may carry over into some of our transacting, and reflection is never completely free from bias and the rest. Furthermore, when we are actively reinterpreting a situation, we are to a degree transcending that situation. Whenever we reason about a situation, we represent it to ourselves and in *re*-presenting it, we transcend it. We are not swallowed up in its immediacy.

If we wish to emphasize our responsibility for what we do, if we wish to highlight the element of distance that reasoning may place between ourselves and the causal forces operating in our situation, we will take the act of reinterpretation, regardless of whether it is active or reflective, as the key element in our freedom. But if we wish to stress the difference between reinterpretations which are grounded in our own reasoning powers and experience and those which we allow to be imposed on us through the expectations and demands of others, then we will take reflective reinterpretation as our paradigm of freedom and see in active reinterpretation only a more rudimentary form of freedom. In reflection, we are better positioned to overcome any bias by which we favor someone else's judgment over our own in deciding whom we shall become. Since our concern in this book is with experiential learning that is functional, especially in the sense of deepening our autonomy, we shall be thinking of freedom in terms of our powers to reinterpret reflectively. We shall think of autonomy as directing our lives on the basis of reflective reason and of our own experience.

Our account of the interrelations between response learning, situation learning, and freedom carries the danger that we may seem to be separating what should only be distinguished. When we speak of our environment controlling our behavior, we may seem to be leaving out of account that our behavior is the action of ourselves as whole persons whose behavior is shaped as much by our interpretation as by the reaction to it by persons and things in our situations. Whether we find a response to what we do desirable or undesirable will depend on the meaning we give to that response, the place it has in the kind of life style we are seeking to enact. It is important for us to bear in mind that we adopt an interpretation only when we embody it in our behavior. Thinking is a part of acting; we act with a sense of the meaning of what we are doing; we act as whole persons.

In situation learning, we break up the flow of experience by applying various concepts or categories of understanding to it, turning it into a sequence of situations. Being placed in the box is a change of situation for the pigeon, for example. Because we organize experience in terms of situations, we are able to learn specific responses for each specific type of situation. We learn those responses that are inherently rewarding or lead to consequences that we desire, and what we desire depends on how we see the situation. We may work hard in a course in literature, for example, because we either enjoy it, or want the reward of a high grade and praise, or are fearful of failing the course.

The way we look at one situation, however, tends to affect the way we look at others. This is sometimes called *transfer of learning* or *generalization*. Because we generalize, we develop a dominant outlook on life. We become basically passive or assertive, dependent or responsible, cowardly or courageous, careless or careful, and so on. These things define what we call our character. It is by situation learning and the response learning it leads to that we develop and change our character structure.

A psychotherapist, for example, aims to facilitate situation learning in his client. Commonly, his client will see his basic situation in terms of dependency on another. He may not think of it as dependency, but he frequently aims at outcomes to which that term properly applies. He sees responses as meaningful only if they appear to have some likelihood of maintaining or fostering his dependency. Of the alternative responses which he tries, he retains those that achieve the desired response from one upon whom he depends, e.g., instructions on what to do or believe, monetary support, or the like. The therapist will seek to encourage and facilitate a reinterpretation by his client of his situation, a change in interpretation from dependency to autonomy. As the client learns to see his situation in this new way, it becomes, in effect, a new situation, and a new set of possible responses now begin to appear as viable alternatives, namely, those which, among other things, seek values that are self-chosen. Those alternatives would not have seemed viable from his old, dependency point of view. Asked about one of them, he might well have said, "Oh, I couldn't do that."

To use the terms of transactional analysis, the client learns to interpret the situation from the point of view of his adult self rather than interpreting it from that of his adapted child self. The ways we learned to interpret situations when we were children stay with us, alongside the interpretations we learn on the basis of the information and experience we have as adults. While our childhood understandings and responses may be quite useful to us, say, when we want to have fun or to be imaginative about something, they create problems if we use them in situations calling for adult judgment.

Often we are not very much aware of the ways we interpret many of the situations which comprise our lives. We've gradually developed them in the process of transacting with our world, and we may never have stepped back away from some of these involvements to look carefully at our interpretations and to say to ourselves just what they are. Raising our consciousness about them is often an important step in changing them, for we often discover that these ways we've been looking at things have been causing us needless difficulties.

To facilitate situation learning in their patients, Bateson indicates that therapists may attempt:

(1) To achieve a confrontation between the premises of the patient and those of the therapist—who is carefully trained not to fall into the trap of validating the old premises;

(2) To get the patient to act, either in the therapy room or outside, in ways which will confront his own premises;

(3) To demonstrate contradiction among the premises which currently control the patient's behavior;

(4) To induce in the patient some *exaggeration or caricature* (e.g., in dream or hypnosis) of experience based on his old premises.[7]

Of these ways of raising consciousness, that in which we become aware of a viable set of premises that contrast with our own is fundamental. The others, in fact, are successful only if they lead to this. *Contrast*, we may say, is a key to situation learning. We become conscious only of those things which we contrast with something else. A highly intelligent fish would not know it was submerged in water until it leaped above the surface and gained the contrasting experience of being in the air. If we lived in an all-green world, we would not know it until another color came into being. All meaning, in fact, depends on contrast. "My little dog has fleas" conveys meaning because in place of each word at least one with a contrasting meaning could be used: "your" in place of "my," "big" in place of "little," "cat" in place of "dog," "had" or "hates" in place of "has," and "mange" in place of "fleas." The richness of our experience depends on the number of contrasts and, so, on the number of meanings we use in interpreting it. We add much to the quality of our experience by knowledge of cultures different than our own, of persons different from ourselves, of modes of consciousness other than the everyday, of philosophies contrasting with ours. These may be important considerations in selecting a learning situation.

Because all meaning depends on contrast, all learning depends on the possibility of error. We learn only when we select from alternatives and the selection makes a significant difference to us. Unaware of alternatives we may feel trapped by a situation, an emotion, a way of life. Becoming aware of contrasting possibilities, we expand our freedom.

Since all meaning depends on contrast, it is also true that any meaningful interpretation of a situation contains the seeds of one or more contrasting interpretations. If, for example, we see our basic situation in terms of dependency on another, the status of the other as one who can be leaned on in this way is also part of the situation and, so, represents the possibility of another perspective on it. There is also present in this situation a side of us that, if we activate it, will develop this alternative perspective represented by the other and may also transmute it into yet another perspective. This part of us seeks autonomy and will see being depended upon as a step closer to autonomy than is being dependent. But from this part of ourselves, we may also see there is something dependent about needing to be depended upon in this way, and so we may transmute being depended upon into responsible freedom—the ability to be responsive to the genuine rather than the neurotic needs of another.

Perhaps you noticed that in talking of the patient's interpretation of his situation, Bateson spoke of the patient's premises. Our interpretations are usually complex and involve many inter-related concepts (sometimes the relation is one of conflict). Seldom are we in the extremely simplified situation of the pigeon in the experimental box, for whom the factors of hunger and food define the essence of the situation (pigeons are seldom in so simplified a situation either). None of the concepts we use, in fact, can be grasped apart from their interrelations with other concepts. To understand "freedom," we must understand its relation to "choice," "responsibility," "limit," "order," and all the many other concepts that we may also use in situations where freedom is involved. We can see from this that if we enlarge our understanding of one of these concepts, our understanding of "freedom" will also be enlarged. Similarly, each premise in our interpretation of a situation is interrelated with each of the other premises involved, so that as we modify one we affect the meaning of each of the others. As children, our interpretation of our family situation may have included the premises, "father and mother care for me as a person" and "father and mother will always set limits for my

behavior so that I will be safe and be able to handle whatever I am doing." Later, as we move into young adulthood, the second premise
may be replaced by "father and mother expect me to be fully responsible for my own behavior." This change, in turn, will affect the
meaning of the care we believe our parents have for us. Most situation learning, in fact, takes the form of a modification of our interpretation of a situation rather than a basic change of interpretation,
the latter generally occurring as part of one of those dramatic turning
points that punctuate the chapters of our life stories.

Whether situation learning involves an evolution or a revolution in
our understanding will depend on which premise among those constituting our way of seeing a situation is being changed. One or two
will generally be quite basic so that to change them will mean a basic
change in our whole way of seeing.

Just as the meaning that a situation has for us is a configuration of
the meanings expressed by the various premises involved, the
various behaviors that we learn for a given situation are interrelated.
As we alter or replace one of our ways of acting, we find that this af-
fects our other ways. Perhaps we replace a passive, placating
behavior with an active, assertive one; instead of remaining silent
when our roommate plays the radio while we are trying to study, we
now ask him if he would play it in another room or at a later time, explaining that we find it difficult to concentrate. We may later find
ourselves listening more attentively as our roommate shares experiences he has had during the day.

We have been examining the sense in which response learning
presupposes another sort of learning that we are calling situation learning. To *distinguish* these two sorts of learning, however, is not
necessarily to see them as separate. Certainly they need not occur as
separate events. Implicit in every response is an interpretation of the
response situation, and every interpretation involves a set of possible
responses. As Allen Wheelis has put it, "A young man who learns to
drive a car thinks differently thereby, feels differently; when he meets
a pretty girl who lives fifty miles away, the encounter carries implications he could not have felt as a bus rider."[9] It may be simply that we
are influenced by someone to take on behavior similar to his. In so doing, we may be learning both new responses and a new interpretation
simultaneously. Or we may be influenced by a new interpretation
simply through reading or talking about it, yet not understand it very
well until we begin to act on it.

Then again, we may change some of our transactions in a situation
in a way that tests our interpretation of it. Perhaps we feel that one
pattern in the way we transact with a friend is the nub of a certain
feeling of dissatisfaction with the relationship. We agree with our

friend to behave differently toward one another in this respect and, as
we do so, we find this was really only symptomatic of the basic problem, which lies in another area of our transactions. Here a change of
behavior has changed our interpretation of the situation.

Transsituation Learning

Some people are better able to examine and modify their situation
interpretations than others. With the help of a therapist, someone
may drastically reinterpret his basic situation yet may not have learned to do this on his own. To learn how *to change* our interpretation of
a situation is what we are calling transsituation learning.

Improving our ability to examine and change our interpretations involves both developing the needed skills and deepening our
understanding of what it means to create interpretations. In this process, we interpret our acts of interpretation, we reflect on our powers
of reflection. Through transsituation learning, we gain a sense of
ourselves beyond our interpretations. We live more fully our
autonomy, grasping more firmly our responsibility for ourselves,
understanding more clearly and movingly the meaning of our
humanity, tapping more deeply the resources of our courage to cope
with all that is threatening. Getting in touch with our powers to form
our interpretations, we strengthen the power that lies deeper than
powerlessness.

If we are able to interpret a situation in only one way, then we are in
bondage to that interpretation. But if we are able to create and choose
between alternative interpretations, then we are capable of autonomy
in a fuller sense than in our earlier use of the term. We are able to be
responsible not only for our actions but for the interpretations or meanings on which these actions rest. As we shall consider at a later point,
a key factor in such autonomy of interpretation is the ability to ask
questions of our experience in such a way that alternative understandings are created.

The bondage to one interpretation, which is part of not having
learned to create and choose between alternative interpretations, not
only blocks all autonomy but prevents us from understanding the
point of view of another. To enter into the way another sees a situation, we obviously must be able for the moment to let go of our own
interpretation.

Transsituation learning makes use of the many sorts of understanding that our culture makes available to us. Our natural language includes an enormous variety of concepts, many of which have great in-
terpretative power. The overly dependent person may not use the

concept of autonomy in his perceiving, thinking, feeling and acting, but it is part of our culture and so is available for his use (under the right learning conditions).

Transcendent Learning

From time to time, however, someone modifies one or more of the available concepts or creates relatively new ones, thereby providing new possibilities—new tools—for interpreting individual situations. We are calling the *development* of this ability *transcendent learning*. Einstein modified the Newtonian concept of simultaneity. Second Isaiah, the *Old Testament* prophet, created his concept of the suffering servant, Freud his of the unconscious, Marx his of surplus labor, Tillich his of ultimate concern, Skinner his of reinforcement, Maslow his of *being* values. Interpretations of particular situations rest on these more basic creations in much the sense that particular paintings of a certain style, say, expressionistic, rest on the more basic creation which first brought that style into being.

Since concepts are tools for social transactions, the creation of new concepts is brought to a successful completion only when they become part of the transactions of one or more groups. Transactions are effective only when those involved interpret the situation in fairly similar ways. Visiting a culture that we know little about may present many difficulties, because we do not understand how others see a situation.

Whether or not we develop the ability to create at this fundatmental level, we can all develop the ability to understand these acts of creation. We can come to see that human creativity touches those structures of meaning which make it possible for us to become persons and to transact with others. When we do this, we gain a new sense of the meaning of being human. We see another side of the relativity of our categories, and this may deepen our sense of the flow of experience and of the fuller reality our categories fail to express. The more we understand that our concepts are not absolute, not somehow given in the very nature of things, the more we can be receptive to the perspective of others and be accepting of change.[10] We can live more fully the conviction that we have not been made for the law, but the law for us.

Above all, it is through creativity that we have power to be a person. We must organize our experience in ways that enable us to make a significant differrence in our life-situations. These acts of creation give unique expression to our selves and are the means by which we can struggle against all that threatens our personal existence. Through the courage they make possible, we can face anxiety about our being and not be crippled by it. In living creatively, we find a courage and a power that takes us beyond powerlessness.

APPLYING THE MODEL

We turn now to consider the specific needs of those who are preparing for a project of experiential learning as part of their formal education process. In light of our model of four kinds of learning, what considerations may help in selecting and effectively utilizing a learning situation?

Our model may help us to learn more effectively in several ways. First of all, distinguishing these four kinds of learning enables us to ask what sort of learning we are seeking from our experience. Getting clear about this can contribute importantly to our success in learning. Second, we can ask what conditions and skills are necessary to each type of learning and then work to create them. Notice that each type of learning is a type of change, and change takes place only under certain conditions.[11] Third, in seeking to learn more effectively, we can develop understanding and skills which will serve our learning needs in the future as well as in the present. Life has always required continued learning, because the individual must cope with the new demands and opportunities of the successive stages of life. Living in a time when change becomes more and more rapid places an even greater premium on the ability to learn.

What this all adds up to is that we can become more autonomous in our learning and in conducting our lives. The more we understand how we learn from experience, the more responsibility we can assume for that learning. We can seek to modify or simply cut loose from situations which tend to distort or needlessly limit our learning. We can select, or even design, more helpful learning experiences. Above all, as we become better situation learners, we have more choice about what we want life to mean for us.

Our effectiveness in learning from experience will involve how we *prepare*, the *conditions* we encounter, and how we later assess or otherwise *reflect* on what we've learned. First of all, then, as we prepare for our experiential learning, it may be helpful to reflect on our learning needs. Because each of us is unique and because the manner in which each of our lives is unfolding is unique, each of us will have somewhat different learning needs and opportunities in the present. We may think of life as a series of stages or situations that we go through. The sort of learning we most need while we are in a given stage will differ from the sort we most need in a time of transition to a new stage.

Transition to a new stage involves a change of interpretation of our situation. The way we looked at our previous situation was developed to cope with certain factors basic to that situation. In a time of transition, we are facing a new set of factors and our old perspective simply won't do. What we most need in such a time is situation learning, with its emphasis upon the reflection on experience.

As we gradually enter a new stage and begin to see things in a new way, we especially need to develop a set of responses by which we put that new perspective into action and, in acting on it, come more fully to understand it and develop it. Here we seek to learn the connections between situation, action, and consequences. Any interpretation remains incomplete until we develop all the responses or ways of acting needed to apply it to the full range of circumstances comprising our situation. In the process, we will add new premises to our way of looking at things and drop or modify some of our original ones. Failure to develop an interpretation in a way that becomes adequate to the full range of needs and opportunities inherent in our present stage leaves us with unfinished business and interferes with our transition to and development of our next stage.

Those who have not yet given careful attention to this idea of stages will probably find it helpful to spend some time on this. One of the more influential treatments is that of Erick Erickson.[12] According to Erickson, "anything that grows has a *ground plan*, and . . . out of this ground plan the *parts* arise, each part having its *time* of special ascendancy until all the parts have arisen to form a *functioning whole*."[13] The first part of a healthy personality the human being must focus on developing is a sense of basic trust in himself and others, one that will outweigh the sense of mistrust that develops from disappointments, frustrations, and the like so that he or she can be reasonably relaxed and outgoing toward the world. The conviction that develops in this stage is, "I am what I am given."

In the next stage, the need is to develop a basic sense of autonomy in the face of experiences which lead to feelings of shame and doubt about oneself. The child seeks to develop some command over himself so that he has some choice about what he does and what happens to him. To accomplish this, he needs to have developed enough trust in his world to feel confident that insisting on having a choice will not make his world untrustworthy. His conviction in this stage is "I am what I will."

Having developed a sense of being a person with a will of his own, the child must next concern himself with what sort of person he will be. "I am what I can imagine I will be." He seeks a sense of unbroken initiative on which to develop ambitions and independence.

Subsequent stages focus on industry (a need to learn how to do things), identity ("the accrued confidence that one's ability to maintain inner sameness and continuity . . . is matched by the sameness and continuity of one's meaning for others"[14]), intimacy, generativity ("the interest in establishing and guiding the next generation)"[15], and integrity ("the acceptance of one's own and only life cycle and of the people who have become significant to it as something that had to be"[16]). Our learning needs will vary, then, in part according to the stage we are in. It may be helpful to consider this in planning our learning experiences.

Secondly, in addition to how we prepare, our effectiveness in learning from experience will involve the conditions we encounter. All of us probably have areas in our lives in which we feel inept, uncomfortable—even fearful or anxious. Very often this is because our early learning experiences in these areas were painful. Similarly, we come to feel competent, comfortable—even enthusiastic—in areas where our initial learning has been pleasurable. In selecting a learning situation, then, it will be helpful to consider whether its conditions will facilitate functional learning.

Foremost among conditions that encourage and support functional learning are those which we find supportive and validating. Carl Rogers, for example, has long maintained that for our personal growth it is necessary to be understood and valued by persons who also relate to us in a genuine way. Such relationships become sources of the courage that is often vital to productive learning. When we feel misunderstood, manipulated, discounted, our learning is apt to be dysfunctional. We may learn premises and responses which distort our perception of ourselves and our world, lead to hurtful consequences for ourselves and others, and undermine our ability for constructive learning. When this happens, functional learning in these areas will be blocked until we begin to unlearn these dysfunctional lessons. We often find it difficult to unlearn such things, because they are usually accompanied by feelings of threat or inadequacy that were part of what we learned. In such cases, a supportive environment is especially important. Sometimes we may need the conditions and guidance of professional therapy. More often, we require simply the conditions found in any supportive, healthy adult relationship.

A set of such supportive, validating relationships may be thought of as an informal learning community, and we shall give attention to learning to enlarge and maintain this sort of network of friendships and intimacies. Obviously, this has important implications for how we interact in our college classes and similar groups. Even rather limited relationships may embody or contradict the conditions which facilitate functional learning.

The informal learning communities that seem typical in our culture involve many dysfunctional conditions. For example, game playing of the sort described by Eric Berne in *Games People Play*[17] contributes to dysfunctional learning and seems to be very widespread in our transactions. If our transactions in one or more groups can help us unlearn some of these dysfunctional behaviors and learn others which are functional, this will be a major contribution to our ability to learn from experience.

When we select a learning situation, there are two sets of factors for us to consider. First, in what ways will the situation encourage and support functional learning, and in what ways will the opposite be true? Second, what opportunities for learning and what limitations to learning does the situation present?

Considering first the question of functional or dysfunctional learning, if we are enjoying validating relationships elsewhere, we may be able to override the effects of negative relationships within the learning situation. But it is not only the quality of our personal transactions that may lead to dysfunctional learning. Suppose we are thinking about an apprenticeship in a primary or secondary school. What are we likely to find? The prevailing interpretation of the school situation by a great many teachers and administrators will involve as a major premise a belief that students are the enemy. Another likely premise is that the authority conferred by one's status in the institution is by far the most important factor in any transaction and that the formal channels of communication and decision making are rigidly to be adhered to in all matters, large and small. Many will judge that a situation of this sort in which one is transacting with persons who are perceiving and acting within the framework of interpretation just suggested will strongly encourage and support dysfunctional learning. Whether this is the sort of learning that results will, of course, depend in part on what we bring to this situation in the way of maturity, personal autonomy, conceptual theoretical preparation, participation in an informal learning community, utilization of a course in experiential learning, and so on.

Second, there are the opportunities for and limitations to learning contained in the situation. How these will affect us, of course, will differ from person to person, depending on background, ability, interest, and the like. What each of us can learn in a given situation is different from what any other would learn. The more we know about ourselves—our learning needs, abilities and vulnerabilities—the better able we are to determine the learning conditions best suited to us. Do we learn best independently or in dialogue with others? Are we easily threatened by authority? Do we need to work with one thing at a time, or are we comfortable with and stimulated by complexity and surprise? Do we rely more on what we see or on what we hear or feel to understand a situation? Has our work in academic disciplines given us perspectives which may be useful in opening up new learnings concerning institutions, behavior problems, stages in living, or other areas of potential learning?[18]

In view of our differing learning needs, some of us may select a learning situation conducive to conceiving and trying out new responses, while others of us may seek conditions which will help us to generate and explore new ways of seeing ourselves and our world or to modify some of our present ways of seeing. Generally, this difference will be a matter of emphasis, since response and situation learning are so intertwined. Assertiveness training and sensitivity training provide clear examples of this interrelatedness. Some may wish to reflect on the learning portrayed by Hermann Hesse's *Siddhartha*, which involves a revolution in perspective and provides a profound contrast to our Western ways of seeing.

You may have noticed that our use of the term "situation" has taken on both a broad and a narrow sense. In its broad sense, it refers to our existential or life situation. The interpretation involved is what we often call our philosophy of life—the overall *meaning* we see our lives to have.

In its narrow sense, it refers to a specific set of circumstances which take on significance in terms of certain goals or *values* involved. In one circumstance, the value of intimacy will be foremost in our minds; in another, our concern for justice; in another, our need for recreation; and so on. The way we live our philosophy of life may be thought of as our style of life. The way we transact in each of our specific, everyday situations will reflect our overall life style, and changes in this life style will generally be initiated by marked changes in our way of seeing and responding to one or two specific situations.

Thirdly, our effectiveness in learning from experience will involve not only how we prepare and the conditions we encounter but also how we later reflect on it. By "*reflection*," we mean the process of interpreting our experience. Even as we are undergoing our experience, we are giving it some sort of interpretation. John Wild has called this *primary thinking*.[19] From time to time, we remove ourselves from the action to reflect more carefully and clearly on what has been happening. This Wild has termed secondary reflection. T. S Eliot suggested that experience is like a partially developed role of film. By secondary reflection, we develop the film more fully. Changing the metaphor, through the primary thinking carried on as we transact with our world, we may sow the seeds of greater clarity, enrichment, or alternatives in our ways of seeing and understanding. Secondary reflection helps us to bring these beginnings to fruition and to clear the way for further beginnings.

But primary thinking also embodies our prejudices and other dysfunctional premises. They become self-fulfilling prophecies as we experience what we expect to experience. Our biases and other distortions are part of the lenses through which we see ourselves and our world. Consequently, our secondary reflection has an important critical function. We need it to cleanse the lenses of experience, to correct the partialities, the distortions, the hasty generalizations that render our learning dysfunctional.

More than a few persons in our time have turned away from developing their powers of reflective reasoning because they are suspicious of reasoning in any form. They fail to see that without reason we not only would have no freedom but would not be human at all. We can all too easily think of reasoning as acting like calculating machines. We often see it used for manipulation and dominance. We know how easily reflective reasoning can fall into a game of detachment from life when we do not keep it closely related to our primary thinking. Even autonomy itself may be confused with a life style in which one acts without regard for others. But without reason in its larger sense, we would not be able to regard others at all. Without reason we could not know another, and without knowledge there could be no intimacy. It is only by reason that we grasp meanings and understand ourselves and others. This means that it is only by reason that we are able to love, make commitments, strive for justice, create culture. Reflective reason is our only tool for keeping ourselves honest and relatively free of distortion in even the most personal aspects of our lives. At a later point, we shall argue that reason is even at the heart of our emotions.

Also at a later point, we shall consider keeping a journal as one of the more helpful means of reflecting on our experience. We will, further, examine the skills basic to secondary reflection and how they may be improved. Obviously, college courses can be a major resource in improving our powers of reflective reason.

SUMMARY: KINDS OF EXPERIENTIAL LEARNING

We have been considering four different levels of change that take place, either separately or in combination, when we learn. We engage in the first two, response learning and situation learning, when we are transacting with our environment. We learn the behaviors that our environment rewards and, by primary thinking, we learn to look at ourselves and our environment in a certain way. Situation learning may also take the form of secondary reflection, in which we examine the way we interpret our environment and create alternative interpretations. We undergo the second two levels of change, transsituation learning and transcendent learning, when we disengage ourselves from our transactions and examine our processes of interpreting these transactions, thereby changing our ability to interpret.

We may think of these kinds of changes as different levels of change, because each creates opportunities for change in the level immediately below it. For example, when we reinterpret a relationship, bringing to it a desire for autonomy instead of a desire for dependency, it becomes possible for us to learn a whole new set of behaviors, namely, those which constitute being an autonomous person. We can display these relationships between levels of change in the following way:

(1) Transcendent learning = change in ability to do transsituation learning (i.e., change in creativity)
(2) Transsituation learning = change in ability to do situation learning (i.e., change in autonomy)
(3) Situation learning = change in ability to do response learning (i.e., change in interpretation)
(4) Response learning = change in repertoire of behavior

We are what we do, and so it is in response learning that we become what we are. We are free when we are able to change in self-chosen ways, and it is in situation learning that we create alternatives to choose between. Alternative ways of looking at our lives open up the opportunity of learning alternative behaviors. We increase our autonomy when we deepen our understanding of situation learning and develop its skills, and so it is in transsituation learning and transcendent learning that we enlarge our capacity to lead self-chosen lives. Each level of learning, then, contributes importantly to our freedom. We are free only if our values are self-chosen, but that freedom would be a poor thing if we were ineffective in realizing our values. At the same time, we are fully responsible for our choices only if through transsituation learning we come to know what we are doing in making them. Our lives are self-chosen only when they are grounded in self-awareness. In concluding, we may round out our delineation of experiential learning as follows: *Experiential learning occurs when direct interaction with our world or ourselves results in a change in behaviour, interpretation, autonomy, or creativity.*

CHAPTER THREE

Mapping Experience

Much learning is primarily a change in our behavior. Much of it, too, is primarily a change in our understanding of the situation within which that behavior takes place. But each of these types of change finally involves the other. We develop our sense of each situation and of the world as a whole as we transact with it. We come to know our world as providing and limiting possibilities for our action and experience, supporting and resisting our efforts, validating and invalidating our worth. We find it seeking and fearing our presence, inflicting pain and giving pleasure, calling, sometimes articulately, often mutedly, for our affirmation. These are the things we learn as we add to or modify our repertoire of behavior, create and recreate our beliefs and evaluations. We turn now to consider how we formulate and test these beliefs and evaluations.

All learning is finally from experience. The experience may be our own, or it may be that of others. We begin life, as William James put it, in a world of blooming, buzzing confusion. Gradually we get things organized and experience becomes communication. Mother sounds happy, brother looks angry, sun feels warm, candy tastes good, toe hurts—in the messages come.

We continue the work of organization, sorting out these communications, ignoring some, drawing lessons from others, storing these lessons to guide our future behavior, thought, and enjoyment. Our use of these lessons settles into fixed routine. We think and feel and act—and even see and hear—out of habit, relying again and again on what has worked for us or given us pleasure and meaning in the past.

But the routine has its frontier, the growing edge of our sense of who we are, what we can do, and what sort of world we live in. This may be a narrow, anxiously limited frontier or a broad, courageously expansive one. But to some extent we continue throughout our lives to learn from our experience.

There are three skills which we develop and use in formulating these lessons from experience: *generalization, selection* and *interpretation*. In generalization we seek out recurrent patterns in our experience. As we discover regularities in our world and develop them in ourselves we are more and more able to anticipate the future. Billiard balls always "behave" in the same way. People very often do. Three times John promises something and each time he does what he promised. We generalize that John keeps his promises. At the same time, we realize that for John, as for anyone, there will be exceptions to this, times when he is unable to or when he gives precedence to something of greater importance. All reasoning about the future on the basis of past experience involves generalization.

A second skill by which we formulate lessons from our experience is selection. Of all the things to which we could give our attention at any given moment we select a few upon which to focus. Absorbed in thought, we don't hear the conversation around us. Looking at the magician's right hand, we don't notice what his left hand is doing. This ability serves us well in reducing our conscious experience to something manageable. We simply can't deal with everything in our experience and so we constrict the scope of our concern and interest. Some people note subtle features of interactions in an organization. Others capture nuances of life in the desert. Still others attend to fine discriminations concerning snow. In learning from our involvements, we abstract from the incredibly rich manifold of experience.

The third ability we use in organizing and recording the messages of our experience is interpretation. When we interpret, we see connections between things, pulling them together into a meaningful pattern, and we assess their value or disvalue for us. We record our way of seeing such things in terms of spatial and temporal relations, what things cause other things to happen, the kinds of purposes that give shape and meaning to our human life and the means available to pursue those purposes.

By these processes of generalizing, selecting, and interpreting we gradually create and recreate a complex set of beliefs, knowledge, and evaluations of ourselves and our world and our interrelations with it. We bring these beliefs and evaluations together in a way that gives us an overall picture or image or map[1] of the many situations that comprise our lives. The term *map* suggests the practical nature of our beliefs. We may find enjoyment or security in simply holding them or in reflecting on them; but if they are genuine, we use them fundamentally as guides to the future. They locate us in our world in such a way that we can anticipate what will happen under certain conditions. If our beliefs are true, then what they lead us to expect concerning the future is what really happens. True beliefs are reliable guides concerning the future. Conversely, false beliefs are unreliable guides. What we anticipated is not what happens. Our map needs to be corrected.

A true belief, then, functions as a reliable guide concerning what, under certain conditions, we will experience. Suppose I say, ''The battery in your car is dead.'' If you believe me, how will this affect your anticipation of your future experience? Obviously, on the condition that you get into your car and turn the key to activate the starter, you will expect that the engine will not turn over. You will also expect that the radio will not play when you turn it on, the cigarette lighter wil not work when you push it in, and the lights will not go on when you pull the light switch. Then, too, on the condition that you charge the battery, all these anticipations will be reversed: the engine will turn over, the radio will play, and so on. If what I have said is true, these anticipations are reliable. But if, when you turn the key, the engine does turn over or the radio does play, then you know that what I said to you was false; it involved unreliable anticipations of future events.

These maps by which we live involve knowledge as well as belief. Those parts of a map which are so well established that it would be unreasonable not to place our full confidence in them are things which we don't just believe but know. Our knowledge is not only a reliable guide, but we have such good evidence for it that we are sure it is reliable before we act on it.

Our beliefs, however, we hold only with some degree of probability. We cannot be entirely sure that they are true or, in other words, reliable. A certain amount of risk is involved in acting on them, but the way life is it often makes sense to act on them anyway. We wouldn't be able to do very much if we didn't.

There are three basic components, then, to our system of belief, knowledge, and evaluation: the *map*, the *anticipation*, and the *experience*. As we learn from experience, we either correct our map or add to it.

An important characteristic of our map is that the beliefs it formulates are not particular but general. They are not about an event at a particular moment in time but about events of that type. The illustration we used in discussing the practical nature of belief was a particular belief about a dead battery. But it would mean nothing to us to be told that the battery in our car is dead unless we already held some sort of general belief about the way batteries function in cars. It is this general belief that is part of our map of our world and enables us to chart the meaning of the information that our battery is dead. We can represent this by the following diagram:[2]

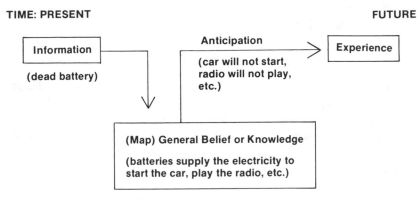

Figure 1

Given some general knowledge about batteries, the information (particular belief) that our battery is dead carries with it the anticipation that we will not be able to start the car, play the radio, turn on the lights, and so on. If that is what, in fact, happens, it supports the truth of the information and it also further confirms the reliability of this part of our map.

In our earlier discussion of types of learning, we referred to response learning and situation learning. Situation learning changes our map of general beliefs. At times response learning also does this. We also referred to transsituation learning and transcendent learning. These create and make changes in a map about our map. We may call this a *transcendence-map*. Our present discussion presents just such a transcendence-map.

Each of our general beliefs is based on either our own experience or what we learn from others, or a mixture of the two. The reliability of our map will depend on the adequacy of its basis. It will help us to bear this in mind if we add it to our diagram. (See Figure 2.) To most of us, the basis for our general belief about the function of car batteries will be a number of experiences with dead batteries, together with some things we have been taught about electricity, the way batteries generate it, and the way cars use it. Each experience we have with dead batteries either strengthens or weakens the basis for our general belief about them.

When we apply one of our general beliefs to a particular situation, there are usually a number of things we must take into account in using it to anticipate the future. If the battery is dead, our car will not start *unless* we get hooked up to the battery of another car. If John

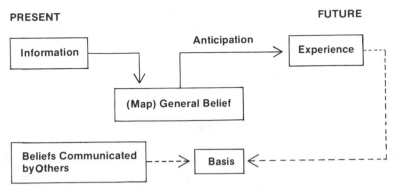

Figure 2

promised to come over, he will be there unless he is physically unable to or a matter of overriding concern comes up. We apply our beliefs, then, with certain qualifications. I *probably* won't be able to get my car started. John *almost certainly* will be there. Behind these qualifications are certain conditions which would make the present case an exception to what usually happens. Adding this to our diagram, we get the model in Figure 3.

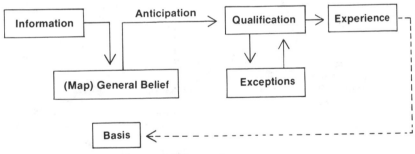

Figure 3

What we are calling "information" may be about a present event (or state of affairs), a past event or a future event. Our illustrations have concerned present states of affairs: our battery is dead, John has promised to come (the promise is in force at the present time). Believing something to be true of the present, we are concerned to anticipate the future.

Sometimes, though, we seek not to anticipate the future but to understand the present by obtaining information about the past which led up to it. We are looking for information about the past which will explain the present. This is anticipation in reverse: what, if it had happened, would have led us, if we had known about it, to anticipate the present state of affairs.[3] In terms of our diagram the situation can be seen in Figure 4.

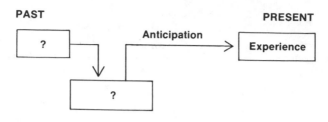

Figure 4

John has not come. Perhaps he has had car trouble, or an accident or been required to work late. One of these possibilities may seem more likely than the others, and we may very tentatively adopt it until we have more information. Our diagram now looks like Figure 5.

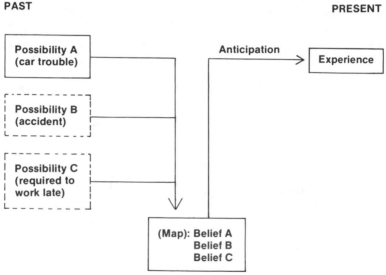

Figure 5

We formulate such hypotheses to enable us to relate the present to parts of our map that will let us see the fuller meaning of our situation and possibilities for responding to it. Our map provides us with ways of dealing with ourselves and our world. When, on occasion, what happens contradicts our anticipations, we don't know how to respond to it, and so we look for the explanation which will enable us to respond. John calls and needs our help. Now we know what to do. Martha explains why she is so excited, and then we know how to react.

Obviously our ability to understand is limited to what can be charted on our map. As our map changes through what we have called situation learning, our ability to understand changes. We can understand a medical explanation only if the necessary medical knowledge is included on our map. We can understand an explanation given by someone from another culture only if we grasp the beliefs of that culture on which the explanation is based.

At still other times, we are concerned to anticipate the outcome of events which may take place in the future. For example, we may be trying to decide between several courses of action. We try to anticipate the likely outcome of each so that we may select the most desirable one. Our reasoning is hypothetical. If I do A, then B is the likely result; but if I do C, then D is likely. Our diagram becomes Figure 6.

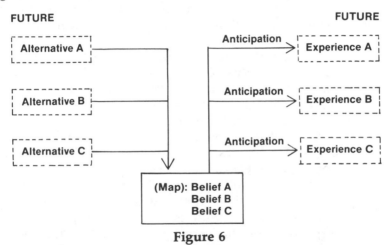

Figure 6

The importance of reliable maps for getting on in the world is evident. We can make decisions and act purposefully only because we can anticipate with some confidence the likely outcomes of our behavior. Then, too, it is in knowing persons and things that we make contact with them. If we do not know the other, we are really isolated from her. David Reisman writes of the lonely crowd. We are most fully in touch with another when our knowledge of her is brought together with a moment of direct experience of her—a moment when we see-hear-touch-feel.

We began our consideration of maps by characterizing them as complex sets of beliefs, knowledge and evaluations of ourselves and our world and our interrelations with it. But our discussion has focused on beliefs and knowledge, and we must now turn to consider evaluations. Facts and values may be distinguished, but in the process of our everyday lives they are inseparable. As we interact with our world we do not first experience things, persons, events, or situations in a purely descriptive way and then add our judgment about their significance for us. Rather, we see everything which comprises our world in terms of our purposes and needs, our likes and dislikes. This pen, this room, this woman, this social gathering—we experience them all in light of their significance in our lives.

More specifically we see them in relation to our needs and wants such as those for survival, bonding, meaning, pleasure, and a sense of worth. This does not mean that we necessarily relate to any of them only or even primarily as a means to our survival or enjoyment or enhancement. Indeed pleasure, fulfillment or a sense of worth are often better realized as a by-product of our pursuit of other goals than in being aimed at directly. But even when these things are not our immediate concern they are in the background of our experience and constitute the basis of something's or someone's value for us.

Aaron Beck thinks of these evaluations and beliefs by which we direct our lives as rules.[4] These rules have to do with either danger versus safety or pain versus pleasure. Danger and safety concern both physical and psychosocial harm. Psychosocial harm "covers the varieties of hurt feelings, humiliations, embarrassments, and sadness that occur after a person has been insulted, criticized, or rejected."[5] In other words, it refers to damage to our self-esteem or sense of worth. We use these rules to determine the likelihood and seriousness of the harm. For example, we might think: "it would be humiliating to fail in front of a group." This might be coupled with the judgment: "I am unable to speak adequately before a group." The risk felt in speaking to a group is the product of both the threat we believe is posed and our ability to cope with this threat. In the case we are considering, the sense of risk would be very high.

The basic test of these danger-safety rules is whether they avoid making us either overly cautious or reckless. As Paul Tillich has said, life requires a balance between fear and courage.

The pleasure-pain rules guide our efforts to achieve happiness or a sense of fulfillment or well-being. Some of these rules are intimately related to those governing psychological safety because our self-esteem is an important factor in our happiness. Happiness seems to be the sense that, in one way or another,[6] our lives are filled more with pleasurable than with painful states of mind or being, and self-esteem produces a pleasurable state of mind. One such pleasure-pain rule that is prevalent in our society is this: "To be happy, I must be accepted (liked, admired) by all people at all times." Another is: "It's wonderful to be popular, famous, wealthy; it's terrible to be unpopular, mediocre."[7]

The basic test of pleasure-pain rules is the extent to which they help or hinder us in achieving happiness or a sense of well-being. They may be unrealistic and so create a needless sense of failure and frustration. The belief that we need to be liked and admired by everyone is obviously unrealistic. Once we reflect on it we see that it's just not going to happen that way and that many people seem reasonably happy who aren't all that much liked. Pleasure-pain rules may also distract us from other sources of happiness and may interfere with other needs or desires that we are trying to meet. We may be so driven to achieve popularity or wealth that we damage our health or undermine our chance of achieving intimacy with others. These rules function properly when they enable us to maximize our happiness and sense of worth in ways consistent with the happiness and sense of worth of others.

It is on the basis of these "safety versus danger" and "pleasure versus pain" rules that we make those judgments that constitute the core of our emotions. We judge ourselves diminished by one thing, threatened by another, wronged by a third. Believing that we must be admired and liked by everyone we become angry or depressed when someone isn't responsive to us—angry if we see it as his fault, depressed if we see it as our own.

From all this we can see that mapping and testing our evaluations differs from mapping and testing our beliefs, although we must again remind ourselves that our evaluations and beliefs are complexly interrelated. The basic test of beliefs is *correspondence*: does what we experience correspond to what we anticipated on the basis of our belief? The basic test of evaluations is *pragmatic adequacy*: do they work in enabling us to achieve happiness and a sense of personal worth?[8] To emphasize this we thought of evaluations as formulated rules. Rules are not true or false but adequate or inadequate to the purposes they serve.[1] We test them by whether they avoid making us either overly cautious or reckless, are realistic, do not distract us from other sources of happiness, do not interfere with other needs and wants, and maximize our happiness and sense of worth in ways consistent with the well-being of others.

Because our interpretations involve complexly interrelated beliefs and evaluations, we cannot establish one way of looking at a situation as clearly superior to all others. But some interpretations are clearly less functional than others, so that skill in testing them is important to our well-being.

In addition to correspondence and pragmatic adequacy, we also test our interpretations by the criterion of *coherence*. On the one hand, we test their *internal* coherence: are the beliefs and evaluations which comprise an interpretation mutually consistent and meaningfully interrelated? Although oars appear bent when part of them are in the water, we reject this as illusory because it is inconsistent with most of our experiences of oars. John appears to have betrayed our friendship, but it will take a lot to convince us that this is true because it contradicts what we know of John from many years of shared activity and experience.

On the other hand, we test the *external* coherence of our interpretations, the way each is related to the others: are they mutually consistent and meaningfully interrelated? Only insofar as this is true do our situations come together to form one world and our character traits come together to form an integrated self. Recall, for example, Allen Wheelis's contention that the way we are in one area of our lives will tend gradually to permeate other areas as well.

We have been considering the system of beliefs and evaluations by which we orient ourselves to the world and anticipate the future. Changes in our beliefs and evaluations were examined in chapter one as situation learning. In that chapter we emphasized the intimate relation between situation learning and response learning, and we are now ready to relate response learning to the way we map our interpretations.

Our maps represent ourselves and our situation in terms of possibilities both for enjoying and being enjoyed and for acting and being acted on. If we think of a road map, the roads are ways we know how to act. They also represent the way we anticipate how someone or something in our situation will respond. They may represent, then, a possible action on our part together with an anticipated response by someone or something in our situation. Or they may represent a way a person or persons or some other part of our world may act toward us and a way we have of responding to that. The roads on our map are for two-way traffic. They represent our interactions or, as Eric Berne has insisted, our transactions. Things we know about ourselves and our world are generally related to actions we know how to take.

Our roads range from unpaved ones to super highways. Some are direct; others wind and twist; some are being planned; others are under construction; some are risky, others are not. When we open up a new road, we open up new possibilities for experience. As our behavior changes, our map does also.

There are two ways in which a change in behavior may change our map. New ways of acting may make possible new results and so open up new values. Perhaps skills necessary for a new job or career are learned and so the possibility of a new way of life with its unique set of values is opened up. But new ways of acting may also be experienced as valuable in and for themselves. They don't lead to something of value but are themselves valuable. Music takes on new meaning when we learn to dance to it. In this case, learning a new behavior is what we have called situation learning, a change in the meaning a situation has for us.

The new meaning that is created in learning how to dance is understood by us much less in terms of words than in terms of the experience of our physical movement. Our experience, then, is sometimes mapped in ways other than by words. We also map by means of sights, sounds, and feelings—the three main forms in which we receive sensory information about our world (and ourselves). John Grinder and Richard Bandler refer to these as visual, auditory and kinesthetic respectively.[10] Even though each of these forms of representation is available to all of us, we tend to use one much more than we do the others. We may orient ourselves primarily in terms of what we see rather than what we hear or feel. This will be reflected in our use of words by a tendency to use visual terms. Consider the following passage in a recent book:

> The concept of Contact can serve as a mirror in which you can see yourself and your encounters with others reflected distinctly, perhaps for the first time. Making thought and theory, feeling and behavior symbolically serve as mirrors is not an unusual endeavor. Whenever we illuminate with awareness an activity or phenomenon which has previously been habitual, automatic, or merely taken for granted, we give ourselves the opportunity to replace "overlooking' with "looking at." For example, just by realizing that most of our contacts with others open with a four-minute prelude, during which connections are made either successfully or not so successfully—just by realizing that fact we begin to "see it happen." In the fresh light of this new awareness, we can perceive our behavior with others as we interact, a mental process not unlike the reflected view of ourselves offered by a mirror.
>
> In this chapter I want to introduce some supplementary tools of perception, in this case useful for looking "into" ourselves—as through windows—for the purpose of self-assessment.

Such terms as *mirror, see, reflected, illuminate, overlooking, looking at, looking into,* and *windows* show clearly the writer's visual orientation. The book you are now reading also has a number of visual terms in it, such as *show* in the immediately preceding sentence.

If two people are using different sorts of maps or representational systems, communication may be difficult. With practice, we can learn to switch over to the same sort of map the other is using and significantly improve both our communication and sense of rapport. Grinder and Bandler give the following examples from a workshop for therapists:

> *Client* (visual): My husband just doesn't see me as a valuable person.
> *Therapist* (kinesthetic): How do you feel about that?
> *Client* (visual): What?
> *Therapist* (kinesthetic): How do you feel about your husband's not feeling that you're a person?
> *Client* (visual): That's a hard question. I just don't know.
> This session went around and around until the therapist came out and said to the authors, ''I *feel* frustrated; this woman is just trying to give me a *hard* time.'' . . . The authors took the therapist back into session and proceeded to elicit the following information.

The woman knew her husband didn't *see* her as valuable.

> *Therapist*: How do you know he doesn't see you as valuable?
> *Client*: I *dress up* for him and he doesn't *notice*. (The client is assuming her husband also has a visual model of the world, as she does.)
> *Therapist*: How do you know he doesn't notice?
> *Client*: He just paws me and doesn't even look. (He responds kinesthetically and doesn't stand back far enough to see.)[11]

The client was unable to respond about her experiences in kinesthetic terms but was readily able to ''cooperate'' when asked in visual terms. At the same time, she was unable to empathize with her husband, because he tended to use a kinesthetic map and so behaved accordingly, while she assumed that he used a visual map, just as she did. As Grinder and Bandler put it,

> Typically, kinesthetics complain that auditory and visual people are insensitive. Visuals complain that auditories don't pay attention to them because they don't make eye contact during the conversation. Auditory people complain that kinesthetics don't listen, etc.[12]

In the following chart (Table 1), the meaning the speaker wishes to convey is presented in the left hand column and the ways of expressing it in kinesthetic, visual, and auditory terms are given in the other three.[13]

Table 1. *Representational Meaning*

Meaning	Kinesthetic	Visual	Auditory
I (don't) understand you.	What you are saying feels (doesn't feel) right to me.	I see (don't see) what you are saying.	I hear (don't hear) you clearly.
I want to communicate something to you.	I want you to be in touch with something.	I want to show you something (a picture of something).	I want you to listen carefully to what I say to you.
Describe more of your present experience to me.	Put me in touch with what you are feeling at this point in time.	Show me a clear picture of what you see at this point in time.	Tell me in more detail what you are saying at this point in time.
I like my experience of you and me at this point in time.	This feels really good to me. I feel really good about what we are doing.	This looks really bright and clear to me.	This sounds really good to me.
Do you understand what I am saying?	Does what I am putting you in touch with feel right to you?	Do you see what I am showing you?	Does what I am saying to you sound right to you?

Not only do we have three representational systems in addition to that of our natural language, or natural languages if we are multilingual, but Marshall McLuhan has been emphasizing the importance for the way we receive information of the many extensions of our senses provided by technology. Television, radio, telephone, hi-fi sets, motion pictures, computers, drugs, and the like can powerfully affect the way we map our world.

Remembering that there are several types of maps may lead us to make fuller use of some we presently neglect. New forms of information about our world, new ways of orienting ourselves to it, will enhance our understanding.

Both our beliefs (or knowledge) and our evaluations, then, may be mapped in visual, auditory, or kinesthetic terms as well as by words. We may know the way to a friend's house in terms of what we see along the way or recognize someone's footsteps when we hear them or enjoy the feel of a well-executed golf shot without being able to put any of these things into words.

There are two more characteristics of our maps that it will help us to bear in mind. First, we construct, change and use parts of them quite unconsciously. It is as though we are sitting in the dark and must use a small flashlight to examine our maps. Just as we cannot shine the light on every area of the map at once, so we cannot give our conscious attention to everything at once. And just as there may be areas of the map that are always in the dark, so there are some things we seem never to give our conscious attention to.

Second, our maps are not the same as the situation we are mapping. Not only are they partially inaccurate and incomplete, but they represent only certain aspects of the situation. Think of some of the maps that we make in the literal sense of that term: road maps, railway maps, airway maps, trail maps, contour maps, population maps, treasure maps, and on and on. Each represents certain aspects of the world but ignores all the others.

The same is true of maps in the metaphorical sense in which we are using the term to refer to our belief systems. Not only are our various sets of beliefs partially false and incomplete, but they represent only those aspects of reality which are of interest to us, and they impose a system of organization on our experience. Some things can be said in one language but not in another. Eskimos have a rich, complex language concerning various kinds of snow, while ours is comparatively crude and simple in that area. Many nuances experienced and mapped by them escape our attention.

Our language functions as a system of organization for our experience by grouping things according to certain similarities which are of interest to us and connecting these groups in various ways. Most of the words we use *classify* things. For example, we group certain activities together as work and others together as play. In doing this we draw attention to the similarities between the activities we call *work* and to the differences between those activities and the ones we call *play*. At the same time, we blind ourselves to differences among the activities we call work and also the similarities between some work and some play. Some forms of work, for example, are pleasurable, take us out of our everyday world for a while, and so on.

A subtle but powerful imposition of our language is its representation of the world as either static or dynamic. Most human languages have a form which presents a static picture. Something *is* something else. John is honest. The book is red. In using this sort of language, we see our world as comprising a very large number of things, each having various characteristics. The world is experienced very differently by those whose language presents it as dynamic. Everything is seen as a process, a sequence of happenings. The red book here before me is a momentary event which gives way to another event and that to another. When experience is shaped through a static form of language both ourselves and our world appear less open to change than they are. We find ourselves saying, "I can't help it. It's just the way I am."

If we keep in mind that our maps are not the world, we can be more open to testing and revising them. We can also be more sensitive to differences between our maps and those used by others in our mutual transactions.

CHAPTER FOUR

Resistance To Learning

Both survival and quality of life depend on our ability to learn from experience. Yet often we resist learning or misuse the learning process. First of all, learning means change, and we tolerate change only to a point. Secondly, we both need and fear the truth. We torque into some aspects of reality yet evade or disguise others. While illusion is unreliable, it is often comfortable and socially expected. Far from being listened to, the little boy who cries out that the emperor has no clothes on is told he is mistaken, is perhaps even punished, and is quickly trained to see that the emperor does have clothes on. We turn now to examine our resistance to learning and to truth.

Despite the importance to us of reliable maps, we often refuse to test them by our experience. We have powerful motivations to shield our maps from change. One such motivation is our desire to leave our sense of identity undisturbed. Any belief that is important to our sense of who we are is difficult to examine. Religious beliefs are of this sort. In a sense, we *are* these beliefs. They become embodied in our behavior. Beliefs concerning our childhood and youth are also often given importance to our identity, especially beliefs about our original family situation. Sister is good, I am bad, mother should never be questioned. We may continue to see ourselves in terms of this ancient history.

We may even cling to beliefs that cause us pain if they are important to our sense of self. Sidney Jourard tells of a client with a problem in overeating. As she gained control of her eating, she found her success unbearable and reverted to her old pattern. Central to her sense of identity was her belief that she was weak-willed. As she stopped behaving that way, she felt something slipping away that seemed vital to her sense of who she was.

Part of the task of maintaining an identity for ourselves is sustaining a sense of worth or self-esteem. Much of our emotional life revolves around this need and it is not easy for us to examine those judgments we make that involve our self-esteem. Our anger, for example, may be a way of avoiding responsibility for a failure or mistake by blaming another, and this makes it difficult to consider whether the anger is justified. Or our basic stance toward life may be that of a martyr or victim, so as to conceal from ourselves a painful sense of inferiority; the accompanying need to find persecutors would make objective judgment unlikely.

Closely related to, and indeed overlapping, beliefs involving our sense of identity and self-esteem are those we hold largely because we think they gain us approval from others, or at least did so in the past. To consider altering or surrendering them seems to us to risk being rejected. We believe others will accept us only if we believe certain things and behave in certain ways. We become so oriented to their approval that we may not even be conscious of this pressure to share their beliefs. Nor do we realize that these beliefs are theirs rather than beliefs that have grown out of our own experience and judgment. The voice of conscience, for example, may seem to be our own when often it is really the voice of a parent or other authority in our past.

A lingering sense of the authority of our parents or other early parent figures can be especially difficult to stand up to. The child in us lived so long and in such formative years under the power of these people that it may seem to him unthinkable to challenge their right to make the important decisions for him. Even to question the values and beliefs they instilled may carry a sense of being rebellious and stir deep-seated feelings of guilt. The early Greeks expressed this in dramas in which the hero's struggle toward autonomy brought an onslaught by the Furies.

A number of writers have been commenting on the hypnotic-like way in which we often hold these early beliefs. Many beliefs, especially those basic to our self-image, were implanted by suggestion. R. D. Laing sees this happening especially by someone attributing some quality or characteristic to us. Perhaps our father said, "You're bad." In telling us what we *are*, he, in effect told us how to behave. But he seemed not to be doing this because he immediately added, "Mind me." Since we were bad, we weren't able to mind. Being told who or what we are is much more powerful than being told what to do. The weak-willed woman Jourard speaks of may have been living under the spell of a suggestion of this sort. Beliefs held in this way are protected from examination because we normally have little or no awareness of them.

We often feel great pressure to accept beliefs which are basic to the identity of groups to which we belong. If we question these beliefs, we risk losing membership in the group. As employees, we commonly feel pressure to accept certain ways of looking at the organization in which we work; although, again, we are often not conscious of this. These beliefs we accept frequently contradict our own experience, but we become so preoccupied with what is expected of us that we scarcely notice this. Speaking of two forms of discrepancy between our own experience and the expectations of an organization we are involved in, Samuel Culbert expresses it in this way:

> We avoid the first type of discrepancy, in which the system expects something unnatural from us, by going along with their demands and pretending not to notice that we're doing something inconsistent with our nature. . . .
> We avoid the pain of the second type of discrepancy, in which we learn that doing what came naturally creates problems, by rejecting our own perspectives, and internalizing norms and expectations of the system as if they were our own. For many of my colleagues in academia, this means publishing two or three articles a year without much personal concern for their actual relevance. The consequences of both these defenses is the same: we subordinate our pictures of reality to those of the system. . . .[1]

More generally, we may say that a major obstacle to subjecting our beliefs to the common test of experience is that, as we change our beliefs, we also change our way of relating, and so the other must change his way of seeing and relating to us. Our own learning and growth, in other words, require a reasonable confidence in the ability and willingness of the other to learn and grow or, failing this, a readiness to seek out those who will be responsive to our growth.

We may also resist testing those beliefs about society and government which justify current social and political practices and situations. If we gain privilege by a certain form of social organization, we tend to protect it and to find a way of seeing it as just. Even if we do not benefit from it, even if it harms us unjustly, we may cling to ideological beliefs which justify it. For one thing, we may not wish to face up to the injustices we are subjected to if we feel we cannot do anything about them. It may be less painful to attribute our difficulties to our inadequacies or unworthiness. For another, we very likely have been taught a not-too-discriminating obedience to authority and so find it difficult to question "authoritative" social and political beliefs.

Another motive that we commonly have for not testing our beliefs is a desire to avoid enlarging our freedom and responsibility. It takes courage to accept full responsibility for ourselves, and there is a child in us who wants to be taken care of. The more areas in which we have choices, the greater is our responsibility. Let's examine ways in which we fail to take hold of freedom available to us.

Our map may be not only unreliable in places but also impoverished. Since our map is an abstraction from the reality we live, and is based on limited experience, it is necessarily incomplete. But sometimes it is needlessly incomplete, failing to represent distinctions and possibilities for action which are important to human freedom and well-being.

Our map is unreliable or impoverished in places where its basis is either inadequate or utilized in a faulty way. This basis is made up from both our own experience and what we have learned from others. Because our experience is limited we need to supplement it. We fill in our map with scientific reports, news telecasts, literary explorations of human nature, tips on good places to fish, and on and on. But to be fully responsible and to maintain our significance as persons there are things we need to know from our experience. However much we may benefit from the experience and understanding of others, it is by our own experience that we need to shape the use of our personal and interpersonal powers and evaluate the consequences. To some extent and in more complex ways, this is also true of our impersonal powers. Responsibility requires judgment based ultimately on firsthand experience. This is one aspect of our significance as persons. Another is that no one else experiences the world the way we do, or can make of that experience what we make of it. The basis of our map, then, is inadequate insofar, as we make do with the experience of others where only our own experience is appropriate. In addition to giving our map an inadequate basis, we also may utilize it in ways that distort our understanding and reduce our freedom. We may use it to hide the truth from ourselves, rationalizing unjust privilege or immature behavior, creating comforting illusion or dysfunctional defenses of ourselves and our sense of worth. In everything from science to religion, we may find ways of buttressing our personal fortresses.

This creates a double pitfall. Not only may we map experience in distorted ways, but what we learn from others may involve similar distortions by them. We may even welcome their untruth as they in turn may be acting on untruths from still others. We could scarcely become so skillful in the games we play without considerable collusion. Perhaps a child is told by her parents that she is stupid or that she is exceptionally gifted, for reasons that have little to do with her. She makes this part of her map, and all of her experiences of herself get filtered through this belief so that she is conscious only of those which support it. Her entire family may act in ways that give credibility to the pretense. As a woman, she may continue to indoctrinate herself with this belief and may seek others who will cooperate with her in exchange for her cooperation in similar projects of their own.

But how, exactly, do we accomplish these distortions? Earlier we considered three abilities which we use to map our beliefs. Each of these abilities may be misused in ways that impoverish our maps.[2] The first way in which we project our experience onto our map is by generalization. Three times John has promised something and each time he has done what he promised. We generalize that John is a person who keeps his promises.

When we misuse this process of generalization we overgeneralize. Joan has a bad experience with both her third and fourth grade teachers. She concludes, "Teachers don't like me." Among a number of the things John attempts, he has some failures. He thinks, "I'm a failure." Joan and John are disconnecting their beliefs from their experiences. Each is losing sight of the specific experiences he or she is talking about, and each is failing to distinguish what is true of those experiences from what is true of other experiences he or she has had in the same area: Joan, her experiences in first and second grade; John, his experiences in things he's attempted with success. Further, in grossly exaggerating problems they are having, they make it needlessly difficult to find a constructive response to them. They unrealistically curtail their options and so their freedom.

We are especially susceptible to overgeneralization because some of our experiences make a much deeper impression on us than do others. Often we have one or two experiences that seem to us to reveal the basic truth about some aspect of our lives. One experience of failure comes with traumatic force and seems to show us what we're really made of. Our successes, we tell ourselves, are just a matter of luck and aren't very significant anyway. Or the apparent attitude of one person toward us overshadows all of our other relationships. We are what he has somehow told us we are. Events which come to us with this revelatory power are the tip of the iceberg, making us conscious of a direction in which our thought subconsciously has been moving for some time. Things which don't lend themselves to this movement easily get left behind.

The second way in which we formulate our general beliefs from their bases in experience is by selection. In the process of selection, we restrict our attention to a certain part of our field of experience.

When we misuse our ability to give selective attention to our experience, we map by deletion, placing some details of our beliefs on the unconscious areas of our map with the result that we needlessly limit our grasp of the options available to us. We remain unconscious of roads that we might find useful to take. When this happens, we may form the general belief that "I can't be open about myself," deleting any reference to just what it is we can't be open about, with whom we feel this way, and what (if anything) really stops us. It may be that we are open about some things about ourselves with certain persons, and that what is stopping us in other cases is our unconscious beliefs about what would happen if we did become more open.

The third ability we use in creating our maps is interpretation. When we interpret, we see connections between things, pulling them together into a meaningful pattern, and we assess their value or disvalue for us.

Sometimes our interpretation is a distortion of the way things are related or of their true value, and this reduces our control of our lives. We commonly think, for example, of one person as causing another to have a certain feeling or emotion. We say, "John makes me angry" or "You make me happy" or "I'm sorry when I upset you." But just because an action and a feeling occur together does not mean that one is the cause of the other. In seeing our emotions as caused by someone else, we are locating the control of them in that person rather than in ourselves. We picture ourselves as a kind of marionette with others pulling the strings for our emotional dance. But not everyone gets angry at the kinds of things we get angry at. In fact, it is often true that even we do not *always* get angry at those things. Getting angry is a response we have decided to make. We may have been making it for so long that it has become a habit with us, but it is a habit of our own making. We are likely to respond with anger to certain actions of John's because it is our habit, a habit which we apparently find useful, and not because John can cause us to make this response. To map the relation as causal is to distort it. This distortion results in our needlessly feeling out of control.

Another common type of distortion is what Albert Ellis calls catastrophizing. We may be overly concerned about something because we tell ourselves if that happened it would be terrible. That's the way we've mapped it, but if we examined it objectively, we would realize we're making a gross exaggeration. If it happened, we wouldn't like it; perhaps we would feel some pain, but it wouldn't be a catastrophe. We could cope with it. Perhaps we are going to speak to a group and feel really tied up in knots about it. We are telling ourselves if we don't do well it will be terrible and, in the process, we are making it very hard to do well. Exaggeration of this sort may make us needlessly fearful of doing things and so rob us of options that we otherwise would have.

Yet another common sort of distortion is mapping what is really an ongoing process as though it were something static and finished. It makes a difference whether we believe it is simply our nature to be liars, or whether we are liars because we continue a long-standing practice of telling lies. If we think of ourselves as dealing with an ongoing process, something we are continuing to do, we have something to say about whether we keep doing it. But if we map our lying as though it were just something given and fixed about our nature, we seem to ourselves not to have any control over it. As is true of the cause-effect and the catastrophizing types of distortion, distortions which misrepresent processes tend to reduce our sense of having options concerning our behavior.

These considerations about how our general beliefs may be impoverished as well as unreliable underline the value of learning, not only to add new beliefs and behavior, but also to correct and enrich old beliefs and behavior. We change our old beliefs both by reflecting on them and by checking these reflections against our ongoing experience.

Reflection is necessary because we often manipulate our experience to fit our beliefs. We perceive selectively and we tend to experience what we expect to experience, hope to experience, or fear to experience. In this way, the anticipations that our beliefs involve may become self-fulfilling. We may simply project our maps onto our experience. We know how unreliable even the most honest reports of eye witnesses tend to be. Those who have tried to proofread a paper know how difficult it is not to overlook misspelled words by simply seeing these words the way we expect them to be spelled.

Psychologists are studying intensely this process of reading our anticipations into our experience. The following is an account of one of the better-known experiments being conducted:

> Bruner and Postman asked experimental subjects to identify on short and controlled exposure a series of playing cards. Many of the cards were normal, but some were made anomalous, e.g., a red six of spades and a black four of hearts. Each experimental run was constituted by the display of a single card to a single subject in a series of gradually increased exposures. After each exposure, the subject was asked what he had seen, and the run was terminated by two successive correct identifications.

Even on the shortest exposures many subjects identified most of the cards, and after a small increase, all the subjects identified them all. For the normal cards these identifications were usually correct, but the anomalous cards were almost always identified, without apparent hesitation or puzzlement, as normal. The black four of hearts might, for example, be identified as the four of either spades or hearts. Without any awareness of trouble, it was immediately fitted to one of the conceptual categories prepared by prior experience. One would not even like to say that the subjects had seen something different from what they identified. With a further increase of exposure to the anomalous cards, subjects did begin to hesitate and to display awareness of anomaly. Exposed, for example, to the red six of spades, some would say: That's the six of spades, but there's something wrong with it—the black has a red border. Further increases of exposure resulted in still more hesitation and confusion until finally, and sometimes quite suddenly, most subjects would produce the correct identification without hesitation. Moreover, after doing this with two or three of the anomalous cards, they would have little further difficulty with the others. A few subjects, however, were never able to make the requisite adjustment of their categories. Even at forty times the average exposure required to recognize normal cards for what they were, more than 10 percent of the anomalous cards were not correctly identified. And the subjects who then failed often experienced acute personal distress. One of them exclaimed: "I can't make the suit out, whatever it is. It didn't even look like a card that time. I don't know what color it is now or whether it's a spade or a heart. I'm not even sure now what a spade looks like. My God!" . . .

Either as a metaphor or because it reflects the nature of the mind, that psychological experiment provides wonderfully simple and cogent schema for the process of scientific discovery. In science, as in the playing card experiment, novelty emerges only with difficulty, manifested by resistance, against a background provided by expectation. Initially, only the anticipated and usual are experienced even under circumstances where anomaly is later to be observed.[3]

Bandler and Grinder describe the way one client manipulated his experiences to fit his belief:

A man who was convinced that he was not worth caring about

complained to us that his wife never gave him messages of caring. When we visited this man's home, we became aware that the man's wife did, indeed, express messages of caring to him. However, as these messages conflicted with the generalization that the man had made about his own self-worth, he literally did not hear his wife. This was verified when we called the man's attention to some of these messages, and the man stated that he had not even heard his wife when she said those things.[4]

Even when these caring messages were pointed out to him, however, he did not allow them to count against his belief that he was not worth caring for. "Each time that he heard a caring message that he had previously been deleting, he turned to us, smiling, and said, 'She just says this because she wants something'."[5]

Another way in which we shape our experience to fit our beliefs is by acting in ways which tend to bring about whatever we anticipate. If we believe someone does not like us, we may avoid him, and so discourage friendly behavior on his part. If we believe we are on a lucky streak at cards, we may play with confidence, alertness, and energy, and so outplay our opponents. Our behavior is often an important factor in learning from our experience.

We may also tailor our experience by manipulating our environment. In a position of power, we may surround ourselves with "yes" men. Conventional and narrowly conservative in our social outlook, we may live in the suburbs and read only conservative magazines and newspapers and so shield ourselves from contact with poverty, injustice, and other unsettling aspects of our society.

The major way in which we manipulate our environment to conform to our beliefs is by what Eric Berne called games and scripts:

> Berne defines a *psychological game* as "a recurring set of transactions, often repetitive, superfically rational, with a concealed motivation; or, more colloquially, as a series of transactions with a gimmick." Three specific elements must be present to define transactions as games:
>
> (1) an ongoing series of complementary transactions which are plausible on the social level,
> (2) an ulterior transaction which is the underlying message of the game, and
> (3) a predictable payoff which concludes the game and is the real purpose for playing.

Games prevent honest, intimate and open relationships between the players. Yet people play them because they fill up
time, provoke attention, reinforce early opinions about self and
others and fulfill a sense of destiny.

Psychological games are played to win, but a person who
plays games as a way of life is not a winner. Sometimes, a person acts like a loser in order to win a game. For example, in a
game of *Kick Me* a player provokes someone else to a put-down
response.

Student: I stayed up too late last night and don't have my
   assignment ready. (ulterior: I'm a bad boy, kick me.)
Instructor: You're out of luck. This is the last day I can give
   credit for that assignment. (ulterior: Yes, you are a bad boy
   and here is your kick.)

Though they may deny it, people who are used to this game
tend to attract others who can play the complementary hand
and are willing to "kick" in response.[6]

The games we play are part of a script or life plan which most of us
unconsciously follow in leading our lives. According to Eric Berne:

Nearly all human activity is programmed by an ongoing script
dating from early childhood, so that the feeling of autonomy is
nearly always an illusion—an illusion which is the greatest af-
fliction of the human race because it makes awareness, honesty,
creativity and intimacy possible for only a few fortunate individuals. For the rest of humanity, other people are seen
mainly as objects to be manipulated. They must be invited,
persuaded, seduced, bribed or forced into playing the proper
roles to reinforce the protagonist's position and fulfill his script,
and his preoccupation with these efforts keeps him from
torquing it with the real world and his own possibilities in it.[7]

We may fail to learn from experience, then, because we mold our
experience to fit our beliefs instead of letting our experience be what it
is and testing our beliefs against it. To break this pattern, it will be
helpful, and perhaps even necessary, to obtain feedback and to use
both this feedback and our knowledge of the cognitive structure of
belief to reflect on our beliefs and experiences. We need (1) to check
our perceptions and interpretations with other persons who do not
share our personal biases and blind spots; (2) to obtain suggestions

about questions it may be helpful to ask; and (3) to look at our beliefs and experiences from a perspective that helps us gain new insight.

Whether or not feedback is useful to us will depend not only on what it is but on the way in which it is given. We refuse to test our beliefs because we are trying to avoid something we sense as threatening or at least discomforting to us. Feedback that conveys a negative attitude toward us may contribute to our being *dis-couraged*—less able than ever to find the courage needed to learn in an area in which we feel threatened—compelled to explain and defend our behaviors and interpretations. Feedback which conveys a positive attitude toward us may contribute to our being *en-couraged*—more able to generate the courage needed—less needful of defending our way of being and so more free to examine it.

Because we tend to perceive selectively and to read into our experience what we expect it to be, it is important for us to check our experience by asking others about theirs. It is basic to scientific method that it involves procedures which can be repeated by others so that the originally reported results can be checked against their experience. Our everyday checking procedures won't be as precise or reliable. But if our experience finds confirmation in that of another, it increases our confidence in it and, incidentally, our confidence in our ability to experience in an open and accurate way. And if, on the other hand, the report of the other leads us to see inaccuracy or incompleteness in our experience, we may be less likely to repeat that same mistake in the future. In the experiment referred to, by Bruner and Postman, for example, we may recall that after someone discovered his mistaken perception in the case of two or three of the anomalous cards, he was generally able to avoid this mistake with the others.

We may not gain greater reliability for our experience if feedback is given in a situation where we feel pressure to agree with the report of the other. It is important that both of us maintain and encourage attitudes of openness about our experience and willingness to disagree.

Feedback concerning our perception of another or our perception of ourselves deserves special attention. We very easily misperceive the behavior of another, especially when it is directed toward us or toward someone or something important to us. If, for example, we have a poor image of ourselves, we will expect negative reactions from others and tend to read this into their behavior or facial expression or other body language. The ways the other behaves and appears are important sources of our belief about what he is thinking or feeling or intending. But what he *says* he is thinking or feeling or intending is often an even more important source. To feel that we have full knowledge of these things without asking the other is what Bandler and Grinder call mind reading.

Earlier we said that life requires a balance between fear and courage. We may create very different maps, depending on whether we map with an emphasis on fear, on courage, or on a balance between the two. If our style is that of fear, we will be overly cautious in what we believe and reluctant to accept invitations to fuller relationship, preferring safety to that creative expansion of our horizons and involvements that requires reasonable risk. Our maps will tend to be impoverished, especially in ways that conceal from us our freedom and responsibility.

If our style is that of unexamined courage, we will be too uncritical in what we believe and needlessly vulnerable to manipulation and betrayal, seeking the fullest possible experience even at the price of illusion. Our maps will tend to be unreliable and even self-contradictory.

The ability to examine and correct or enrich our maps while striking a balance between fear and courage is necessary if our life style is to be reasonably open rather than closed. We can be open in communicating with others (or with other aspects of our world) only if our belief system is open to change in light of their messages.

II

*Learning In Three
Areas Of Life*

CHAPTER FIVE

Changing Our Emotions

Success in living depends especially on emotions and attitudes. Take away hope and fear, joy and sorrow, love and anger—remove all devotion and disappointment, all compassion and indignation—and life would be impoverished indeed. But some emotions enhance or even ennoble our lives, while others reduce or degrade them.

Important as emotions are, there is a widespread tendency to think there is little one can do to change them for the better. Reason and emotion are often seen as enitrely separate from one another and emotion is commonly equated with feeling. In part, this is a legacy from eighteenth-century faculty psychology that sorted mental activities into thinking, feeling and willing.[1] The idea that emotion *is* feeling finds frequent reenforcement by such forms of expression as "How do you feel about it?" or "My feelings of annoyance rose higher and higher." As a consequence, there is a strong tendency to think of emotion as something that just happens, something for which the individual is not responsible. Reason, then, often seems to stand in opposition to emotion or to have little or no relevance to it, and this discourages any effort at evaluating and perhaps changing particular emotions.

This idea that emotion is devoid of reason, however, seems to me not to withstand careful analysis. Emotions do not just happen to us but are ways of responding that we develop through situation learning and response learning.

If we can come, then, better to understand the nature of our emotions, the purposes they serve, and the way they are learned, we can increase our control of them. Often, having control of our emotions is taken to mean determining how we express them and act on them. But here something more fundamental is meant; namely, the ability

91

to evaluate them and to change them, modifying some, outgrowing others, and adopting still others.

EMOTIONS, FEELINGS AND JUDGMENTS

Among the philosophical and psychological views which identify emotion with feeling, the most famous and still not without influence is that of William James and C.G. Lange: the feeling state which accompanies various visceral changes as they occur *is* the emotion.[2] This led to two important lines of criticism, one by psychologist W.B. Canon, and the other by philosopher John Dewey. We shall look at each briefly.

Canon argued that emotions cannot be the sensations produced by visceral changes because:

(1) The total separation of the visceral from the central nervous system does not alter emotional behavior.

(2) The same visceral changes occur in very different emotional states and in nonemotional states.

(3) The viscera are relatively insensitive structures.

(4) Visceral changes are too slow to be a source of emotional feeling.

(5) The artificial induction of visceral changes that are typical of strong emotions does not produce the emotions.[3]

The last point was based on a study by George Marañon who found that adrenaline injections produced no emotional experience in a large majority of his patients and only a kind of "as if" experience ("I feel *as if* I were afraid") in most of the others.[4]

To Canon's first point that persons who have lost bodily sensations continue to act emotionally, James's defenders have replied effectively that behavior learned before this loss may be continued in appropriate circumstances without the corresponding feelings. This is suggested by G.W. Hohmann's study of paraplegics and quadraplegics who have lost varying degrees of visceral sensation.[5] The following is typical of their reports:

> It's sort of cold anger. Sometimes I act angry when I see some injustice. I yell and cuss and raise hell, because if you don't do it sometimes, I've learned people will take advantage of you, but it just doesn't have the heat that it used to. It's a kind of mental anger.

If Canon's second and third points are correct, emotions cannot be identical with feelings because they cannot be differentiated from one another or from nonemotional states simply on the basis of feeings. There is a great variety of possible emotions—someone has listed 550—while a drastically smaller number of sensations is experienced. The distinction between our emotions may also be rather subtle—embarrassment and shame, guilt and remorse, annoyance and indignation, for example—yet that between sensations is comparatively crude. As George Mandler, following Canon, has recently put it, the receptors available by which to perceive visceral happenings "are essentially insensitive and few, thus resulting in a perceptual system that can register only gross changes in either variability or intensity."[6]

Many researchers have attempted to discover patterns of sensation unique to individual emotions. The results are especially impressive in being so meager in comparison with the effort. But some results there are, so that the theory of Stanley Schachter, Mandler, and others that visceral arousal is for all practical purposes the same in *any* emotion—often called the general arousal theory—must be qualified for several cases.

The problem here for the defenders of James is how, if it is so difficult to establish differences in feelings for a few emotions, to make it plausible that there are similar differences for the hundreds of other emotions. Generally, they contend there are a few basic emotions and all the rest are combinations of these few. But to evolve so many from so few would be exceedingly difficult even if there were adequate evidence and rationale for establishing which emotions are basic. The weakness of evidence and rationale is such that theorists agree very little about which and how many emotions are basic, the number ranging from five to fifteen.

The other line of criticism of the James-Lange theory is that indicated by John Dewey. Dewey pointed out that emotions have an object. Whatever emotion we have—joy, sadness, fear, anger—it is always an emotion *about* something, so that to have an emotion we must look at its object in some way. But feelings or sensations, taken by themselves, are not about anything. A thumping heart is simply a thumping heart.

Several other differences between feelings and emotions have also been noted. We shall mention only two.

First, it is characteristic of our emotions, but not of our feelings and sensations, that we can and often do evaluate them in various ways. We can ask whether or not an emotion is warranted, reasonable, appropriate and the like, because these criteria have to do with the relationship of our emotions to whatever they are about.

Secondly, we may be mistaken about our emotions but not about our feelings or sensations. Robert Solomon puts it this way:

> We deny that we are angry when there is every reason to sup-
> pose that we are; we laugh at the idea that we are in love
> when even the laughter itself, hysterical and defensive, is fur-
> ther proof of our affections. We feign anger and fool even
> ourselves; realize after years of apparent tenderness that what
> seemed to be love was not love; believe that we are self-
> righteously indignant when we find that we are envious or
> resentful. We sometimes think ourselves depressed when we
> are really angry, sympathetic when we are being vicious, lov-
> ing when we are jealous and possessive; merely sad when in
> fact we are guilty or depressed.[7]

In contrast, our feelings and sensations, as such, are simply experiences. We may feel sore, tense, excited, drowsy, or sluggish, and
all of this is comparable to experiencing a color or a sound. We can be
mistaken that the *book* in front of us is red, but not that we are having
the *experience* of red. Similarly, we can be mistaken about an emotion
but not that we are having the experience of soreness or tenseness.

Many psychologists have long neglected the philosophical point
that emotions are about something—a point arrived at by reflection
rather than by experience—and consequently have worked to
establish some version of the Janes-Lange theory. As a result, experimental work by Schachter and Singer in the early sixties,[8] which
has drawn attention to this referential nature of emotion, has had a
major impact on psychological thought. They injected persons with
epinephrine, an adrenaline extract that arouses the sympathetic nervous system, producing "palpitation, tremor, and sometimes a feeling of flushing and accelerated breathing"—symptoms that much
research indicates are characteristic of emotional states.[9] Some were
then placed in situations where a stooge was acting in a playful,
euphoric way, and others in situations involving a questionnaire that
was personal and insulting and a stooge who reacted to it with increasing anger. Those placed in the former reported feeling euphoric
and appeared that way to obervers. Those placed in the latter situations interpreted the same sensations as feelings of anger and also appeared to be angry. The important exception was those persons who
had been told the truth about their injection—that it would be arousing. They did not experience these sensations as feelings of emotion.

Schachter and Singer see these results as strong support for their
belief that emotional experience involves both arousal of the sympathetic nervous system and a labeling of this experienced arousal in
terms of whatever information subjects have about their situation.
Persons who know that their arousal was caused by a drug have no
need to account for it by an emotional label. The experiment has its

critics. But, all things considered, the evidence is impressive, as is its impact on psychological thought. It strikingly displays emotions as essentially about something.

William Alston cites somewhat related findings in the case of emergency emotions:

> Thus bodily changes typical of fear have been induced by suddenly tipping a chair in which the subject was seated. When this was unexpected the subject reported having been frightened, but when he was warned in advance what would happen, he reported not being frightened. Nevertheless the recorded bodily upset in heart action, respiration, glandular and digestive secretions, and so on, was indistinguishable in the two cases.[10]

Feelings, by themselves, are not emotions.

Evidence that the feeling can occur without the emotion can also be found in our everyday experience. A typical case is that in which the feeling outlasts the emotion. For example, we wait a very long time for someone to show up for an appointment. Our irritation grows at the thought of his apparent carelessness and inconsiderateness. We become aroused physicially. Then we get word that he has been in an accident. We no longer have any thoughts about his action being wrong. We are still aroused but we are no longer angry. To take another example, someone bumps us and we fall. We look around in anger only to see our supposed assailant sprawled on the ground. The bump, we see, was unintentional. We may be flustered or upset but we no longer feel wronged, angry. In both cases our bodily arousal continues beyond the emotion.

To summarize, there are many reasons for concluding that emotions are not identical with feelings. Two of the fundamental reasons are:

(1) the same feelings occur in very different emotional states, such as anger and euphoria, and in nonemotional states;

(2) emotions are about something—anger about an alleged wrong, fear of an apparent threat—but feelings, taken by themselves, are not.

What happens, typically, when we have an emotion such as anger? It may be that we are reading a letter from Z and begin to think that he is being unfair to us and to have a sense of being hurtfully attacked. Our heart begins to thump, our stomach and neck muscles tighten and our face tenses. We say to a companion, "Just listen to this," and as we read he notices the anger in our voice, in our face, in the fist with which we hold the letter. Soon we are pacing the floor. We think again of how wrong it was of Z to say those things. We become more aroused than ever. Our companion asks whether we aren't letting this bother us more than we should. As we ponder this, we also think about the long relationship we have had with Z and the things we each value in it, and alongside our anger there arises a fear that these things may be in jeopardy or damaged beyond repair. What to do? We will call Z on the phone and express our chagrin but also see if a door can be opened to some sort of reconciliation through apology or discovering some misunderstanding or the like. No, we handle such things better by writing. We take pen and paper and with strong, fast strokes we express our anger and ask for an explanation. That evening we are irritable and restless. We go to bed and dwell once more on the situation, remembering other times, some long past and not involving Z, in which we felt wronged. Later in a dream we strike out at someone.

All of this is called being angry—saying things to ourselves, talking with our companion, evaluating, informing, expressing, questioning, reflecting, weighing options, writing a letter, pacing the floor, dreaming. It is a changing, many-faceted *process*, including moments of tension both with a competing emotion and with doubt about its appropriateness. We may think of this as enacting a scenario or script. We have learned a plot for being angry: when anger is justified, what its body language is, the various roles that are played by oneself and others, and the options one has about what to think and say and do in these various roles.

An emotion, then, is not just one sort of thing but several. Keeping this in mind will be difficult unless we avoid a common mistake. Words are often seen as pointing to particular things; "tree" is used to denote particular trees, "table" to indicate particular tables, and so on. What, then, one may wonder, does "emotion" point to? If not to feeling then to what? Yet we know that such words as *university, nation, government* or *story* refer to something complicated. Thinking of emotions as scenarios may help us with this.

Analysis shows an emotional scenario to involve three different things: a judgment about the object, a feeling, and one or more actions. In the example of the letter from Z, the scenario began with the judgment that Z had made a "hurtful attack" and that this was "unfair." Next came feeling: heart pounding, stomach and neck muscles tight, face muscles tense. Finally, there were various behaviors typical of being angry, such as reading in an aroused tone of voice, pacing the floor, writing about the anger with strong, fast strokes.

I use the term *judgment* for the evaluational aspect of our emotions in order to avoid terminology that is more technical than is necessary for our purposes here. It can be misleading, however, in implying that our emotional evaluations are always separate, consciously experienced events. Often the cognitive appraisal that characterizes an emotional scenario is simply implicit in one or more aspects of it or even in the scenario as a whole. As George Pitcher has put it:

> I consider it reasonable to include under the heading "evaluations" such otherwise quite different things as evaluational modes of behavior, inclinations to them, wants, desires, assumptions, beliefs, and judgments. Some emotions include evaluational beliefs or judgments predominantly—namely, the "calm passions," like envy. Some emotions include desires or wants predominantly—for example, love. And still others—"hot passions," like anger—include actions or inclinations to them predominantly. But . . . most emotions, including those just mentioned, very often include evaluational elements of different kinds. . . . .[11]

We frequently become frightened without time to think, angry the moment someone strikes us, elated the instant the winning shot is made.

Since emotions involve evaluations of objects, they are about some aspects of those objects—those objects looked at in a certain way. Our evaluations direct our attention.[12] Often we are not directly aware of them, and it is rather by means of them that we perceive and engage our world. Frequently, our emotional evaluations are the spectacles through which we see.

In addition to evaluational judgments, our emotional scenarios involve those general body tones and sensations that we call feelings. Feelings alone are not emotions but they are obviously an important part of them. Our emotional judgments characteristically generate feelings.[13] In most cases, these feelings are caused by the introduction of adrenaline into our system.

It is also characteristic of our emotions that they typically carry implications for action. Exceptions are a few contemplative emotions, such as wonder or a feeling of the sublime or the mystical. Joyful about our achievement, we may wish to shout, leap, embrace our teammates. Sad about something we believe has diminished us, we may withdraw. Fearful of something we perceive as threatening, we may run. Angry about an action we see as both hurtful and wrong, we may strike or denounce.

This intimate connection between emotion and action accounts for our extremely rich vocabulary concerning the emotions. It is often important to others to be able to anticipate our actions, and information about our emotional state helps them do this. By comparison, our vocabulary for the body sensations generally accompanying our emotions in meagre. For the most part we refer to these sensations by using the name for the emotional states which they often become part of. We speak of feelings of anger, joy, love, and so on. Doubtless this characteristic of our language usage encourages our tendency to identify emotion with feeling.

Of the three components of an emotional scenario, it seems to me it is judgment that is basic, basic in the sense of identifying what specific emotion the scenario is.[14] We have seen that feeling cannot do this because the same feeling may occur in very different emotions. The same is true, although to a lesser extent, of behavior. In the case of the letter from Z, for example, either a sense of unfairness or a concern that the relationship might be in jeopardy would have resulted in bodily arousal and could have led to such behaviors as reading with an aroused tone of voice, pacing the floor, and writing in an agitated manner. Such feeling and action is experienced by ourselves, and others who observe us, as the feeling and action of anger if the situation is appraised in terms of wrong-doing, but as the feeling and action of fear if the appraisal is one of danger.[15]

Since emotion, then, cannot be identified *by* our behavior alone, it cannot, as behaviorists have tried to do, be identified *with* behavior. The same physical activity may be part of very different emotional scenarios. It is our evaluation of the situation that gives our physical movement its meaning.

It is often true that we ourselves, as well as others, become aware of what emotion we have by means of our behavior. In such a case, our evaluation of this situation does not take the form of a separate event in which we tell ourselves the evaluation, but rather is a part of the behavior. Our behavior becomes the language by which we formulate an evaluation. When this happens, we can distinguish our evaluation from our physical activity, although these things are not separable.

Another way of seeing the basic role played by evaluation in our emotional scenarios is to consider that we may react to a situation in terms of a scenario, without activating the prescribed feeling or behavior. Ordinarily, both feeling and behavior are important components of an emotional scenario and, if they are absent without any apparent reason, others, or even we ourselves, might well doubt whether we really do look at the situation in the way necessary to that emotion. We sometimes are mistaken about our emotions. But we also may be unable or unwilling to take appropriate action; and in some circumstances the customary feelings are not forthcoming.

Concerning feelings, it may happen that we have become so accustomed to something that it usually fails to arouse us as once it did. Or we may be so preoccupied with something else that, for the time being, an occurance that we ordinarily would respond to with feeling has little effect.

Once we understand emotion as basically an evaluative judgment with implications for action, we can see that learning our emotions involves both situation learning and response learning. Situation learning we defined as a change in how we interpret a situation. When we interpret, we bring things together into a meaningful pattern, seeing connections between them and judging their value or disvalue for us. Those judgments we call emotional are a fundamental part of the way we interpret situations.

We have also said that response learning is often determined by our interpretations. The meaning of a situation is, at its heart, what we seek in it—what is at stake for us there—and we learn those behaviors which are most successful in getting us what we seek.

Consider love. We're not born able to love. It's something we have to learn. We must learn both a certain way of looking at someone or something and behaviors that enable us to give effective expression to that way of seeing. We must learn to see another as an equal, to prize her, to identify with her, to delight in her, to enjoy sharing with her.

From this we can see that love or other emotions will vary from person to person because interpretations or judgments differ. Not everyone, for example, will have a well-developed sense of equality between persons, and those who do may differ considerably in the way they understand this. Obviously a child's love is a very different emotion from that of most adults. Pets do not have the emotion of love at all because they do not possess human concepts.

Emotions also vary from person to person because abilities to act on those emotions differ. It is when we embody an emotion in our actions that we come fully to experience it and to make it part of us. We scarcely regard someone as loving who does not act in loving ways.

Another characteristic of our emotions is that, while some are judgments of particular situations, others are broader in scope; some are ways of responding to or giving meaning to life as a whole. As an emotional habit permeates a significant part of our lives and becomes a steady influence on our transactions, we call it an attitude. Generally we become angry about specific occurrences, but some among us focus such keen awareness on injustice and inhumanity that anger becomes a basic evaluation of life as a whole. We often love a specific person, but we may also come to have a love affair with life in general, a great many encounters carrying the potential for a sense of delight and belonging. If our lives are pervaded by a sense of guilt, whatever we do we find ourselves wanting; if by anxiety, everything is masked by a sense of threat; if by judgment of duty, our actions take on dignity from moral purpose; if by hope, we move forward expectantly toward a time of brotherhood or some other ideal. If life is to have a meaning for us, we must interpret it as having that meaning. Our interpretations may or may not be supported by the objective world, but the world we experience, our subjective or existential world, *is* the world as we interpret it, and in this sense our emotional judgments and attitudes create the meaning of our lives.

At the heart of every religion or philosophy of life, then, is one or more emotions or attitudes which give basic structure to one's way of transacting with his or her world. Christianity generally embodies love, hope and guilt as basic judgments about life and destiny. Yet the meaning of and emphasis on each of these terms varies from one version of Christianity to another so that radically different approaches to life are called Christian. Guilt, for example, may have an authoritarian meaning in which we judge ourselves as of little or no worth because we have failed to fulfill moral demands imposed by another. The voice of conscience is then a condemning voice, and the only hope we experience may be the judgment that, although we will never become persons of worth, the authority may act toward us as though we were of worth. Love, in turn, may be a kind of idolatry in which we see the authority as possessing all the qualities that we would need to have to be of worth and in which we also see our own signifiance as inhering solely in having a relationship with that authority.

In sharp contrast, guilt may have a humanistic meaning in which we judge ourselves as partially failing to live up to the full meaning of being human as we understand it from our own experience. Conscience, in the words of one philosopher, is then "the voice of our own being calling us to become what we truly are." Hope may become the judgment that we are capable of continuous growth toward a full realization of our humanity, and love may be, at its heart, the judgment that both we and the other are of unconditional worth.

Typically our dominant emotional stance toward life is triggered by or anchored in a particular event or set of events. Often these are subtle messages we received in the early years of our lives together with those happenings we took to be decisive confirmation of their truth. Are we really bad? Well there are surely a lot of times we are reprimanded for something or other; at one time in the past by father and mother, but now by their voices within us and perhaps also by someone who plays parts of their role with us. As we said in discussing the function of generalization in mapping our subjective world, some of our experiences make an especially deep impression on us. They seem to reveal the basic truth of things and so exert a life-shaping power.

These life-shaping events may be not only private but social or historical as well. We find commonality and communion with others when we share an emotional orientation rooted in the same events. In religion, events of this sort are called revelations. For example, the exodus of Jewish tribes from Egypt; the return of Jewish peoples from exile; and the life, death and resurrection of Jesus have determined the emotional structure of the basic approach to life of countless millions.

Our emotions, then, are not simply experiences but ways of being in the world. They involve feelings, interpretations, and ways of acting. We may think of them as scenarios we have learned, scenarios which tell us how we may justifiably look at and act in a situation, what intensity of feeling we may appropriately maintain, and how we may expect others to respond.

FUNCTIONAL AND DYSFUNCTIONAL EMOTIONS

Emotions, I have argued, are, at heart, evaluative judgments. But the question arises as to what sorts of evaluations are emotional. We may evaluate a hand of cards, the meaning of a comment, or the weather, without any of these involving emotion.

I call emotional those judgments we make in existential matters—matters that most vitally concern our existence as a self. We have said that we become selves by both response learning and situation learning. Our emotional scenarios provide us with ways of being a significant self in situations that are most important to us. Typically we may learn anger or fear where our physical existence is threatened, love or jealousy where our need for bonding is concerned, pride or resentment where our personal worth is at issue, a sense of beauty or of discord in our search for wholeness in ourselves and our world, a feeling of the infinite and of the finite in our quest for ultimate meaning and courage. Often, more than one existential need is involved in the same situation and so may be served by the same emotion. Both intimacy and worth, for example, may be served by love, or by fear, or by joy.

Because our emotions involve interpretations and actions whereby we seek to maintain or enhance our existence as selves, we may evaluate them as functional or dysfunctional according to how well they fulfill this role. If we can see more clearly why our emotional learning becomes functional or dysfunctional, we may be helped to learn to use more functional emotions.

More of our emotions seem devoted to situations involving our sense of worth than to any other sort. Our lives take on their meaning through our emotional interpretations, but we do not find our lives meaningful, it seems to me, unless we see them as having worth. Worth and meaning rise and fall together. Because of its centrality, we shall focus on this side of our emotional lives.

To be functional in giving us a sense of our worth, it seems to me that our emotional judgments must (1) be significantly related to our transactions; (2) be justifiable to one or more persons whose opinions matter to us; (3) carry implications that we are of (unconditional) worth; (4) (where an interpersonal relation is directly involved) be based on a genuine, non-game-playing way of relating. They must, first of all, be significantly related to our transactions, because we are what we do. Only if we see our worth reflected in what we do—in our creation of meaning and value—does it really come home to us as ours. We cannot experience being something simply by dreaming about it, hoping for it, or even planning for it. Dreams, hopes, plans may be important, but only because they may lead to action. Others may treat us as of worth, based upon our distinctively human potentialities and ways in which we realize them, however poorly; they may defend and respect our basic human rights. And yet this worth remains for us an abstract thing unless we live it in significant ways.

The danger is that we use our emotions to deceive ourselves or others or both. Supposedly, they are ways of being a significant self, but they may be merely a pose. We may whip up feelings of love for all humankind yet translate none of this into our ongoing transactions. We may react with indignation at an injustice we see on television news but do nothing to correct it or similar injustices close to home. We may apologize frequently for something we do, yet make no effort to change that behavior. Not infrequently we become emotional as a way of seeming to be something, a substitute for genuine action.

We relate our emotional judgments significantly to our transactions in two principal ways. In the first, our transactions are based on those judgments—are enactments of our emotional scenarios. Consider joy. In being joyful we have a sense of well-being or fulfillment, generally grounded in the use of one of our distinctively human powers. We create, we understand, we care, we generate meaning in the exercise of our freedom, we deepen our knowledge of good and evil, and in each of these ways we make real something of the power of our being, gaining a sense of worth not from the approval of another but from qualities inherent in our human nature itself. Typically a sense of joy may well up in us as we use these powers.

The second principal way in which we relate our emotional judgments significantly to our transactions is by using our emotional responses to appropriate more fully for ourselves the meanings of our transactions. For example, we may respond with joy not only while we are using our powers but also in looking back on these transactions. We may share with another our sense of delight by letter or telephone or over dinner. We may drive home humming or singing to ourselves. We may run a victory lap or throw a party. By reliving moments of heightened feeling, often with the help of ritual and other forms of sharing and celebration, we both enjoy and more fully appropriate for our sense of self the significance of being able to create meaning and value and to express in other ways our distinctive humanity.

To be functional in giving us a sense of worth, our emotions, secondly, must be justifiable to one or more persons whose judgment carries some weight for us. Generally they will be persons with whom we are or have been involved, although they may also include persons we know only through reading or even through our imagination—representations of our values and ideals. We are *selves* because we participate in a social drama. Our part in that drama cannot make sense to us unless it also makes sense to one or more of the other players. Emotional scenarios related to self-esteem are of little help to us unless they connect us with others, providing a way for them to be significant selves in response.

Thirdly, to help us feel significant in a functional way, our emotions must carry the implication that we are of significance. This seems a trivial thing to say and indeed it would be were it not for the fact that we typically learn many emotional scenarios that do the opposite. Envy, resentment, authoritarian guilt, idolatry, adoration[16] are among these emotions that are based on a low estimate of ourselves as selves.[17] Some reinforce a de-centered approach to life, others are a reaction to the burden of this condition, but all provide a way of salvaging something in our quest for significance.

Emotions that implicitly call our worth into question are, of course, rather contradictory ways of trying to establish or renew or strengthen a sense of our value. Yet whatever their cost to us and to our personal relationships, however many twists and turns and self-deceptions it may take us, we derive from these self-defeating emotions something of use in our struggle for worth. Were this not so we would not adopt them. Acquiesce though we may in the questioning of our value, there remains deep within us the refusal to be nothing.

To understand these dysfunctional emotions, we may simply line the need for self-esteem up against relationships of dominance and submission—relationships in which power is highly unequal. What kind of emotions, for example, can be permitted a slave in his transactions with his master? How is he to feel significant in that relationship? We can easily see how deceptive or twisted or pathetic it all must be.

It seems to me that this sort of thing exists, in varying degrees, throughout our society. Where social injustice is strong, social control must become excessive. As we have considered earlier, we are more easily controlled if we come to believe that our worth as persons depends on meeting the expectations and demands of others. We absorb this belief in many ways, not the least of which is through many of the emotions we are taught.

In teaching us authoritarian guilt, for example, the family and other institutions lay the foundations for unquestioning obedience to authority. In this form of guilt we are taught to judge ourselves as lacking in worth because we have failed to be obedient to another or, indeed, are deemed utterly incapable of true obedience. We learn to seek approval through acts of contrition in which we judge ourselves as negatively as possible, complete self-condemnation being the ideal. Again and again we are rewarded when we place subservience to authority ahead of our need for autonomy, and punished when we do not. When we are secure in our own value, we respond to authority with appreciation for insight and understanding that our own minds and experience can attest to as enhancing human worth. Uncertain of our value, we respond with deference in exchange for being made to feel some sort of significance.

Similarly, in learning to idolize someone, we are taught that the value we yearn for but lack is preeminently possessed by that person and the best we can hope for is whatever modicum of worth comes to us in having some sort of tie to him. This often characterizes, or at least contaminates, our face to face relations with family, friends, lovers, or those in positions of authority. But it is also an important feature of our response to the heroes generated by our more distant societal life. Very commonly we become someone's fan, the word *fan* coming from "fanatic." This movie star or that sports hero is everything we're not, but we must be a little something after all, we persuade ourselves, because we identify ourselves with him or her and base our significance on his achievement. This makes understandable the old saying "they never boo a bum." Only the one into whom we project our ideals can at first support and then shatter our illusions that we can receive from him a value we lack in ourselves. When we are secure in our own worth, we can take pleasure in the achievement of another without turning him into an idol—without demanding that he remove from us the task of existing as a unique person. In providing idols, our society compensates us for undercutting our sense of significance, by the illusion of being personally involved in something great and by being a part of a large body of fellow fans.

Authoritarian guilt and idolatry, then, are closely related. They rest on the belief that our worth depends on our subservience to or identification with someone of marked superiority.

Other emotions can be seen as primarily a reaction to the burdens of a de-centered life. We may indulge in envy; moments of fantasy about how wonderful it would be to be another provide respite from feelings of inferiority and unworthiness. Or we may adopt one of the most destructive of all emotions, resentment, seeing others as the cause of our failure to be. If it weren't for them we'd really be something. This child, we say, with all his dependencies, keeps us from a career and from really being our true self. It's her success, we tell ourselves, that keeps us in the shadows, obscuring our real qualities. If only our parents had been different, we mourn, we could be the person life intended us to be. Dwelling on all we somehow truly are but are wrongfully prevented from showing, we achieve a kind of escape from our situation, another excursion into fantasy. When conditions frustrate human needs, a variety of means of escape are created.

Whether they reinforce the message of unworthiness or provide respite from it, all of our dysfunctional emotions provide some semblance of self-esteem. They fall short of meeting our true needs because in them we must try somehow to reconcile our need to experience a sense of worth with our belief that we are seriously lacking in worth, a belief originating in messages from early childhood and perpetuated by a variety of ways in which we, often with help from others, reindoctrinate ourselves with those messages.

When we engage in such contradictory, self-defeating emotions, we use others as mere means to our purpose. We use authorities and idols to bestow on us a significance we feel lacking in ourselves. We cannot get past our own sense of need to see what and who they are apart from us. We must project onto them our ideals or the capacity to judge and determine our worth. Or we may use others to make self-serving comparisons with ourselves. Resentment, for example, may masquerade as a kind of morality in which we judge others for their sins, carefully composing the list of *do nots* and *dos* so that, although lacking in some degree, we will look good by comparison. When others join us in this venture it is called gossip. Or, in the case of guilt, we may give great attention to our own transgressions. True, we are unworthy but at least we confess it and are penitent, while others, equally unworthy, do neither. We may not be much, but precisely in making this judgement about ourselves we become a little something after all, at least by comparison. In these and similar ways, we purchase some sense of self at the price of relating destructively to others and forfeiting the fulfillments of a life based on genuine affirmation of our mutual worth.

Functional emotions, ways of seeing ourselves and our world that enable us to experience an unqualified sense of value as persons, must be based not only on a belief in our own worth but also on a belief in the equal worth of others. As we have said, we are selves only because we participate in a social drama. Our very identity is created by us out of our myriad relationships. Considered apart from them we are mere abstractions. Since we are our relationships, impoverished relationships make us impoverished persons. If we discount the worth of the other, treating him or her only as a means to our purposes, how can our relationship be anything but a poor one and so lead to a diminished sense of ourselves? It is in relating to persons of value that we experience value in ourselves. It is only in celebrating the humanity of others that we affirm the value of our own. The value in being human applies either to everyone or to no one.

This means, fourthly, that to be functional, our emotional judgments must be based on genuine, non-game-playing ways of relating. In his *Games People Play*,[18] Eric Berne has explored at length the many ways in which we substitute games for genuine relationship. When we relate by game playing, we are interested in the other only insofar as he or she plays in our game a part that will result in our making the kind of emotional response we want to make. Such emotional responses, then, are completely phony because we have simply manipulated others to behave in ways that allow us to indulge in that emotion. At the same time, the other is using us in a similar way. We become angry at behavior we have demanded of the other. He is scornful at behavior he has required of us in return. In contrast, our emotions are genuine in situations free of any manipulation on our part. In our ongoing personal relations, we are nonmanipulative when we see the other as he is quite apart from us and what we would like him to be and affirm his right to determine for himself who he will be.

When we see our emotions as scenarios that we adopt to serve our existential needs for a sense of worth, bonding and the like, we thereby see ourselves as responsible for them. Not everyone makes the particular judgments that we do. Love, fear, anger, and the rest come in countless varieties, are described very differently from person to person. Others do not become jealous or depressed or joyful in the kinds of circumstances that we do. Some may not use at all an emotional scenario that we find very important. Since others may not make the emotional judgments we do, there is no necessity for us to make them either. But here, as always, there are conditions that must be met if we are to have freedom to change our emotions, to base them on our own experience of genuine relations with others.

Those emotions which are basic to our way of life define for us, subjectively, what it means to have self-esteem, intimacy and the rest. Our very identity rests on them. A sadistic person, for example, will experience his or her deepest significance only in subjugating others to himself, reducing them to extensions of his being. In such cases, it is in emotions of hostility, resentment and the like that one feels most alive, most real, most important. All other emotions are judged in reference to the experience afforded by those which are basic to our identity. Emotions in which others most truly affirm themselves may mean little or nothing to us because we are oriented so very differently in, what Erich Fromm has termed, our basic character structure. Decentered or narcissistic ways of being tend to be self-perpetuating because what is valued is defined in decentered or narcissistic terms, and also because these perspectives are widely shared by others. It often takes intense suffering, generated by the deficiencies inherent in these orientations, for us to open ourselves up to alternative possibilities of what we may be.

This helps us to understand why we tend to think of our emotions passively as things that just happen to us rather than as judgments we make. It often seems as though we just couldn't be any other way. This passive stance is also encouraged by those occasions when our feelings cause our emotions, as when irritability from overwork, illness, or overstimulation causes us to become angry where ordinarily we would not. Yet another reason for thinking we can have no control over our emotions, is that they, like any movements, thought patterns, or ways of perceiving that are repeated sufficiently, become matters of habit. We then make these judgments automatically, and it is as difficult to break such habits as it is to break any others. Whether owing to habit or to some kind of resistance, we are sometimes not aware of making our emotional judgments. It may be the experience of certain feelings or certain things we find ourselves doing that leads us to realize that we even have an emotion. Similarly, we may discover that we have given up a certain emotion when we find ourselves not feeling or acting in ways we would expect to if we were still making that judgment.[19] A final factor in explaining our sense of passivity, may be seen in connection with those emotions which render us more susceptible to control and manipulation by others, for certainly those persons and institutions that seek to exercise control will tend, although perhaps not consciously, to reinforce the belief that it is simply natural and inevitable to have such emotions.

It is not surprising, then, that objective examination and restructuring of our emotional lives is generally rather difficult. The deficiencies in our present structures may have to become dramatically apparent to motivate us sufficiently to change. Seeds of such change may be found in emotions we have about our basic emotions. Anger about being resentful or guilt about being hostile point to a certain instability in these structures of resentment and hostility, one part of us warring with another. And yet it is usually the emotions we have emotions *about* that are the most deeply rooted. Often both our emotions and the emotions we have about them spring from messages we received in childhood, the former being messages about who we are that were most strongly reinforced and so entered most deeply into the construction of our identity. The others generally were delivered with less power. We developed some emotions in responding to these weaker messages, and for periods of time these emotions may predominate. But they tend to carry little conviction and, commonly, we are relieved when we, often with the help of games, can return to those closest to our hearts.

The emotions most central to our sense of identity both open up and foreclose possibilities of what we can be and do. To judge and act justly or to truly know another, the emotions we engage in must presuppose an equality of worth between us. Resentment, envy, idolatry, demeaning forms of guilt, and the like scarcely allow the balance and objectivity necessary to render each person his due or the sensitive independence required to take the point of view of another. Fundamental to our sense of identity and worth, the central emotions we adopt represent our most important decisions about how we are going to transact with ourselves and our world.

Emotions, we have said, are scenarios which are learned by a combination of response learning and situation learning. We use these scenarios to respond to situations in which we believe our project of being a person is significantly involved. In Chapter 3, we considered Aaron Beck's analysis of many of the general ideas or rules that lead us to adopt dysfunctional scenarios of the sort we are now calling emotional. By asking ourselves what ideas or rules have led us to adopt those emotions with which we are dissatisfied, we may open the door to some helpful experiential learning in our emotional lives.

CHAPTER SIX

Learning to Know Other Persons

There is a kind of knowledge that serves us well in relating to one another and yet is not enough. It allows us to negotiate our routine transactions, to anticipate reliably the way our behaviors will mesh in these circumstances. But it is impersonal. It does not necessarily demean; it simply keeps us uninvolved and out of touch with each other as persons. If our transactions are not to leave us utterly isolated, islands of unfulfilled yearning for intimacy, we need to bring to some of them knowledge that is personal. We need to see the other in her behavior, to sense her in her touching. And yet there is something here that may disturb and haunt us. Personal knowledge can seem so elusive, our efforts so disappointing.

Can we ever know another, really? Sometimes we ask this in a mood of aloneness or estrangement or disappointment in which the answer fairly shouts itself at us, "No." Each of us is an island. We exclaim our joys unheard, suffer in separation, die alone. "Is anybody there? Does anybody care?" The words echo dishearteningly within us.

At other times, moments of wholeness, we know the answer is "Yes." None of us is an island. Nothing human is alien to us. No matter how terrifying our path, there is one who stays with us. Our lives touch, our minds meet, our bodies merge. In ecstasy, beyond words, we know, and we are known.

Again and again, we lose sight of other persons as our world becomes for us a world of things. We are detached, uninvolved, uncommitted. We see the other person as merely a potential sale or an information giver, the tree as so many cords of firewood, the poem as something to be analyzed for an assignment. We experience nothing more than objects, means to our ends, threats to our being, while we in turn become simply a means, a threat, an object in the world of another.

More often our world is neither this world of things nor that at the other end of our universe, a world of persons, but something inbetween. In what we say and do, there is a kind of recognition that falls short of entering into the life of the other and yet somehow affirms the potential value of doing so. If the other is a means, he is not only that. If he is an object, he is a subject as well.

But then there are those moments when our world becomes a world of persons. We are fully involved, responsible, changed by our encounters. The other person becomes a responsive presence sharing with us the meanings of our transactions; the tree becomes akin to us, moving us by its vitality and beauty; the poem speaks to us of our lives, our fears, and our dreams. In Herman Hesse's novel *Siddhartha*, Vasudeva says to Siddhartha:

> I have taken thousands of people across and to all of them my
> river has been nothing but a hindrance on their
> journey. . . . However, amongst the thousands there have
> been a few, four or five, to whom the river was not an
> obstacle. They have heard its voice and listened to it, and the
> river has become holy to them, as it has to me.

In this world of persons, we neither dominate nor submit but create a mutuality in which we find meaning and strength.

There are moments when the full meaning of being in this world shakes the very foundation of our being. Martin Buber tells of an event which was a turning point in his life:

> What happened was no more than that one forenoon . . . I had
> a visit from an unknown young man, without being there in
> spirit. I certainly did not fail to let the meeting be friendly. . . .
> I conversed attentively and openly with him—only I omitted to
> guess the questions which he did not put. Later, not long after,
> I learned from one of his friends—he himself was no longer
> alive—the essential content of these questions; I learned that he
> had come to me not casually, but borne by destiny, not for a
> chat but for a decision. He had come to me, he had come in
> this hour. What do we expect when we are in despair and yet
> go to a man? Surely a presence by means of which we are told
> that nevertheless there is a meaning.[1]

We have all experienced the depth of these moments when we seek in one another a presence, a human understanding.

As we move from the world of things to that of persons, our knowledge also changes. Having related impersonally, we may know much *about* her, her habits and preferences, her abilities and vulnerabilities, her life history and goals for the future, and yet not know her as a person, not know what it is like to be her having those habits and preferences and the rest. But then something happens, and we give our attention not simply to what she says or does but to who she is; what we know about her begins to come together in a new way.

Carl Rogers has said that we often seem like prisoners locked in a dungeon who send out faint messages by tapping on the wall. For months, perhaps years, we hear nothing in return. Then, suddenly it happens. The silences are broken, our isolation overcome. Someone begins a tapping in response to our own. The sounds of our self-disclosure no longer fall on empty spaces. At long last we are being heard. "Time and time again in such moments," Rogers says, "I have seen a moistness come to the eyes." We deeply need to know and be known as persons.

Despite our feelings of isolation and rejection, then—indeed implicit in them—we recognize the fact of personal understanding. What greater difference is there for us than that between the contact we have when we understand another, and the heedless passing by we endure when we merely use him. Because we can know someone else, we can pretend to be her, act her life on the stage, give an account of how she lived an event in history, help her to feel understood. Our experience of knowing and being known plays a basic role in our understanding of such fundamental human problems as alienaton, insanity, and aggression. Erich Fromm, in his major study of human aggression, maintains that a "nonjudgmental understanding can lower aggressiveness or do away with it altogether."[2] Taking strong exception to a recommendation that we promote personal acquaintance and friendship as a means of lowering aggression, Fromm contends that

> "Acquaintance" and "friendship" cannot be expected to lower aggression because they represent a superficial knowledge *about* another person, or knowledge of an 'object' which I look at from the outside. This is quite different from the penetrating, empathic knowledge in which I understand the other's experiences by mobilizing those within myself which, if not the same, are similar to his.[3]

Then, too, Carl Rogers has long contended that a person will grow when he has "a relationship in which he is prized as a separate person, in which the experiencing going on within him is *empathically understood and valued,* and in which he is given the freedom to experience his own feelings and those of others without being threatened in doing so.''[4]

The fact of personal knowledge, then, lies at the heart of our lives as persons, as does its difference from impersonal or "objective" knowledge. Yet our uncertainties about personal knowledge persist. The impersonal knowledge we have about ourselves and our world seems to be the real thing; its outlines stand out so much more clearly. By contrast, our talk about things personal sometimes seems merely a matter of subjective feeling. Do we ever really know another, especially one of the other sex? Differences arise between us. She sees it one way, we another. Perhaps she is right. A number of things seem to point that way. And how well do we know the self we are? How sure can we be that we're not projecting our feelings into her, seeing things the way we want to see them rather than the way they are? And yet how well does she know herself? And how often have we felt her unable to see things through our eyes, to feel things through our flesh? And so, around and around we go. Perhaps this time we decide she is closer to the truth than we are. On another occasion, we decide she is not. How desperately arbitrary it all can seem. Is our search for truth in personal relations anything more than a contest of wills? We know how to find the truth about our car batteries, but do we for human hearts?

Our problem here does not lie in our lives having an impersonal side. These doubts and confusions about personal knowledge, and the feelings of lostness and estrangement that underlie them, are not the inevitable outcome of belonging to two worlds. That we are citizens of an impersonal world need not make us aliens in a world of persons. Rather our difficulties with personal knowledge are rooted in the way we live in and move between and give shape to these worlds.

Sometimes our difficulties stem from confusing the personal and the impersonal, acting in matters that belong in one world as though they belonged in the other. Someone may come to us seeking a personal presence, but we, perceiving unclearly, only advise, explain, analyze. An organization we are part of may do something that threatens our well-being, yet clinging to innocence at the expense of power, unwilling to claim citizenship in any world other than the personal, we fail to assert ourselves. Like the flower child before the national guard or the uncounselled defendant before a judge we become needlessly vulnerable through behavior that is inappropriate or inept in the impersonal world.

Let's emphasize the point. There is nothing inherently second-rate or unimportant or impoverishing about our impersonal interrelations and knowledge. It is our very nature as persons to have needs, interests, problems on both sides of our lives. On the impersonal side, we need to survive and to live a sense of physical well-being. We need to keep our less-important interactions routine so that we have more energy and time to invest in those relations that matter most. We need to shield ourselves from experiences we are not prepared to deal with. We need to create those material conditions and social procedures that are the impersonal foundations necessary to support and even to enhance and to enlarge the opportunities for our growth and fulfillment as persons.

On the other hand, there is nothing inherent in our capacity for personal knowledge—our ability to enter into another's life with feeling—that prevents us from misusing this capacity or otherwise disappointing ourselves and the other. How easily we violate the world of persons, entering it carelessly or under false credentials. Well intentioned, we are deaf to the word behind the words. Appearing to offer understanding and love, we really seek knowledge by which to dominate and control. Much of our disorientation and uncertainty about personal knowledge may be rooted in fear of betrayal, or of failure, or of impotence—an inability to understand. The world of persons is a world of risk; personal knowing demands courage even as being known makes courage possible.

Doubtless, then, we will be helped to see personal knowledge more clearly and to attain it more fully as we come to live more honestly and courageously. Doubtless, too, we will be helped by the creation of economic and social conditions that support and encourage such knowledge. But we may also find help by reflecting carefully and sensitively on those experiences of knowing and being known—and of failing to know and to be known—which we already share in common. Indeed, the clarification we may attain by thinking together about these experiences can help us significantly to achieve the greater honesty and courage and care which we need if we are more fully to make of our lives—our way of being—a way of being in touch. By reflecting on our personal knowledge of others and of ourselves, then, we may come to see more clearly what that knowledge is, the requirements for it, obstacles to it, creative and destructive forms of it, and how we may better attain it.

After we have examined these aspects of personal knowledge we shall look again at the doubts about it that are so commonplace in human experience. Their very persistence suggests that their sources must be deeply embedded in our lives and that they cannot easily be uprooted to clear the ground for more effective personal learning. So far we have touched on one source, the painful things that may happen to us in our efforts to get close to people. We may be tempted to say "We never really know anyone else" because we are disappointed or injured or feel little ability to understand. But another powerful source is the typical way we have been taught to see our nature as persons. We need to take a brief look at this, here, because our account of personal knowledge will present an alternative conception.

We may have doubts and perplexities about personal knowledge because we are under the spell of that picture of ourselves as separate, self-contained individuals which has played such an important role in western culture since the Englightenment. From this view, we are who we are, quite apart from or prior to our relationships. It is impossible to have personal knowledge of another because the self is something inner and we can never get past the outside. We are condemned to know only appearances, locked out from the person who lies behind them.

We shall explore the contrary view that personal knowledge is possible because we are not essentially isolated, self-contained beings who then happen to engage in certain transactions and contracts with our world but, rather, interrelated, socially constituted beings to begin with, formed by our interactions. We do not first become persons and then enter the world of persons; we become persons in that world and are mere abstractions apart from it. In a word, we really *are* our relations with others.[5]

If we see clearly what personal knowledge is, then we can see how this knowledge is possible—how we attain it. My basic aim will be to give an account of personal knowledge that is based on what we all experience, one that lets us see more clearly how we are able to have such knowledge, and one that may help us to live more fully and effectively in the world of persons.

EMPATHIC KNOWING

What does it mean to know another person? What is it, not just to know about him, but to reach out and touch the person he is? As we reflect on what it means to be in touch we shall be sketching a picture of our nature as persons, for we can scarcely know a thing without knowing what sort of thing it is. And since it is our nature as persons to have both an impersonal and a personal side, we shall begin by considering the place in our lives of both impersonal and personal knowledge of others and then ask what distinguishes the one from the other.

We need to know persons and things in order to anticipate correctly what our future interactions with them will be like. Both knowledge of persons and knowledge of things, then, involve the reliable anticipation of what, under certain conditions, our future experience of the person or thing will be. Suppose I say "The battery in your car is dead." If you believe me, how will this affect your anticipation of your future experience? Obviously, on the condition that you get into your car and turn the key to activate the starter you will expect that the engine will not turn over. You will also expect that the radio will not play when you turn it on, the cigarette lighter will not work when you push it in, and the lights will not go on when you pull the light switch. Then, too, on the condition that you charge the battery all of these anticipations will be reversed; the engine will turn over, the radio will play, and so on. If what I have said is true these anticipations are reliable, while if what I have said is false they are unreliable. If, when you turn the key, the engine does turn over or the radio does play, then you know that what I said to you is false; you know it is false because it involved anticipations of future experience that turned out to be unreliable. Knowledge, we may say, gives us a map of the future by which we select the route we wish to take.

This reliable guidance that knowledge provides concerning the future is obviously fundamental to our ability to get on in the world. Imagine what it would be like to be unable to anticipate the consequences of our actions with some reliability, actions such as turning the car key, charging the battery, or acting in a friendly way toward someone. When we have a picture of ourselves and our world that provides adequate guidance concerning the future we have a grip on reality. We begin to lose this grip when our anticipations become unreliable. Consider such things as prejudice, fanaticism, superstition, and paranoia, which masquerade as knowledge. When we become paranoid about something, for example, we twist our experience to fit our fear-ridden beliefs rather than testing our beliefs by our experience. Perhaps a fully blown paranoid tells himself that the entire hospital has joined his family and friends in a plot against him. He appears to anticipate that his future experiences will be of one sort rather than another, but he really doesn't do this. No matter what he experiences he continues to "believe" everyone is against him. No one harms him. Well, they are biding their time. Many are friendly and helpful to him; they, of course, are simply trying to throw him off his guard. His belief fits everything that happens and so is not functioning as an anticipation that certain things will happen and that other things will not. It is comparable to telling ourselves the battery is dead even though we just started the car and the radio is playing. Explanation? Well, the power must be coming from some other source.

Genuine knowledge of persons and things, then, is tested by experience. We anticipate certain things and so we rule out everything that is incompatible with these things. In knowing what we will experience we also know what we won't experience.

Adequate guidance concerning future experience is fundamental to our relations to persons as well as to things. We need to be able to anticipate what others will do under all sorts of conditions, especially when our own actions are an important part of those conditions. Much of our anticipation of the behavior of others takes the form of impersonal or objective knowledge. This generally serves us well in routine transactions in which we are each playing our more public roles or otherwise acting in ways that have become habitual or culturally standardized. Every culture, for example, must provide a complete assortment of types of behavior, personal appearance, and setting for use when persons meet so they can quickly communicate what each expects of the other and what the other may expect of him in the ensuing transaction. By his uniform, body language, manner of speaking and the like, a complete stranger can readily show his intention to be a casual conversationalist, religious proselytizer, prostitute, information giver, political campaigner, salesman, policeman, and so on. But as our transactions involve us more fully as persons, our knowledge of the other as an impersonal role player or as otherwise employing a familiar repertoire of behavior becomes inadequate to guide us. Not only does the other's behavior become less routine and standardized but what we now want to anticipate is not just what this behavior will be but the way he will be as a whole person. As we move to deeper levels of relating we must rely increasingly on the sort of anticipation which personal knowledge involves.

Personal and impersonal knowledge differ in the kind of anticipation involved. In personal knowledge, we anticipate being able to recognize the other person in whatever he does. We gain this knowledge of the other by empathy; and it is by empathy that we are later able to recognize him, to cognize or know him again. Empathy is the use of our feelings to try to do what every good actor must be able to do—take the other's point of view, enter into his experience, his way of being in the world.

In Dorothy Canfield's "Sex Education," Aunt Minnie was finally able to do this:

"What do you suppose *he* felt, left there in the corn? He must have been sure I would tell everybody he had attacked me. He probably thought that when he came out and went back to the village he'd already be in disgrace and be put out of the pulpit.

"But the worst must have been to find out, so rough, so

plain from the way I acted—as if somebody had hit him with an ax—the way he would look to any woman he might try to get close to. That must have been———'' she drew a long breath, "well, pretty hard on him."

In trying to take the other's point of view, we seek to stand in his shoes, to grasp what it's like to have his goals, values, beliefs, feelings about things. We want to sense what it's like to relax to his rhythms, ache with his nerves, fear with his past conditioning, exercise the skill of his hands, and dream his dreams. In other words, we seek to put on and wear for a time his personal history and the sense of himself and of his world which grow out of it. We try to get in touch with him as a whole person.

In describing personal knowledge of another in terms of sensing both what it's like to be him and how he sees himself and his world, I am relating it both to what is often called *self* as *subject* or *process* or *knower* and to what is often called *self* as *object* or *structure* or *known*. Chad Gordon, for example, defines the self as

a complex *process* of continuing interpretive activity—simultaneously the person's located subjective stream of *consciousness* (. . . perceiving, thinking, planning, evaluating, choosing, etc.) *and* the resultant accruing *structure of self-conception* (the special system of self-referential meaning available to the active consciousness).[6]

When we sense what it is like to be another we experience what he does or says as he experiences it, namely, in the context of his way of seeing himself and his world. Self as subject cannot be separated from self as object. If we think of the self-as-subject as a stream of consciousness, then self-as-object is part of the channel through which that stream flows. Our awareness of the stream involves the width of the channel, the direction it takes, and some sense of its depth. The more we know of the channel, the richer our sense of the stream. The more we understand the other's structure of self-conception, the richer our sense of what it is like to be him.

Having such empathic or personal knowledge of the other we anticipate that we will be able to recognize this person in whatever he does. Our sense of being in touch will be renewable in our future transactions. We are confident that what he says and does, and how he appears, will be expressive of the person we see him to be—the goals we understand him to have and the way he sees things. What we anticipate about the other's behavior, then, is not what it will be specifically—not what an impersonal observer would hear and see—but that we will be able to relate it to the fundamentals of the special outlook we know him to have. It will make sense that someone with his goals, beliefs, feelings, and the rest would act in that way. By placing our experience of what he does in the context of our knowledge of his personal outlook we are able to grasp the personal meaning which that act has for him. The place of that act in his way of seeing things *is* that meaning. We are in touch not just with the action but with the one who is acting.

Life is growth and change and so what we anticipate is not a static sameness but a pattern of development coherent enough to sustain a sense of personal identity—a theme we shall return to in a subsequent section. Much as the later passages of a symphony flow from what has come before, or the later moves in a game develop from those which preceded, so the growth and change of the other are a continuation of her life story.

Personal knowledge of another is based on our knowledge of ourselves. We can understand or stand under the other only by relating his point of view to our own experiences of ourselves and of our relations to our world. What the other says or does, or the way he looks, activate in us experiences that we had in doing or saying similar things; it is in terms of those experiences that we give our attention to, or stand under, his. We can do this insofar as we have come to realize that nothing human is alien to us. Has the other lost someone close while we have not? Well, we know at least in lesser ways the threat and pain of separation.

Empathic knowledge does not necesarily involve sympathy. Sympathy means *feeling with* the other; empathy means understanding or sensing the feelings of the other. We have sympathy when we identify with the feelings of the other. We share those feelings, are in harmony with them. In empathy we maintain just enough distance to experience those feelings as his and not ours; our feelings are involved only in the way they must be to understand or sense what the other is feeling.

In saying that we seek to see the other person and his world as if we were that person, the words *as if* need to be emphasized. In empathizing, we do not forget that the point of view we are taking on is another's and not our own. The good actor does not forget he is not the person he is portraying. He understands the way his character sees something, but he may also sense that this character is blind to certain things about what he sees. Or he may understand the terror that his character feels yet may also regard it as unrealistic. In understanding the blindness, the overreactions and other things the character is not aware of about himself, the actor can portray him more fully.

In empathy, then, we take up residence in two countries, seeing the other and his world from both his point of view and from our own simultaneously, although it is his point of view that is dominant, our own functioning only as the means by which we understand his. His friend was fatally injured in an accident, he struggles with feelings of self-doubt, he yearns to be understood, he has found new meaning in his life. We listen and find ourselves getting a sense of these things. Something in our own experience enables us to step into his. We need not be aware of what personal experience we are drawing on in this way; it is there in the back of our mind and by means of it we begin to understand what his experience must be like for him. Bereavement, self-doubt, feeling unheard, finding new meaning are experiences we too have had in some form and to some extent. Only by means of our own experience can we empathize with that of another.

Our own experience, then, is the background against which we focus on his. As we give our attention to his experience as such, rather than to that part of our own of which it reminds us, we place his experience in the pattern that we sense his life to have for him. We enter into the way he lives this experience, the meaning it has in the context of *his* life. We understand him, we might say, by also standing by him, for in standing by him we see the world from his vantage point but with our own eyes.

Because empathy involves this dual standpoint, personal knowledge of another cannot be *equated* with seeing things from his point of view. Our own point of view is always there as an element in the experience. We know him from inside and outside simultaneously. We see things from the other's point of view, but we also maintain a certain psychic distance between him and ourselves.

If we fail to maintain this distance we confuse the other's identity with our own and distort our knowledge of him. We feel responsibility for his commitments, pride (in ourselves) for his achievements, validation in the love he receives. But our knowledge of these things is then distorted because it must serve certain needs of ours and so does not let the other appear simply as he is in himself.

It is because knowing has an outside-inside structure—involves a dual standpoint—that it appropriately may include more than how the other consciously sees things.

Personal knowledge of another has two additional features of importance. First, it allows for freedom and creativity in the other; there may be genuine novelty in what he does or becomes. A Picasso may begin painting in a new style. Those who know him best, indeed he himself, could not have anticipated that style because it didn't exist before he brought it into being in his act of painting. In this sense, this new style comes as a surprise. But for those who truly know him it nonetheless makes sense that he would do this. They are able to see it as an expression of the person they know him to be.

Similarly, in personal transactions the other may surprise us by what he does and yet we may then find it perfectly understandable that he does it. Perhaps neither of us had previously even conceived of that particular way of responding to his situation and yet we find that response perfectly in keeping with the person he is. This seems to me, for example, to express the sort of expectations we have when we place our deepest level of confidence and trust in another. It is not that we rely on her always to do a specific thing, such as always to tell us the truth, but that whatever she does we are confident it will be expressive of her care, understanding and the like.

Each situation in which we act is at least a little different from any previous situation. We may not take any notice of what is new about that situation and so may act rather mechanically or routinely. But when, as in personal interactions, we are responsive to what is new, then whatever we do will have at least a slightly different personal meaning than anything we have done previously. When we know another in a way that is largely impersonal this element of novelty slips through the net of our understanding.

We may find it very upsetting when our world changes or we ourselves change and we are unable to respond in those familiar ways in which we feel at home. At a time when Whistler was learning to paint in a new style a woman became quite indignant in looking at one of his canvasses. "Well," she exclaimed, "I never saw a sunset that looked like that." To which Whistler replied, "But Madam, don't you wish you could?" In thinking about this story I've sometimes imagined a modern day Heraclitus maintaining that we can't come home twice to the same person. Perhaps one of us exclaims, "Oh come now, I do it all the time," to which Heraclitus replies, "But Sir, don't you wish you couldn't?" In resisting change we lose touch with the frequently changing, ever-unique being of the other.

Personal knowledge thrusts us into a world of continuous change. It shows us others not as routinely functioning parts of a system but as essentially free beings who need not remain as we see them or ask them to be. Even if they seem to have renounced their freedom, the potential for it is there. A strength may be quietly growing within them, through which they will move from their accustomed place. Perhaps our biggest difficulty in knowing, much less enjoying, the other may be a reluctance to accept his freedom. Perhaps the same is true of knowing and enjoying ourselves.

The second additional feature of personal knowledge is that it involves possible *tests* of the extent and depth of our knowledge of the

other. This is easily overlooked. Because the anticipations of our personal knowing are much less specific than those *typical* of the impersonal, we may sometimes think of our sense of the other as purely
subjective—something for which there are no reliable checks. But anticipations *are* involved and, so, what we experience may contradict
them. Granted, then, that in our personal knowledge of a particular,
unique person we anticipate not one specific experience but the often
rather wide range of possible experiences in which we would
recognize that person, nonetheless, there is generally a much wider
range of possible experiences in which we would be unable to
recognize him. Such experiences would count against the truth-
fulness of our picture of him. A Picasso, for example, is continually doing new things none of which may contradict the expectations of one who knows him really well. But, aside from extraordinary circumstances, these expectations do rule out, say, his painting pretty little sentimental pictures or acting in support of fascist
governments. Because the process by which we test our personal
knowledge is often subtle and complex, it may be helpful to reflect on
our experiences of failing to understand certain actions of someone
we know—of being unable to relate these actions to the person we
believe her to be.

What happens when we fail to recognize the other in what she says
or does? To begin with, we may simply let it pass. Perhaps we are
tired or preoccupied with something else. For one reason or another it
doesn't seem worth pursuing at the time.

In some cases we may want not to understand. What the other says
or does is really clear enough but we do not let ourselves hear it or see
it because we want to avoid facing the truth about something—perhaps about the other or about ourselves or about a third person—and
perhaps also because we want to avoid having to change the ways we
ordinarily respond to her. In this case we will find some way of side-
stepping the difficulty. Those of us who are men might say to
ourselves, and even to her, that she's just not making sense, but of
course she never is very logical. Or we might say that she's not
herself right now and it's probably that time of the month. Those who
are women might say that he doesn't really feel that way but he has to
tell himself that because he's a man, or the problem is he just doesn't
remember things very well. As R.D. Laing has said, we often maintain our illusions by invalidating the other; she is illogical, his
memory is of no account. We may also do it by invalidating ourselves.

In other cases, what the other says or does is not entirely clear, but
we do not want to ask her about it because of the risk that her answer
might require us to change our image of her and so to respond to her
differently than we are accustomed to. In this case, we may turn our

eyes away from the fact that we are unsure of what she intends and pretend to ourselves that we see a meaning there that we're comfortable with.

But often we will want to understand the other. What will happen in those cases, when we are unable to relate what she says or does to the person we believe her to be? Persons are so complex and are so often undergoing significant change, and the situations in which they must act often vary so greatly, that we can have no simple answer to this question. In many instances our failure to understand does not mean we are going to have to revise our image of her. All we need is more information. Perhaps we simply ask her to explain or we talk with someone else about her situation. We learn she is not feeling well or is under unusual pressure of some sort and that clears it up for us. Under these circumstances her behavior fits the way we see her. But even if what we learn does not help us to understand we may simply dismiss it as unimportant or tuck it away in the back of our mind hoping for new clues in the future whether from our own subconscious processes or from external events. In either case—whether we now understand or remain puzzled—our image of her remains unchanged.

At times, though, as we listen to her explanation we begin to feel that we don't understand because we just don't know her well enough. We may be seeing something of who she is that is missing from our picture of her. As we talk with her we begin to reexamine that picture. If the conviction grows on us that *this* is our problem we try to revise our image of her in a way that fits the actions or words we are trying to understand, while continuing to make sense of all of our prevous experience of her.

Our knowledge of the other may be inadequate in different senses and degrees. First, it may be incomplete. This is a side of her we had not seen before. We revise the way we see her accordingly, and if we do this correctly we find our anticipations are more reliable than before. Our knowledge may simply be more comprehensive if we have now experienced her in a wider range of circumstances.

Seeing a new side of someone we know often involves the fact that, in a sense, each of us is more than one person. Eric Berne referred to this as having different "ego states," each being "a consistent pattern of feeling and experience directly related to a corresponding consistent pattern of behavior."[7] Sometimes we feel and behave the way we saw our parents do, sometimes the way we did as children, and sometimes the way we have learned as adults to deal with present reality. In coming to know ourselves or another, then, we need to distinguish different outlooks, and how they are interrelated. We may be quite familiar with someone in one or two of her ego states, and yet have little or no awareness of her in a third.

Second, our knowledge may be inadequate in the sense of not being deep enough. In this case we have come to see something that is fairly central to who she is so that in making it part of our image of her we do not just add to that image but significantly reorganize it. Certain experiences in the past now seem more important to who she is, others less so. Perhaps we see new connections between aspects of her personality. We shall consider this more fully when we come to consider the nature of self identity.

It may also happen that what we took to be knowledge of the other may be not simply inadequate but deeply mistaken. If her actions seem to be in fundamental contradiction to the way we saw her we may begin to doubt whether we really know her at all. We are faced with the prospect, not of enlarging and deepening our knowledge, but of disillusionment about our relationship with her. We are more likely to conclude that we really haven't known her at all if we have been acquainted a relatively short time than if we are old friends. In the latter case, when our picture of her has the confirmation of many years of experience we may continue to place our faith in it, even though we don't know how to account for actions which seem so completely out of character for her. Surely there must be some explanation, some extraordinary circumstance which, if only we could discover it, would bring even those actions into line with the person we remain convinced we know her to be.

We may or may not finally know the answer. Perhaps subsequent events, although failing to explain those actions, will either strengthen or further shake our confidence in the way we have so long seen her. If events continue to shake our confidence at what point will we seriously consider withdrawing it? At what point will it become simply foolish not to? Obviously these questions involve both individual judgment and risk. Where understanding ends, trusting will often carry on.

That our experiences of the other stand in such a varied and often complex relation to the truth or falsity of the way we see her should not blind us to the fact that these experiences do constitute tests of that picture of her according to whether or not they fit the anticipations involved in that picture. The relation of evidence to belief or theory is often equally varied and complex in our impersonal forms of knowledge—even in its more rigorous, scientific modes. A considerable part of our understanding of all that is impersonal and objective is too complex to be shown to be true or false by one or two experiences, such as failing to start the car. Even the relatively simple statement that the car battery is dead may turn out to be false despite the fact that the engine will not turn over. Perhaps the connection between the battery and cable has become badly corroded, or there may be a short in the starter, or something may be wrong with the starter switch.

In determining whether a belief is true we are determining whether we can rely on it as a guide to future experience. We *know* something to the extent that beliefs concerning it are certain—certain in the sense that our evidence makes it unreasonable not to place *complete* reliance on the anticipations involved. Not to rely on our well-supported beliefs because of a remote possibility they may be in error would be as self-defeating and incapacitating as refusing to trust anyone because we cannot completely eliminate the risk involved. To know something or someone is to have eliminated all reasonable doubt, where what is reasonable is determined by our practical need to anticipate the future reliably. We achieve our knowledge or completely trustworthy belief in one way (or closely related set of ways) concerning things and in a related but not identical way concerning persons. That there are tests is fundamental to both.

Even as we come to understand these things more clearly, however, we may still be uneasy about the idea that personal knowledge has its test in the anticipations it embodies. This uneasiness comes from our experiences of being in touch with someone, moments in which we know not by anticipation but in the immediacy of our contact with the other—moments in which what we know becomes flesh. Such encounters are so important to us, so inherently valuable, that at first thought they may seem to have nothing to do with anticipating. The immediacy of personal knowing is an end in itself—something we find fulfilling—and when we live such a moment it seems so complete in itself that any thought of the future is entirely foreign to it. Such moments, however, are not isolated and self-contained but derive their meaning from the stream of life of which they are a part. When we are in touch with someone there is both recognition and anticipation, for he is not a static, timeless thing but a dynamic, changing organism. That the other comes to this present moment from his specific, unique past and is moving into a future of possibilities unique to him is not something external to the person we are in contact with but is the very stuff of his being who he is.

Feelings are important to our sense of being in touch with another. But knowing is not simply feeling; it is an act of the whole person in which feeling is united with reason. Without reason, we would not know with whom or what we are in contact. Because it is informed by reason, our touching is not an empty sensation or blind feeling but a direct experience of the other's way of being—the unique pattern that is her life as she lives it.

In the present moment, we recognize or *re*-cognize her as we enter once again into the point of view that is uniquely hers. Never simply identical with what it was, we sense it to be a development from her earlier way of seeing things. And the present carries promise that we will continue to see an expression and development of this pattern in whatever she does in the future.

Our present experience sometimes seems to be completely self-contained because so much of the richness of the past and future is present below our threshold of awareness. The meanings which move between us and the other in our personal knowing and being known have a complex history or preparation; some of the threads of this history we can draw together by metaphor. Perhaps we say, "We've been like comrades in arms," and this and similar expressions capture a great deal. But in its full concreteness, this history extends far beyond what we can consciously grasp.

Put in somewhat different terms, the feelings that our personal encounters with another have nothing to do with anticipating, may result from thinking of the self as subject, in abstraction from the self as object. As I have argued, the sense of what it is like to be another is inseparable from our understanding of how he sees himself.

Impersonal and personal knowledge differ not only in the kind of anticipation involved but *also in the purposes and needs* that each serves. Fundamental to personal knowledge is our need to be in touch with each other. Bradley, at age nine, expressed it this way:

> If you touch me soft and gentle
> If you look at me and smile at me
> If you listen to me talk sometimes before you talk
> I will grow, really grow.[8]

The vital importance to children of being touched is all too well documented. "Infants who are neglected, ignored, or for any reason do not experience enough touch, suffer mental and physical deterioration even to the point of death."[9] Touching is an act of recognition. As we grow, our need for touch and recognition develops from the need for being handled and held and smiled at, to being listened to and understood, as well. It becomes harder and harder for us to retain a sense of our significance if no one responds to us as a unique person—communicates with us in a personal way. When we fail to know one another, no matter how closely we crowd together, we are encompassed by loneliness. Neither the noise of words nor a violence of actions can dispel it. At its heart, being a person is being in touch.

Eric Berne calls anything that meets our hunger for recognition a stroke. "Strokes can be given in the form of actual physical touch or by some symbolic form of recognition such as a look, a word, a gesture, or any act which says 'I know you're there'."[10] How deeply recognized we feel by such strokes, of course, will depend upon the history of our relationship with the person giving them. If, in the past, we have been listened to and understood empathically by her, the look or gesture will carry the meaning of personal recognition. But if she has not been in touch with us in this way, her act can carry only a less-personal meaning, a recognition of us only in the role that we play, although somehow affirming that we are more than that. Each of these forms of contact has its value. Each conveys a kind of respect, for "respect" literally means "to look at." But only in personal knowledge does the other see us directly, see us from our point of view.

Personal knowledge, then, involves both touching and seeing. The sense in which knowing is touching is reflected in the *Old Testament* use of "know" for sexual intercourse. Seeing is ordinarily less intimate than touching and yet when we see things through her eyes our intimacy is maintained.

In addition to meeting our need to be in touch with each other, personal knowledge also serves our closely related needs for mutual enjoyment and responsiveness. Possibilities for enjoying one another increase dramatically as we participate in each other's thoughts, feelings, interests, dreams, achievements. Obviously, too, our ability to be mutually responsive or responsible is limited by how well we know each other.

In contrast, impersonal knowing and being known serve quite different needs and purposes, ones that do not involve us in personal ways. We seek not to be in touch but to handle the actions of the other effectively. Here we know the other by observing his role playing, his habits, his ways of performing the more routine transactions of daily life. We generally do not need to know what it is like to be the person playing the role to be able to cooperate or compete effectively with him as he plays it.

On another side, we may seek impersonal knowledge for the power either to protect ourselves from the other or to exploit him. If we are motivated by fear we want to know enough about the other to determine what sort of threat, if any, he may pose, and how we may avoid it or manipulate him so as to undercut it. If we aim to use him we need to know something about his vanities and fears, his gullibilities and guilt, his dependencies and deprivations—points at which he is most susceptible to the external push and pull we can exert.

For the most part, though, our knowledge of others is a mixture of the impersonal and the personal. Our motives are often no less complex than we are as persons. We want to be in touch but we also need distance. Our enjoyment may be laced with fear, our caring with vanity. We need to keep our many roles, especially the more public ones, fairly routine and yet in some part of our minds is at least the trace of a thought that we are dealing with persons and not just role players. The world of things and the world of persons are after all the same world, in different perspective.

The conditions necessary for obtaining an undistorted personal know-ledge of another can be summarized as being able to love. We have emphasized the role of empathy in personal knowledge, and love is essential to true empathy. Without love we use our feelings in a way that is manipulative and distorting and results in dominance knowledge. In this case the knower seeks power to control the other by "getting his number," discovering "what makes him tick." The knower may be motivated by fear or anxiety. Once the other's vulnerabilities and susceptibilities to manipulation are discovered he becomes less threatening. Or the knower may be motivated by sadism. As Erich Fromm has put it, "the essence of sadism is the passion for unlimited, godlike control over men and things."[11] Consider, for example, the mother who required her daughter to inform her of everything about her life—her every experience, every thought, every dream. When the daughter had a decision to make the mother would pray about it and would then tell her daughter the answer she received from God. Or we may contemplate the first grade teacher who impresses by the attentiveness—one friend said "sweetness"—of her listening to others but who once explained, "I've found if I just listen to anyone long enough they'll give themselves away."

Dominance knowledge has a fearful potential in the hands of the state. In the motion picture, *The Prisoner*, for example, it is by gaining intimate personal knowledge of his prisoner (after subjecting him to a long period of isolation) that the agent of the state is able to manipulate him into giving a false public confession. Another example is the tough reform procedures which, according to Robert Lifton,[12] were used by the Chinese Communists on the Chinese intellectuals, among others. The program began with ten-man study groups in which the members were first encouraged just to get to know each other. An increasingly frank sharing of experience, ideas and feelings was warmly encouraged. In time, political lectures were begun and debate by members of the group encouraged, the group leader remaining neutral. In the next phase the student was surprised to find that the many things he had revealed of his attitudes and convictions were now held up to rigorous examination with particular attention to his motivation. Increasingly he was led to self-criticism and to criticism of and by the others in his group. The process culminated in a written summary and public confession of his thoughts and attitudes, usually focusing especially on a denunciation of the student's father. In the absence of love, personal knowledge can become a powerful tool for manipulation and control.

Dominance knowledge is a distorted way of seeing the other. There are two reasons for this. First, to see the other simply as he is we must be willing and able to let him be as he is. If we are secure enough we can take a Taoistic, receptive, noninterfering attitude toward him. We keep our categories of interpretation, expectations, biases, fears, and needs out of the way so we can simply listen and wait openly, patiently, even wonderingly, for the other to disclose himself in his own way. As Siddhartha puts it:

> When someone is seeking it happens quite easily that he only
> sees the things that he is seeking; that he is unable to find
> anything, unable to absorb anything, because he is only think-
> ing of the thing he is seeking, because he has a goal, because
> he is obsessed with his goal. Seeking means: to have a goal;
> but finding means: to be free, to be receptive, to have no goal.

There is a Zen saying that, "A pickpocket in the presence of a Saint will see only pockets." Those who need control over the other see him in terms of what lends itself to that need. The sadist sees the other only as an extension of himself. The knower motivated by fear sees the other only in terms of his need to be safe. His picture of the other comes together around that motif, which may have little to do with the way the other sees himself and the meaning his actions have for him.

When the other is an end, important in and for himself, then knowing him becomes an end in and for itself. What we come to know of him is centered in the way he sees himself. It comes together around his own outlook. To be sure, this knowledge involves reliable anticipations of our future experience of the other. This anticipatory function, though, is not an end outside of this knowledge to which this knowledge becomes a means. Anticipation is simply part of what knowledge is, just as the person's future is part of what or who that person is. But when we place the other primarily in our world rather than his, what we know of him comes together around our goals and needs and outlook as the center rather than around his goals and needs and outlook. If he is an obstacle to our safety or an extension of our person then our knowledge of him is centered in one of these things and becomes a means. Our anticipations have to do with threat and safety or with dominance and resistance, and their reliability is measured in these terms. We anticipate that whatever the other does it will be something we know how to handle for our own safety or manipulate for our own power to control. Of course, as long as we are dealing with the other as merely a role player or as otherwise routine in his behavior, these aims may be served by the anticipations involved in impersonal knowledge. Beyond that point these aims require the anticipations of a dominance knowledge gained by an empathy without love.

The second reason that dominance knowledge is distorted has to do with the effect the attitude of the knower has on the other. When the knower expresses attitudes of respect, care, friendship, and the like he creates conditions under which the other is helped to understand himself and is encouraged to disclose this understanding. But under attitudes of seeking power and control over the other, the other is less free to see himself and becomes defensive.

Something rather similar may be said of self-knowledge. We are helped in learning who we are if we have an accepting and respectful attitude toward ourselves. Conversely, a judgmental, rejecting attitude makes it difficult to see ourselves truly, for we are then unwilling simply to let ourselves be who we are, even for a few moments of reflective self-awareness. We find permission to see ourselves as we are, as Rogers emphasizes, through relationships in which we are "prized as a separate person, in which the experiencing going on within us is empathically understood and valued, and in which we are given the freedom to experience our own feelings and those of others without being threatened in doing so."[13]

Genuine empathy, then, in which we enter into the viewpoint of the other and see her on her own terms, requires love, as does knowledge of ourselves. The *agape, eros* and *philia* dimensions of love each play a necessary role in full empathic knowing. Empathy, that is, includes caring for the well being of the other (agape); finding her likeable, pleasurable, enjoyable (eros); and sharing the mutuality of friendship with her (philia). Empathic knowledge is not fully achieved if one of these dimensions is missing.

An erotic empathy from which agape is absent is an uninvolved sort of relation in which knowledge is only a way of taking pleasure in the other. Knowing the other only in terms of pleasure is comparable to knowing her only in terms of fear. One fails to see her as she is as a whole person, to respond to her at this level. The absence of agape, however, does not necessarily imply an inability to love this way. A mainly erotic empathy may contain the seeds of a fuller relationship just as knowledge motivated by fear may in time evolve into knowledge motivated by love. It becomes more fully personal as we gain a sense of the other as she is quite apart from her relationship with us—a genuine looking at her or regarding her which, as we have noted, is the literal meaning of "respect."

Conversely, agapeic empathy from which eros and philia are missing is a detached sort of relation in which the knower tries to act for the well-being of the other only out of obligation. There is no genuine two-way relationship. But we do not want to become the mere object of another's good deeds. Anyone could serve as well to be this sort of object. We experience genuine relation and understanding only if the other is not only concerned for our well-being but also likes and enjoys us—values her relation with us for what we and we alone can mean to her. Knowing the other without eros we fail to know her as desirable, as one with whom union is enhancing. Knowing the other without philia or friendship, we fail to know her as one in whom something comes alive as we give ourselves—our interests, concerns, experiences and the like—and as one who brings something alive in us by sharing herself. We fail to know her as capable of that sort of relationship apart from which we lose all personal existence. It is in philia that we know truly personal existence as one of full mutuality with another, for as Aristotle noted, philia is a relationsip between equals.

Needless to say, we have been considering abstract types rather than concretely existing persons. For the most part we find ourselves and others to embody a mixture of the things we have distinguished. We often find in our desire to know the other a mixture of fear of and interest in him for his own sake. Our relations commonly are a blend of I-Thou and I-It. Sometimes, to be sure, relations are almost purely I-It, as in the case of Descartes's followers who thought animals other than humans were machine-like and lacked any feelings at all, or in the case of those who see members of another race as utterly lacking in all the distinctly human feelings they know in themselves, or again, in the case of the bombardier who sees in his sights only a military target. Generally, though, we have at least a vague awareness that the actions and appearances of another have an inner side of feelings and all the other intangible attributes of humanity. And conversely, our moments of deepest personal relation are mediated by the objective meanings of what the other says and does.

The major obstacle to being able to love another and, so, to coming to know him in an intimate, personal way is unfinished business from important personal relationships in our past—especially in our childhood. To one extent or another, we all seem to carry into the present unresolved angers, fears, jealousies, and the like, adopted in our earlier struggles for love and survival and significance. As part of these emotional scenarios, we typically continue to harbor unfulfilled wishes that prevent us from torquing into opportunities for love and creativity in the present. Consequently, we may tend to project into the present our perceptions of the past, responding to one or another of our fellow adults—especially our mates or those in authority—as though they were mother or father or perhaps even a brother or sister with whom we were rivals. Such projections, of course, prevent us from seeing and enjoying the other as the unique person he is. Instead, often with little awareness, we try to use him as a means of gaining something that we felt deprived of long ago.

Aside from the frequency with which most of us sense the inappropriateness of emotional responses by ourselves and others, striking—we might even say staggering—evidence of the pervasiveness of projections of the past onto the present is thrust upon us by the phenomena of transference and counter-transference that are basic features of the typical relationship between therapist and client.[14] Not only must the therapist recognize and work with the virtually inevitable transference to him by his client of feelings from the client's past, but he must recognize his own tendency to do the same toward his client. Those who are important to us will often tend to evoke powerful memories of our childhood and perhaps also of later years. *Learning to discriminate what is memory and what is present reality is, I believe, the most important condition for truly coming to know another.*

What we have said of our knowledge of other persons applies generally to knowledge of ourselves as well. Just as we need to anticipate the responses of others, so we need to anticipate our own. Many of our decisions involve our sense of what we will be able to do effectively and what we will find rewarding. Sometimes we surprise ourselves about such things. We may behave in a way we had not anticipated, or feel differently than we had expected to. This may be a pleasant surprise or it may be disappointing to us. But if our unexpected response is not only different than what we anticipated but actually contradicts it, it means what we thought about ourselves was wrong—our belief about ourselves was false. If this happens often enough, we may come to feel that we don't know ourselves very well. Sometimes we may even get the sense that, in some ways, others know us better than we do.

We may also know ourselves in both personal and impersonal ways. In knowing ourselves impersonally, we treat ourselves as an object, look at ourselves as though from the outside. It may be a moment of awkward self-consciousness when we stand outside of ourselves, as it were, to monitor how we are performing. Trying to write or to paint, we may look at ourselves through the eyes of an imagined critic or censor. Or we may feel the embarrassment or shame of being stared at by eyes that seem ever-present and all-seeing. Yet again, we may turn ourselves into an object of condemnation by the voice of our conscience.

Robert Solomon analyzes a large class of emotions in which "we treat ourselves as if we were 'someone else'."[15] These include self-contempt, self-hatred, self-love (narcissism), self-pity, self-"respect", and self-"confidence." According to Solomon,

> The classic portrait of Narcissus admiring himself in the reflecting pool, so transfixed by his image that he is oblivious to the world, devoid of desire and incapable of love or respect for others, is an apt allegory for the irresponsible and paralyzing judgments which admire oneself at a distance, as an object rather than as a subject. What one "loves" about himself is merely the image of himself, not him*Self*. Accordingly, "self-love" is not love at all, but . . . idolatry . . ..[16]

Similarly in self-contempt "one wallows in his self-ascribed repulsiveness just as the man of self-pity wallows in his misfortune . . . without attempting to do anything about it."[17] Of this class of emotions, Solomon contends that "they are all, even self-love and what is so often called 'self-respect' and 'self-confidence' (which are *not* the same as . . . 'self-esteem'), defensive emotions, attempts to salvage our dignity from a distance, as if to prop our images up from behind, as if we ourselves might remain behind the scenes."[18] In such ways as these, we strike a pose not only to others but to ourselves as well. We construct a message *about* ourselves.

In describing impersonal self-knowledge in terms of looking at ourselves as an object, we must not confuse this meaning of "object" with the distinction made earlier between self as subject and self as object. In the earlier meaning, self as object is self as known from the point of view of the one who is known—an object of empathic knowing. In the case of impersonal self-knowledge, the self is object because it is known from the point of view of another—an object of impersonal knowing.

Knowing ourselves in a personal way has three of the features we have emphasized concerning personal knowledge of another. First, it involves seeing ourselves from our own point of view. Second, it allows for genuine novelty in what we say or do or feel. We expect only that we will be able to recognize ourselves in doing or feeling these things. It will make sense to us, in light of how we think about ourselves, that we might respond to these ways. Third, the *anticipation* involved in personal self-knowledge constitutes an ongoing test of the extent and depth of this knowledge. There are things we might do or feel in which we certainly would not recognize ourselves. They would carry the message that something is "off" in the way we understand who we are.

THE CONTENT OF PERSONAL KNOWLEDGE: IMAGES

We shall say, then, that in knowing another we know her images of herself and her world, both *what* those images are and *how* she lives them—the ways she thinks, feels and acts out of habit, her degree of centeredness in her own organism, and her unconscious intentions, feelings and perceptions. Let us consider first the images themselves.

We come to know our world as we interact with it, and we come to know ourselves in this same interaction. Consequently, our images of self and world stand in polar relation to each other. We know ourselves in terms of and, in fact, by means of our knowledge of our world, and we know our world in terms of and by means of our knowledge of ourselves. More specifically, we know ourselves as both subject and object, seeing and being seen, valuing and being valued, acting and being acted on. Correspondingly, we know our world as possibilities for our action and experience and as having certain effects on us by its actions. It provides and curtails our possibilities, supports and resists our efforts, validates and in- validates our worth. It inflicts pain and relieves it, gives pleasure and denies it, seeks our presence and fears it, asks our affirmation and refuses it. These are the things we learn to anticipate.

Consider our interaction with our physical environment. We may feel cramped by kitchen walls or narrow streets, become dulled by suburban sameness or urban rot, grow expansive with wilderness trails or garden spaces, find joy in soaring structures or mountain vistas. Harrassed by heavy traffic, estranged by plastic repetitions, we feel mechanical and mass-produced. Quiet in desert nightfall, moved by brilliant sunrise, we know life pulsing within us, gentle and triumphant.

We are able to be what we are able to do, so that as we make discoveries in our environment we make discoveries in ourselves. A rigid, repetitive environment closes off the flow and variety which are potential in our being, while wilderness may put us in touch with depths in ourselves we could not otherwise know. We may not be able to say what we now sense in ourselves; we may know it only tacitly, only as a responsiveness in us to the unplanned, uncontrolled variety and vitality of the environment. But we do live this knowledge of ourselves and it becomes part of our repertoire of ways of being. And often we become able to say what this knowledge is;

our corresponding knowledge of our environment then forms the background against which we hold this new understanding. We discover our potential as our environment invites its use. There is always a merging between the process that we are and the processes that others are.[19] We are participant beings.

Similarly we know ourselves and others in terms of and by means of our transactions with them. As Eric Berne has noted, we don't simply interact with others, for our meeting is a coming together of our intentions and purposes with those of the other; together we *transact*. Fundamentally, our transactions may validate or invalidate our own worth as persons and in turn the worth of the other. It is in manipulating (and in being manipulated) that we know ourselves as manipulator and the other as a possibility for this action. It is in being manipulated (and in manipulating) that we know the other as manipulator and ourselves as providing this possibility. Equally, it is in empathically relating to and affirming another (and in being related to and affirmed) that we know ourselves as persons and the other as the possibility for—indeed, the call for—this action. It is when another empathically relates to us (and we to him) that we know him as person and ourselves as the possibility and call for this action. When we know the other as a call for an empathic, validating relationship, we experience ourself as being called to become the person we really are. As Martin Buber has emphasized, we are not persons apart from living in I-Thou relationships. That is, we do not start off as persons who then may or may not enter into personal relationships. It is only in entering into such relationships that we become persons.

The way we come to know ourselves in our actions is dependent on the way another knows us in those actions. Consequently, we know ourselves from both inside and outside our own organism, simultaneously. For the most part, actions must be learned. If we want to be a tennis player the flight of the tennis ball reveals our failure or success. If we want to be a humorous person the behavior of others tells us whether we are succeeding. We could scarcely have the image of ourselves as humorous if no one ever smiled or laughed at our attempts.

Similarly, if we want to be a friendly person, we succeed only if another person or persons respond to our attempts in a way that shows they see them as friendly. They may respond in this way simply by speaking of us as friendly. This would validate for us the meaning we intended our behavior to have—an act of friendliness. Another response which would help to confirm our behavior as friendly would be the reciprocation we hoped for from the other and intended to elicit by our behavior. Still another such response would be one in which the other shows confidence that we can be counted on in the future in the way one only counts on a friend. Such a response shows us we have succeeded in behaving in the sort of way that others interpret as friendly, and so we anticipate the future accordingly.

This example points out that we are born into a culture in which it is already established what sort of behavior is taken as expressing any of the personal qualities we seek to take on. Only if we learn behavior of that sort will we be regarded as having that quality and the desired responses be forthcoming. It is these responses which tell us the general meaning of our behavior. As we are gesturing and speaking in a certain way we are also looking at our behavior as we believe another or others are seeing it, and experience its meaning by means of our sense of what it means to them. If we believe they are seeing our behavior as friendly then it can have this meaning for us. In this sense, we live our behavior from both inside and outside of our organism simultaneously. We live it as the behavior of both an "I" and a "you," neither intelligible without the other.

Our behavior, however, not only has the very general or conventional meaning assigned to it by our culture, it also has the more specific and personal meanings given to it by various groups within our culture and the unique and still more personal meanings placed on it by particular persons with whom we transact. In addition to the conventional meaning of "friendship," being friendly with a draft resister during the war with Viet Nam was seen typically in one way by the American Legion, in another by the Society of Friends, and in a third by the Black Panthers—recognizing, of course, individual differences within these groups. This act would have yet another meaning, say, to the mother of the one resisting.

The meaning we experience our actions to have, then, as we look at them from outside of ourselves will depend on whose eyes we look through and whether this other embodies only very general meanings or more specific and differentiated ones as well. At times we see ourselves not as one specific person sees us but as anyone typical of our culture would. Our sense of this imaginary representative of our culture is formed out of our countless transactions with those who are part of it, some face to face, others by way of television, magazine, record, and the rest. Then there are times when this imaginary other is a generalization, to borrow Meade's term, from our experiences of some sort of group—family, school, church, circle of friends, and so on. Caught in heavy fighting at Argonne in 1918, General Patton recounts; "I felt a great desire to run, I was trembling with fear when suddenly I thought of my progenitors and seemed to see them in a cloud over the German lines looking at me. I became calm at once and . . . went forward to what I honestly believed to be certain death."[20]

At still other times we see ourselves through the eyes of one specific, unique person. It may be one with whom we are presently transacting or one we know through other encounters, perhaps even through a book or a play. Allen Wheelis has shared his sense of that:

> My father and I have never parted. He made his mark on me that summer and after his death that fall continued to speak on a high-fidelity system within my conscience, speaks to me still, tells me that I have been summoned, that I am standing once again before him on that glass porch giving an account of myself, that I will be found wanting, still after all these years a "low-down, no-account scoundrel." Whenever a current situation calls upon me to stand forth, to present myself, my father speaks again with undiminished authority.[21]

Our present situation may bring to mind one from the past, perhaps simply by a remark, a glance, a smile, and once again we regard ourselves as we did then.[22] We may also assume that others in the present see us in this same way, sometimes even though it is quite unlikely that they do.

In moments of introspection we may become vividly aware of seeing ourselves as though from the outside. More commonly, we are not aware of this; we simply use it to provide a sense of the meaning of our actions and personal qualities. Just as in empathy our experience is a *means* by which we focus our understanding on the experience of another, so looking at ourselves through another's eyes is the *means* by which we live, from within, the meaning of what we do. We do and think and experience many things without being aware of it, and looking at ourselves from the outside is often one of them. In this, it is similar to our use of certain features to recognize the face. As Michael Polanyi has pointed out,[23] we simply recognize the face without any thought of the characteristics *by means of which* we do it. Asked we might be unable to say how we do it.

Knowing ourselves as not only an *I* but also a *you* or *he* does not necessarily mean seeing ourselves as an object. Perhaps we speak to another of a habit of his which we find annoying. At that moment he is aware of himself from our point of view. We are the subject and he is the object. But as we do this we, too, see ourselves from the outside. We know we are being seen and heard by him. The difference is that the outside perspective is what he is paying attention to, while it is only in the background of what we are paying attention to, namely, his habit.

Because we can see ourselves through many different sets of eyes we are not confined to any one particular way of looking at ourselves.

When we contrast one with another we gain some freedom concerning which we will use. This is even true, to some extent, concerning that *generalized other* who represents our culture. While we remain the creations of the culture of our early formative years, as we learn of other cultures we may be able to see ourselves at times as someone native to one of them would see us.

We are saying, then, that in knowing another we know his images of himself and his world, and that his image of himself includes himself as an *I* and as a *you*. When we enter his point of view, it is not the point of view he has simply as an *I* but as an *I* and a *you*. In seeing himself through the eyes of another he is not adding another point of view to his own. He does not have a sense of being a self, and so of having a point of view, prior to seeing himself from the outside. The way he sees himself from outside is already part of his point of view about himself to begin with.

Consider, for example, the teenager in conflict with his parents. He is aware that his point of view differs from theirs. He sees himself in that encounter through the eyes of his friends. Their way of seeing him has become part of the way he sees himself. Because we are simultaneously an *I* and a *you*, we have an inside-outside image of ourselves.

Whatever be the full truth, we may recall here that B. F. Skinner sees the self as a repertoire of behaviors which have been rewarded by their consequences—especially by the responses others make to them. We know our behavior from the outside as much as from the inside. And Erving Goffman sees the self as a product of a successful performance. We are a friend only as we succeed in behaving in ways that the other interprets as friendly. Our actions could not have the meaning they do for us if we did not see them as having that meaning at least for certain others, whether in the present or in the past, real or imagined.

We are saying, then, that the self is created and sustained in its interaction with its world. We are at once both public and private. Because we have both public and private dimensions, an outside-inside structure, our knowledge both of ourselves and of others has an outside-inside structure. It is in being outside of ourselves that we are also ahead of ourselves, anticipating our future. Our sense of the future is our sense of alternative possibilities; and our sense of alternative possibilities arises from our realization that we may present ourselves to others in more than one way. We may conceal ourselves from them, withholding clues by which they might anticipate our future behavior. Or we may deceive them, providing clues which lead them to an unreliable anticipation of that behavior. But if we can act in more than one way then we can be more than one person.

Because our sense of ourselves is inseparably linked to the way we manifest ourselves publicly we have the possibility of freely choosing who we wish to become.

We have been exploring ways in which we know our world in relation to ourselves and ourselves in relation to our world. Our world is shot full of its meanings for us, possibilities of experiencing, acting, and being acted on. Our eyes fall upon a chair, light, pencil, wall, child, flower—each experienced as it relates to our values, goals, fears, and the like. Each space conveys a meaning: living room (our room, a friend's, a stranger's), bedroom, sidewalk, schoolroom, church, jail, park, home town, ghetto, foreign country, the space immediately around our own bodies, the spaces within our bodies. So, too, we experience time not as neutral, uniform units but as related to our personal histories and values: past, present, future, Friday, Sunday, December, July, birthday, noon, evening, deadline. Faces are especially rich in meaning: female, male, old, young, friendly, indifferent, familiar, strange, black, white, bright, dull, joyful, bored, innocent, jaded, seductive, stern, responsive, placid, ecstatic, anxious, understanding, rejecting.

Equally, we know ourselves in relation to our world. Our feelings, thoughts, and personality traits all relate to our world. Our bodies are ways of being in our world. We see our own hands as our means of caressing, pointing, writing, waving, twisting, striking, carrying, molding. As women, we experience our vaginas in terms of ecstatic love, seduction, rape, becoming pregnant, giving birth, being the second sex in our society. Able to be what we are able to do, we know ourselves in our actions and discover our potential as our environment invites its use. Small wonder that prolonged isolation undermines our sense of self; hungry to get back in touch with ourselves we eagerly reach out for whatever interaction becomes available—a hunger the brainwashers know how to exploit. Certainly an impoverished, sterile, dispiriting environment such as that of Aldous Huxley's *Brave New World* or, as it seems to many of us, of our contemporary suburbs is the best possible context in which to inculcate submissiveness.

Since we act and think and feel in relation to our environment we understand ourselves or another only as we understand that relation. We know the other empathically in knowing how he experiences the various sorts of environments with which he interacts. We misunderstand another so easily because we are far more attentive to what he says and does than we are to the subtle aspects of his environment to which he is responding. We are only now coming to understand the mental patient in light of the subtle meanings that the hospital environment has for him, especially the behavior of the hospital staff, which, in turn, is shaped by the nuances of its perception of that environment. Our understanding of prisons and prisoners has been equally distorted. We are constantly responding to perceptions of which we are unaware. We know them only tacitly as they function as the means by which we focus on our transactions with others.

An especially important aspect of how the other experiences his environment concerns the frequency of response he has come to expect from a certain kind of behavior. If he has come to expect the continual responses we get from putting money in a coffee dispenser his behavior will quickly be disrupted if the expected response is not forthcoming. We may find this difficult to understand if we have come to expect from the same sort of behavior only the very occasional responses we get from putting money in a slot machine. Each of us measures the success of our present behavior by comparing the frequency of present responses to that of responses in the past. To understand the other, we must know whether he is accustomed to frequent or infrequent expressions of affection, or responses to his presence, or rewards for his work.

Even our human freedom, our capacity and opportunity to choose freely between alternative futures, is rooted in our relation to our environment. We experience our freedom only as we act in response to the alternative possibilities we discern in our situation. As these alternatives are reduced, so is our freedom. Equally important, we develop our ability to choose freely between alternative possibilities only under certain environmental conditions. We choose freely only when our choice is grounded in our own experience and, as we shall see, we learn to be this sort of person only when another responds to us with empathic understanding and affirmation of our worth. Unaware of these environmental conditions, we think of our own freedom as our ability to lift ourselves by our own boot straps, and we expect the same of others. Aware of these conditions, we can seek to create an environment in which the other may become free.

Self and world, then, are inseparable. It is in interaction with our world that we both create ourselves and are created. It is in this same interaction that we both create our world and find disclosed the self-creations of others. We may emphasize receiving or we may emphasize transforming, but both are present in our interactions. On the one hand, then, we are our relations. As they change, we change; our goals can no longer be quite the same or be unfolded in quite the same way. Indeed, our directions may change dramatically. On the other hand, we transcend our relations. We are able to step back away from them and formulate alternatives to them or ways they may be changed. By empathy and affirmation, our power to transcend may be enlarged.

THE CONTENT OF PERSONAL KNOWLEDGE: STYLE

When we are in touch with another, we know not only his image of self and world but what it is like to be him having those images. In part, this means seeing the place of those images in his life story; the way they unite past, present, and future; the meaning they have for him. But knowing what it is like to be him also means knowing *how* he lives those images. As we shall see, this means that when we enter into the point of view of another, we go beyond his conscious knowledge of himself.

How we live our images of self and world depends on the place of habit in our lives, the degree to which we are centered or de-centered, and the conscious or unconscious way we hold those images. We are one sort of person when we are perceiving and thinking and acting in ways grown stale through repetition, and quite another when we open ourselves to the ever-new qualities of the present. Our sense of ourselves is very different when we determine our lives by the demands and expectations of others than it is when we ground our lives in our own experience and judgment. We live with less freedom and responsibility when we fail to be aware of our true beliefs and feelings and perceptions than we do when we know these things.

First of all, then, in knowing how another lives his images of self and world, we know which are the habitual ways in which he thinks, feels, and acts. In holding our images out of habit, we are different selves than if we test and modify them in light of our unfolding experience. Acting out of habit is a significantly different experience and way of relating than acting out of awareness of the present situation in all its uniqueness and novelty. When we know that another does something out of habit, we know something about how he lives that act from the inside. We also can better anticipate his actions if we know which would be opposed by, supported by, or virtually compelled by a long history of repetition.

On the one side, habit conserves energy, provides stability, and releases attention for other things. With a minimum of effort, we tie our shoes, drink our coffee, take our customary route to work, reach for our door key and flick on the light, and all the while we are giving our attention entirely to what another is saying and to our plans for the day. Similarly, our skills can become more complex as their simpler forms become routine.

On the other side, habit makes change difficult and blinds us to what is new. Hard-won changes in ways of seeing and feeling about ourselves may slip away under the pressure of ways more familiar, comfortable, and deeply grooved. And in responding by habit, we treat the present situation as though it were identical with similar situations in the past.

We may use habit as a defense against seeing and, so, against having to respond to what is new in ourselves or in the other; by protecting our images and concepts from the test of new experience, we maintain our prejudices, projections, introjections, and the like. Such images place a veil between us and reality, frustrating our organismic need for stimulation and growth, diluting our sense of ourselves and of the other and, so, making us more susceptible to the demands of irrational authority. How much and in what areas we live by habit, then, are important questions about ourselves.

In knowing how another lives his images of self and world, we know, secondly, the degree to which he centers them in his own organismic experiences and, consequently, the degree to which he centers his communications and decisions in this way. We act as centered persons when we ground our actions in our own experience and judgment. When we live autonomously, we are guided by our organismic experiences, experiences in which both mind and body fully participate. We center in the worth of our own being. The locus of control of our behavior and decisions is in ourselves. The mark of organismic experience is feeling. We live our feelings when we live our bodies. Taut bodies have little feeling, and we are unable to experience them from within. We are most alive with feeling when we walk, make love, play, work, sing, breath with full, free movement. We are centered in our own organismic experience when we are centered in the flow of movement to which we give ourselves fully.

When we live de-centered from our own being, we try to see and feel and behave as others expect us to. The locus of control of our behavior and decisions is in them. The more importance we give to meeting the expectations of others, and so to gaining their approval, the less attention we pay to our own organisms. We lose touch with our feelings. Our images of self and world come to be based on what we are expected to be rather than what we experience ourselves to be. Perhaps we are told that good people don't become angry, and so we come to see ourselves as persons who have learned to turn the other cheek, responding with love and considerateness—or at least with neutral feelings—rather than with anger. The more our images of ourselves conflict with our experiences—the more our socialized consciousness is in conflict with our organismic consciousness—the less aware we are of these experiences. But we do not stop experiencing organismically even though we stop being very much aware of doing so. The mark of this de-centeredness is that we consciously communicate one thing but unknowingly communicate another at the same time.

When we de-center ourselves our images become closed and often contradictory. As we lose touch with our organismic experiences we surrender those inner resources by which to test the values, interpretations and other things which constitute our images. Either we feel frighteningly empty of inner resources so that we must rely heavily on others to direct our behavior—the other-directed person so typical of our society today (and far from uncommon in the nineteenth century)—or we find in ourselves a strong voice of authority which is the voice not of our own experience but of others—the inner-directed person. The values we then identify with are either the latest messages of significant others reverberating throughout the empty spaces within, or the representations of our congealed past which we impose on the present, selectively perceiving only what fits that mold and can be understood in terms of it. We can only apply these value beliefs rather woodenly and irrationally since we are not in touch with our own experiences whereby we could test the adequacy of these values to the present situation, containing as it must elements of genuine novelty. Indeed we cannot even judge their adequacy to past situations. For the same reason, we may live by conflicting values and interpretations since we cannot call into play our resources for resolving these conflicts, namely, our ability to weigh each value claim against our own organismic experience—to see whether we have really found it valuable in terms of our needs as a total person. We may believe it is good to be honest, something we've learned from our parents, teachers, minister, yet also believe it is good to cheat sucessfully on school exams (or income tax), something we've taken over from our peers. In existentialist terms, these value beliefs are inauthentic in the sense of the root meaning of ''authentic'' which is to be the *author* of. We did not author or originate these values on the basis of our own experience and so we do not express who we are organismically when we apply them.

To be centered in our own organismic experience is very different from being selfish. The selfish person, in fact, is de-centered. As Carl Rogers has long maintained, far from being asocial, as organisms we need creative social interaction, for only thus do we fulfill our need to give and receive love. We are by nature aggressive only when we perceive our vital interests threatened and even then we prefer to avoid the threat when given the opportunity. The possibility that some organismic needs (e.g., for sex or freedom) will threaten the well-being of other persons will be balanced by our organismic needs to give and receive understanding, companionship, affection, and validation.

Our social and individualistic needs may not only balance but also enhance one another. How richly we relate depends in part on how significant we make our lives apart—on what we bring to our relating. Conversely, the quality of our relating carries over into our activities as separate persons. Neither oneness nor otherness are rewarding by themselves.

In knowing how another lives his images of self and world we know, thirdly, his unconscious intentions, feelings, and perceptions. The human is that animal which both resists and seeks awareness of itself. To understand another's behavior we must know whether he is conscious of the purpose and feelings we see in what he does. If we do not know when he is doing something for unconscious reasons we will not empathize with the way he lives this behavior and our anticipations of his future behavior in this area will be less reliable. It will be less reliable because we will put too much confidence in what he says he will do, failing to realize that he may also have another intention that he cannot tell us of because he is not aware of it.

It will be helpful as preparation for our discussion of the unconscious side of ourselves to reflect on something that acting out of habit shows us about purposive or intentional action. Although such action normally involves both a pattern that marks it as purposeful and a consciously held purpose on the part of the actor, we often have purposes or intentions in what we do without being conscious of having them either in the sense of being aware of these intentions while we are carrying them out or in the sense of having thought about them consciously prior to carrying them out.[24] This is frequently true when we act out of habit. That we drove our car while thinking of other things does not mean that we did not intend to drive it. If we were asked, we could readily explain our purpose in driving. Further, anyone seeing us do these things would be likely to see the pattern in them which marks them as purposeful. That our behavior has this pattern and that, under certain conditions (e.g., we do not resist being aware of our intention), we can explain our purpose is what w ᐟ mean in saying we do it intentionally, deliberately, on purpose and the like. Intentional behavior has an outside-inside structure and consequently our knowledge of it does too.

Because of the outside-inside or public-private structure of intention, if we are puzzled by someone's behavior we could either ask him about it or study it more carefully to try to discern a pattern in it, much as we might study a puzzling paragraph or play or historical event to determine its meaning. Of course, here too the outside-inside structure of purposeful action opens the possibility of deception or misunderstanding. The other may wish us to see his behavior as an expression of love while his conscious intention is manipulation. Or we may think we discern one sort of pattern in his behavior but then hear him speak of it differently and perhaps come ourselves to see quite clearly the pattern which corresponds to his account. Perhaps, too, he consciously intended one thing but only succeeded in doing another, much as an artist's work is often not just what he intended.

As we have said, we may intend something without being conscious of it. Our behavior is intentional or purposeful if it has a pattern that others can understand as purposeful and if, under certain conditons, we can say what our purpose is. Where our purpose is something we act on out of habit without any need to think about it, and not something we do unconsciously, we need only be asked and we can say. But where our purpose is something we act on unconsciously (and this may be true of some things we do habitually) it is something we cannot now say, but that we could say under those conditions whereby we become conscious of what is unconscious. Each of us is familiar with becoming conscious of longstanding purposes, feelings, or perceptions for the first time. We come to see that we have been trying to dominate the other or that we have felt desire for her or that we have perceived a fear in some of her body language that contradicts what she has said to us.

In some cases we need only have it drawn to our attention perhaps directly by what someone says or indirectly by a play we are watching or the like. In other cases we must overcome our own resistance to being aware of it. In these cases the experience of being empathically understood by another seems to many of us a necessary condition for us to overcome our resistance; without this sort of relationship we are not able to do it. It may even be that such a relationship, which includes love and openness on the part of the other, is a sufficient condition for enlarging our awareness; with this sort of empathic understanding by the other it may be we are not only able to do it but will in fact do it.

But the point to be emphasized here is that all purposeful action has an outside-inside structure. If the purpose is, say, altruistic, the actor will, under the right conditions, see it that way and others of his culture must be able to see it that way as well.

Perhaps someone claims to have one intention while her behavior appears to everyone else to reveal another. We will wonder whether she is trying to deceive us by her claim, or whether she is unconscious of the intention so apparent to us, or whether we are mistaken about her behavior. We ask her and she gives us an explanation of the apparent conflict. We now are able to see a pattern in her behavior which matches her account and so the conflict is removed. The process here is not unlike that of first seeing the following picture as that of a young woman turned about three-quarters of the way to the left and then being shown that it can also be seen as that of an old woman. The procedure might be to trace around the young woman's whole cheek and jaw bone and say this is the old woman's nose, to point to the young woman's neckband as the old woman's mouth, to point to her left ear as the old woman's left eye, and so forth.

Figure 7

But perhaps we are unable to see her action the way she explains it. Depending on how long and how well we have known her, we may simply take it on faith that we are misinterpreting her action; its puzzling, but perhaps it will become clear in time. Otherwise we will conclude that either she is trying to deceive us or she is unconscious of the intention we see in her behavior. Here, too, which of these alternatives we select will depend, in part, on our prior knowledge of her. It will also depend on whether she appears upset and/or denies too vigorously the way we see her behavior, these things being marks of resistance to seeing what is unconscious.

We have been discussing knowing another's unconscious intentions. Here we use "unconscious" as an adjective. We have also spoken of doing something *unconsciously*, using the term as an adverb. These uses are descriptive, pointing up features of her behavior. Under the impact of Freud's genius, though, the term has also come to be used as a noun, and one speaks of ideas, wishes, fears and the like as being in *the unconscious*. This use as a noun is not to describe behavior but to explain it in the sense of presenting the prior conditions which cause it. Here we get a picture of our minds as something like inner rooms with basements which were populated during childhood with such things as wishes and fears. These things affect our upstairs or conscious minds and our behavior, producing dreams, reveries, associations, compulsive fears, ritual actions, slips of the tongue and the like; but normally we cannot get at them until, with the help of psychoanalysis, the door to the basement is unlocked and they can come up.

We often find pictures helpful in organizing and/or explaining our experience but they may also confuse or mislead us. This picture of an inaccessible inner realm, the unconscious, seems to many of us not to provide a way of explaining our unconscious experience and behavior. Rather it may mislead us so that we confuse describing experience with explaining it.

Along with his theoretical work in attempting to explain neurotic behavior, Freud provided illuminating new descriptions of such behavior. A number of studies show, however, that he frequently confused the two, speaking of unconscious motives sometimes to describe behavior and sometimes to explain it.[25] At times he would speak of an unconscious wish in order to draw attention to a pattern in the neurotic's behavior, a pattern which revealed the purpose of seeking pleasure or avoiding pain. Consider a patient who must constantly wash her hands. Freud would describe her action in terms of the purpose of avoiding punishment and then we would see that sort of action in a new way.

Yet at other times he would speak of an unconscious wish in order to explain a behavior. For this purpose he conceived of the wish as an unconscious mental entity that is the cause of the behavior, "the driving force behind the act." The compulsive hand washer has carried with her in her unconscious both a childhood wish to kill her mother and a resulting guilty fear of punishment.

But how does imagining the existence of such entities in some sort of cellar room in our minds provide causal explanations of behavior? To establish something as the cause of our behavior we must be able to determine its existence without referring to that behavior. Suppose someone maintains that horses win races because an invisible, ever-silent, little green elf rides on them. Everytime a horse wins a race he says, "Ah, that's the one the elf was on this time." But he can't determine in advance of the win which horse the elf is on and this idea is useless. Similarly, unless we can determine the presence of an unconscious mental entity apart from the behavior it is to explain, it is useless as a supposed causal explanation of that behavior.[26]

This picture of an inaccessible inner realm called the unconscious not only fails to explain behavior but may also lead us to disown part of ourselves. There is a world of difference between thinking "something caused me to do it" and "I did it." In the first way of thinking I refer to something external to myself, something alien to me. In thinking "I did it" I own my behavior as originating in me. It is grounded in purposes or intentions which are mine regardless of whether I am now aware of them.

We are maintaining, then, that the distinction between conscious and unconscious is useful and important, but is distorted if we picture it in terms of a private inner room and its underlying basement. As an alternative we may more helpfully picture our experiences as constituting a dark region or field and our awareness as the light by which we illumintae that part of the field which draws our attention. Part of the field is dark because we cannot give our attention or light to all parts of it at once. Yet if we have previously lighted some of those dark areas, and continue to do so from time to time, we know they are there as the environment of the area we are now aware of. They are part of the gestalt or sense of the whole that is the context of our present awareness. But there are some areas which we fear to see. Perhaps long ago we lighted them but at that time they were so frightening we resolved never to notice them again. The movement of our light forms a pattern according to what interests us and what we dread.

Our culture instructs us about a general pattern of movement that our conscious attention is to follow. We are not to be fully aware of death. We talk about it abstractly or, if someone close to us dies, we veil it by our words. We say father "passed on." Nor are we to be aware of homosexual or incestuous feelings, of a distincton between what is best for us and what the organization is asking of us, or even of mystical experience.

Various groups also have rules about what we can be aware of and so what we can talk about. We are learning, for example, that families generally live by scripts in which each member has his or her assigned part but no one is to be aware of this. One child is expected to perform the role of the hero, another the goat and a third the comedian. Yet, as R.D. Laing puts it, there is a rule against knowing that these things are expected and a rule against knowing about this rule. Our light moves across the field of our experiences in the required way. No attention is given to the way it does not move because that would affect its movement. Laing cites the story of a treasure at the bottom of a tree. To find it one must remember not to think about a white monkey, otherwise the treasure will vanish. If we want to avoid thinking about something we must not think about not thinking about it.

These unknown, continuously dark regions of our experience themselves comprise a gestalt the outer contours of which coincide with the outer contours of the lighted regions. The edges of our paths of illumination are also the edges of our dark regions. It may be helpful to use the term *unconscious* as a noun to refer to this gestalt. A Freud or Nietzsche or Marx or Dostoievsky can help us discern many of the inner connections which comprise it, to relate one thing we do unconsciously to another and also to previous experiences.

When we say, then, that personal knowledge of another includes knowledge of her unconscious intentions, feelings and perceptions we are using "unconscious" for purposes of description rather than causal explanation. In personal knowledge we seek not causal explanations of her experience but a richer, more discriminating awareness of it. When Freud brings out a connection between present and childhood experience, that connection finds a place in our personal knowledge not as a causal explanation serving prediction but as revealing still more fully the purpose of that behavior. The anticipations involved in the personal knowledge are based on our understanding not of the causes of her behavior but of her purposes.

We have been discussing personal knowledge of another as distinguished from impersonal knowledge about that person. A second distinction has been implicit, namely, knowledge of a particular, unique person as distinguished from general knowledge of the nature of persons or, technically, idiographic as distinguished from nomothetic knowledge of persons. We know what persons are but we might not know Martin Buber. In this, our knowledge of persons and our knowledge of things is similar. We know what books and symphonies are but we might not know Vonnegut's *Slaughter House Five* or Beethoven's *Fifth*. Yet our knowledge of particular persons is different from that of particular things in that each person has a sense of his own uniqueness—his personal identity—and it is this sense of being just this particular person, of being me, that we are in touch with when we truly know another as a person. We may be able to pick someone out in a crowd and to describe that concatenation of characteristics that differentiate him from others but our knowledge of him is not personal unless we also are in touch with his uniqueness as he experiences it. We turn now to examine, first, the nature of our knowledge of particular persons as distinguished from our general knowledge and, second, the nature of self-identity.

SEEING A PATTERN

The eighteenth-century philosopher David Hume expressed perplexity about self knowledge:

> There are some philosophers who imagine we are every mo-
> ment intimately conscious of what we call our *self*. . . . For my
> part, when I enter most intimately into what I call *myself*, I
> always stumble on some particular perception or other. . . . I
> never can catch *myself* at any time without a perception, and
> never can observe anything but the perception.[27]

Introspection, it seems, discloses all sorts of perceptions, none of
which appears to be a perception of the self.

Perhaps we are watching the motion picture *On the Waterfront*. One
moment we watch Marlon Brando as he first meets Eva Marie Saint.
Later we see him quarrel with Rod Steiger and later still take part in a
waterfront fight. We see these and many other scenes. But in what
way do we see *On the Waterfront*?

Returning from the movie, we enter our apartment. We see furniture, plants, paintings, books, walls, and so forth, but in what way
do we see the apartment?

We talk with another about the movie. We see her body in various
postures, making various gestures, and with various facial expressions, but in what way do we see her?

When we discuss the movie we go over sequences of scenes, the
way one event led to another and related to still others; we reflect on
these and many other connections whereby the whole thing came
together for us. We know the movie not just as a miscellany of
scenes—Hume spoke of "bundles" or "collections" of perceptions—but as a complex pattern or configuration that they form. Until
they all fall into place we feel we haven't completely "gotten hold" of
the movie. It is our ability to grasp many different scenes as interrelated in a pattern or gestalt that enables us to see each scene as a
part of the movie, and it is to this gestalt or configuration that we refer
in speaking of *On The Waterfront*. If, as we are seeing this movie, someone asks us what we are watching, we say *On The Waterfront*. We
see the scene we are watching at the moment as part of that movie
because we see it as part of a developing pattern or whole. Indeed we
see Marlon Brando as Joey because we see him in that context. To
know this particular motion picture is to know the unique pattern
formed by its many scenes.

Similarly when we enter our apartment we experience the various
items as comprising the pattern we know as the living room, and we
experience the living room in the context of the configuration of
rooms we call our apartment. Each scene of the movie is in the same
way a gestalt of its component parts. Here we notice that our experience of the living room is a spatial gestalt and has as its context a

temporal gestalt of what has preceded and what is to come. We are saying, then, that in knowing a particular, unique thing or person we grasp all of our experiences of it or him as forming a pattern or gestalt. *In knowing another person,* we may say, *our experiences of him come together to form a story.*

To see movements and gestures as the movements and gestures of a particular person, then, is to see them in the context of the pattern of our experiences of that person. Even to see a movement as part of an action is to place it in the pattern of the sequence of movements which comprise that act—fighting on the waterfront, for example. Here we must remember, of course, the outside-inside structure of our experiences of the other. We do not hear a groan and then infer that the other is in pain. We simply experience the other to be in pain. In other words, we see him simultaneously as groaning and as feeling pain. This means that our knowledge of the other combines two basic patterns simultaneously, the pattern of our experiences of the other and that of his experiences of himself. In knowing the other we know, from this dual standpoint, the pattern which he forms out of his experiences of himself and his relations with his world. Experiences of clenching his fist, smiling, making love, twisting his ankle, urinating, feeling a toothache, being joyous, memorizing a poem, being spanked, being sarcastic, holding a child, telling a lie, fulfilling a promise, fearing death—all this bewildering complexity of experience of mind and body and interaction with his world somehow come together under the tutelage of the meaning that his culture gives to being a self to form that configuration which gives him his sense of self.

We understand the meaning that the other's actions and experiences have for him by placing them in the context of his gestalt of his experiences of himself, including his relations with his world. We understand the way he lives that meaning by knowing how these actions and experiences are related to his habits, his degree of centeredness and his unconscious intentions and feelings. How far this meaning can be communicated will depend on how well those involved know his sense of self. If someone involved doesn't know him very well the communication can be improved by telling something more of his story—especially those events which are particularly revelatory.

Our knowledge of each unique person and our general personal knowledge of the nature of persons are closely interrelated. We come to understand any concept, including the concept of persons, by relating it to particular instances of it. These include our own experiences, those related to us from the experiences of others and the imaginary accounts conveyed to us by such media as literature, poetry, art, drama, fairy tales, advertisements, and our own powers of imagination. As our experience develops, our understanding of concepts changes. Our attention may be drawn to connections we have overlooked. New instances may take on special importance and some of the things we formally took to be instances we may now reject. We may come to understand love differently, for example, as we experience caring for another over and above her relationship with us. Some of the things we formerly thought of as love we may now see as infatuation or possessiveness or vanity. Similarly our sense of being a person will change. New experiences dislodge our early sense of our parents as infallible or ourselves as magic. It may dawn on us that we could not be the person we are if the other were not the person she is. We may see in another a new way of being a person. Definitions guide us but they mean nothing until we flesh them out with concrete instances.

In our general personal knowledge of the nature of persons some instances of our knowledge of particular persons will occupy a central place. Some experiences seem to us especially revelatory of what all persons are like. Hurt by a few who were important to us we tend to distrust all, focusing on those actions which support this view and pushing into the background those which do not. Healed by relationship with one who validates us through empathic understanding and touch we discriminate those who are trustworthy from those who are not.

As we step into the world of persons we activate this general personal knowledge. In the first moments of meeting someone this enables us to take on a rather general and very tentative sense of his internal frame of reference that goes significantly beyond our meagre experience of him, for in knowing the stories of certain others we know something of what to look for and what is likely in piecing together a new story. Helpful in this way, our general knowledge of persons becomes an obstacle to understanding another if we insist on seeing him only in ways in which he is similar to persons we already know.

Knowing another we know her self-identity, her sense of who she is. Knowing ourselves we know our sense of identity, our feeling of being this particular, unique *me*. We turn now to examine both the identity of things and persons in our world and our self-identity in terms of patterns of experience.

For something to have an identity for us we must differentiate it from other things and grasp its continuity from one moment of our experience of it to another. Each moment we stand in a region of space which we know as possibilities for experience. As we look around we have a complex variety of perceptions. We experience individual things rather than William James's "blooming, buzzing confusion" because we have early discovered, with the guidace of our culture, that our perceptions fall together into clusters, each with its own configuration. Here is a configuration we know as this chair, differentiating it from the many other configurations—table, carpet, lamp, pen, wall—which together make up our present perceptual field.

We see the configurations we have words for so that, in providing a common language, our culture ensures that the configurations we experience conform closely enough with those seen by others that we can effectively communicate and otherwise interact concerning them. These patterns are part of our temporal pattern—the story that is our sense of our life. Our present experience of this chair falls into place in a pattern involving our past experiences of it. It retains its identity for us through time as the same chair so long as the previous temporal pattern that was its identity is taken into the slightly more extensive temporal pattern that includes our present experience. Similarly, in watching a play or reading a book or playing a game we experience it as the same play or book or game throughout by constantly recreating the gestalt to include each new scene or passage or move. Unlike that of physical objects the temporal continuity of many plays and games is not unbroken. The play may have more than one act, the game may be interrupted by the end of a period and later resumed. Nor do they have the unbroken spatial extension of physical objects. Each kind of thing is different because our experiences of it have a different organizing principle or set of principles—for example, the rules of the game or the interrelatedness of the actions of the play or the unbroken spatial extension of the object—and it is the organizing principle which determines the thing's spatial-temporal pattern.

The identity of persons in our world is more complex since, in addition to the outside or public identity that things have, they also have an inside or private identity—a sense of who they are. As we know them impersonally, their sense of identity is not part of their identity for us. As we know them personally, their sense of identity comprises the heart of their identity for us—an identity around which we cluster what we also know of them from the outside pole of this outside-inside way of knowing. Because of this outside pole we know not only their sense of identity but how they live that identity.

This outside-inside structure will be difficult for us to recognize fully if we have not exorcized the picture, discussed earlier in this chapter, of ourselves as separate, self-contained atoms related to our world only externally. Our experiences may seem locked up in our heads. We call them *subjective* and wonder how they are related to the objective reality of the things outside of ourselves we experience. William James has given us an alternative image. Our perceptions of, say, a room are like the point lying at the intersection of two lines; they lie at the intersection of two patterns or processes or histories, that of ourselves and that of the room. The brown we experience is not something in our heads but is the color of the chair; it is part of the gestalt we refer to when we speak of the chair. If we point to it we do not think of pointing to our heads. When we refer to our *subjective* experience of the room we are placing these perceptions in the context of our personal history, the pattern of our ongoing experience. When we refer to the room itself we are placing the same perceptions in the context of the history of that room, the pattern of all perceptions of it—both our own and others'.

That our perceptions are either experience or things experienced, depending on the context in which we place them is somewhat analogous to the dual role of the words we write in a diary recording a conversation. These words are either those of our diary or those of the conversation depending on the context in which we think of them. Analogous, too, is seeing a play within a play, as in *Hamlet*. Here what we see is either the play *Hamlet* or the play within that play, depending on which gestalt we refer to.

Our perceptions of another lie at the intersection of not just two but three lines: our private, internal history as selves; his public, external history as a self; and his private, internal history as a self. When we refer to him as this particular, unique person we are placing these perceptions in the context of his inner history, the pattern of all perceptions of it—his, ours, those of others. Here we must keep in mind what we said about another's conscious intentions: they are both his experience of them as consciously held and our experience of them as patterns in his behavior. All other perceptions that comprise the pattern of the other's self share this same dual aspect of being both public and private. The other's pain is both his experience of it and what we may see of it in his behavior and appearance. Our perceptions of another, then, may be thought of as subjective, objective or empathic, depending on which gestalt we make their context. Subjectively they're our experience, objectively they're the external thing experienced, empathically they're the self of the other.

DOUBTING THAT WE CAN KNOW

My aim has been to set forth an account of personal knowledge that is based on what we all experience, that lets us see more clearly how we are able to have such knowledge, and that may help us to live more fully and effectively in the world of persons. If this account has in some degree rung true, if we've been able to find ourselves in it, we may, in looking back on those times when we—most of us at least—have doubted that we ever really know another, be all the more confused or bewildered by such occasions. We need to look a bit more fully at the sources of this doubt and relate our account to them.

In John Steinbeck's *The Winter of Our Discontent*, Ethan expresses doubt about every really knowing another, in a way that may recapture for us much of our own.

> There was Mary, my dear, to think of, asleep with the smile of mystery on her lips. I hoped she wouldn't awaken and look for me. But if she did, would she ever tell me? I doubt it. I think that Mary, for all that she seems to tell everything, tells very little. There was the fortune to consider. Did Mary want a fortune or did she want it for me? . . .
>
> By money, Mary meant new curtains and sure education for the kids and holding her head a little higher and, face it, being proud rather than a little ashamed of me. She had said it in anger and it was true. . . .
>
> I put the coffee on and sat waiting for it to perk, and it had just begun to bounce when Mary came down. . . .
>
> "What are you doing up so early?"
>
> "Well may you ask. Please to know I have been up for most of the night. Regard my galoshes there by the door. Feel them for wetness."
>
> "Where did you go?"
>
> "Down by the sea there is a little cave, my rumpled duck. I crawled inside and I studied the night." . . .
>
> "Doesn't coffee smell good? I'm glad you're silly again. It's awful when you're gloomy. I'm sorry about that fortune thing. I don't want you to think I'm not happy."
>
> "Don't give it a worry, it's in the cards."
>
> "What?"
>
> "No joke. I'm going to make our fortune."
>
> "I never know what you're thinking."
>
> "That's the greatest difficulty with telling the truth." . . .
>
> "I haven't washed my face," she said. "I couldn't imagine who was rattling around in the kitchen."
>
> When she had gone up to the bathroom, I put my note to her in my pocket. And I still didn't know. Does anyone ever know even the outer fringe of another? What are you like in there? Mary—do you hear? Who are you in there?[28]

The sense that we are utterly isolated, unable really to know what it is like to be the other person may spring from a number of sources. First, it may be an expression of an experience of betrayal or a deeply hurtful misunderstanding of one another. We seemed so undeniably to be in touch with her, truly to know her, only to discover it was not so. How can we ever believe in, trust in, such things again? Our faith in human beings may plummet. Our confidence in our ability to judge wisely or even to achieve intimacy may be deeply shaken. Have we the skills, the depth of perspective, the capacity for care, and the courage needed, or will we be found wanting no matter who our companion? Far easier to believe no one can really know another than to risk such discovery. But whether we look without or within for the explanation, the way toward truly meeting another may seem utterly closed off. And yet it may still happen that a key turns, a door opens, light once again breaks in—this time more fully, more steadily, more powerfully illuminating. Gradually suspicion dissolves into trust, self-doubt into confidence, isolation into knowing and being known.

That our intimacies involve so much risk tests not only our self-confidence and our capacity for realistic trust in another but also our willingness to live with limited certainty. When the voice within us whispers "But do I really know her?" what do we mean by "really"? Isn't it a knowing in which we could never possibly be wrong? At the very least, something akin to mathematical certainty? The problem, of course, is that such absolute certainty is not to be found in every day life (it is not even to be found in mathematics). When we truly know another we have the kind of evidence that warrants our placing full confidence in the way we see her. It is not that we couldn't be wrong but that it would serve no worthwhile purpose for us to withhold our full confidence for this reason. Indeed, it would cut us off from full intimacy with another. It would be as unreasonable and damaging to our lives as refusing ever to trust anyone because there must always be risk involved. To know someone is to have eliminated all reasonable doubt, where what is reasonable is determined by our practical need to anticipate the future reliably so that we can determine what actions to take.

Third, we may expect to, yearn to, know another in ways we never can. Knowing her, even knowing ourselves, is far more fragmentary, for more limited, than we would like for it to be. We want her to be less labyrinthine in her being, less opaque to our seeing, able to share with us more fully. And yet, however tenuous, however limited, moments of being in touch are often profoundly moving and renewing, always needed and important. Recognizing its meaning and value we may give up demanding that such knowledge be what it is not. We may come to simply accept it for what it is, a personal knowing that unites us in ways that are partial and fragmentary and yet have power to become ecstasy.

Fourth, when we reflect on knowing another we may think ''But I can never really have her experiences and so I can never really know her.'' Perhaps this is another form of a desire for absolute knowledge. In any event, it may not occur to us that we cannot give any meaning to the words ''have her experiences.'' We know another by means of our experiences which are not somehow hers but similar to them.

We cannot, of course, understand in another what we have not experienced in ourselves. How much of a limitation is this on our ability to know another? If our experience has been narrowly circumscribed and our awareness of it minimal, our power to understand has a limited range and is shallow even within that range. But the most fundamental features of human experience are shared by us all. In one way or another we all know something of such things as death, sex, freedom, conflict, chance, the polarity of self and world. Perhaps another has suffered a great bereavement and we have not. Yet we know the pain of many lesser separations, remember the fear of abandonment, have felt the anger of being let down by another, have moved from refusing to accept something terribly hurtful to finally making our peace with it. To this extent, then, we can understand, and what matters most to the other is that we stand by him with all the power of understanding that we have. In this simple sharing of ourselves the other finds support and healing. Our power to stand under his experience comes less from our beliefs and evaluations than from living fully and openly our own experience. As an Indian colleague said to me, ''Our mutual understanding and rapport comes from living our humanness as fully as we can in the different ways that our cultures provide.'' Beliefs and evaluations differ and yet nothing human is alien to us.

Fifth, in reflecting on personal knowledge we may also come to doubt its possibility because, without realizing it, we are identifying all of knowledge with one particular kind of knowledge. Perhaps we have in mind our knowledge of tables and chairs. We begin to see that knowing another is not very much like knowing chairs and so we conclude we don't *really* know the other. The chair is so public, so open to inspection, while persons are not, at least not entirely. What is open to public inspection is human behavior. Maybe that is what we really mean, or should mean, when we speak of knowing another, namely, knowing his behavior. Now we are just a short step away from Skinner's definition of the self as a repertoire of behavior—a set of ways we tend to behave. The self, we think, is fundamentally public. How else could we know the other as a self?

Where does this leave us? The idea of personal knowledge of another is gone. All we have is knowledge of behavior or of something we construct out of that—a repertoire. Perhaps we have a sense of something personal merely because we sometimes have warm feelings about some of the behavior we experience. But now we may wonder if we're not leaving a lot out of account. What has become of the one who behaves that way, the one for whom that behavior has certain meanings, the one who thinks of that behavior as his own—as something for which he is responsible, the one who sometimes reflects on that behavior and decides to change it?

When we raise these questions we shift our attention to our experiences of being a subject, the agent of our thoughts and actions. Rejecting the idea of the self as solely public, we may dismiss the public side of the self altogether and think of the self as solely private. There is much in our present culture and in our cultural heritage that teaches us to picture the self in this way. From this point of view, we see the self as subject, not object, something that lies hidden from view, residing like a ghost in our bodies. The self, we may think, is something that causes our behaviors but is not in any sense made up of them. To take an example from a preceding section, our intentions may seem to us to be only something that we say to our selves and not also a pattern that may be seen in our behavior.

If we try to think of the self in this way, as something completely private, what becomes of our knowledge of other people? If the self were somehow completely private we could know about being a self only from our experiences of *our* self—only from our own case. We could only infer that others must also be selves because they behave much as we do. We would first come to know that we are selves and then infer that others are as well.

Does this picture succeed where the picture of the self solely as public failed; namely, does it fit what we all experience in knowing others? There are many reasons for concluding that it doesn't. We shall look only at one that is fundamental.

We could not possibly come to know what a self is from our own case alone and then extend what we know to others. Our sense of being a self is a sense of belonging to a class of entities to which the term *self* applies. This is because when we learn to use any predicate, such as *self* or *chair* or *red*, we learn to use it as applicable to a group of things. The very idea of a predicate is inseparable from reference to such a group. We can come to know that we are selves, then, only if at the same time we come to know that others are also selves. Since we only experience directly the public side of others our sense of self is from the start a sense of something both public and private, both object and subject. I cannot learn to say *my* and *me* without learning to say *his* and *hers* and *him* and *her*. I cannot apply a term to myself if I have not learned how to apply it to others. The concept of self, then, is the concept of something that is the subject of both first and third person statements—a concept in which inner experience and public behavior are indissolubly related.

If, in reflecting on what it means to know another, we sometimes conclude the self must be something public and at other times that it must be something private we are partly right on each occasion.[29] On the one side, we attend to some features of our experience of being and knowing selves. On the other side, we attend to other features of this. Attending to the public side we focus on the evidence we have for our knowledge of another—his behavior, body language, and the like. But evidence is not identical with the thing it is evidence for. Consider that our evidence concerning who Julius Caesar was and what he did is quite different from Caesar himself. Attending to the private side we focus on the way we organize and give personal meaning to the evidence we have of the other. It is our experience of being subject (as well as object) that is the model by which we organize our experience of the other.

Since selves are both public and private, our self-knowledge also has these dimensions to it. We come to know ourselves through our thoughts and feelings and also through our behavior. At times we surprise ourselves by our responses, acting and feeling contrary to our firm expectations. We then realize that something is "off" about the way we think of ourselves. Others may experience both a similar surprise at our responses and similar doubts about their idea of who we are. It makes no sense to subscribe to a picture of ourselves that is contrary to the way we behave. We are what we do, and our behavior, of course, is public. Even our feelings have their public aspect and others may see some of them more clearly than we do.

Our fullest sense of being both subject and object derives, of course, from our interactions with others. We are relational beings. As our relations change we change. We do not know our self as an *I* apart from our self as a *he*. Our experience has no meaning apart from the meaning we share with others. Nor do we know the other as a *she* apart from a sense of her as an *I*. We can know her because she truly is her public self. Yet her behavior has no personal meaning for us unless we see it as hers, as something intended by an *I* and expressive of that *I*. Mind and body, first and third person, private and public, subject and object, in these and other ways we refer not to separable things but to dimensions of a single organism. When we know the other we see her in her actions, we hear her in her speaking, we sense her in her touch. However fragmentary, our life together resides in knowing and being known. However dangerous, life is worth little if we are not in touch. However difficult, we can learn together to know each other more truly, more deeply.

CHAPTER SEVEN

Learning and Life in the Organization

The learning process in a one to one personal setting is quite different from that in a corporation, university, hospital, social work agency, or other organization in which we work. There are features of our organizational life which make it very difficult for us to function as truly responsible, autonomous persons in that context, basing our behavior and decisions on our own experience and reasoning. Samuel Culbert introduces the problem in this way:

> The other day I heard a speech given by the outgoing deputy director of a medium-sized public organization. As he stepped forward to speak, tears began streaming down his face. . . . He frankly admitted his tears were of pain and disappointment for allowing himself to be chewed up by the system. . . . He had compromised himself and now felt he had achieved little. He saw himself falling into established ways of doing things, even when he sensed they were outmoded. He knew change was needed, but he never could quite come up with practical alternatives. . . . And worst of all, . . . he was sure he couldn't have done a better job.
>
> The dilemmas that seemed to get the best of this man are the ones that face all of us who work in large organizations.[1]

Reflecting on these dilemmas, Culbert concludes that "We've created an organization world in which the system defines the man rather than one in which the nature of man determines the system."[2] "In effect," he maintains, "we've lost control of our organization life. The images that determine what we want and how we act to get it are too often externally imposed."[3] In language we have been using, the situation learning that typifies our life in the organization is decentered.

Culbert's aim is to help us "learn how to learn from our experience" in the organization so that our learning will work for us rather than against us. His conceptual approach, including his indebtedness to Carl Rogers, is virtually identical to the one we are using and it will be a natural extension of our discussion to consider some of his ideas.

Education has three main components: training in skills; development of our distinctively human powers to create, to care, to be self-directing, to shape and test our own ethical norms; and induction into the outlook of a group. The organization provides training and induction, and it is this latter process of socialization that Culbert argues is the root of our problem. We undergo intensive situation learning about the organization and what it means to succeed in it and yet our awareness of what we've learned is minimal and decreases the longer we are in the organization. "Only after those who are responsible for us believe that we see things a certain way do they leave us alone to act independently."[4] The process is especially powerful because it operates "behind our backs," as Erich Fromm would express it. The boss himself "is unaware of how he's controlling us. From his point of view, he's merely giving us positive direction."[5] When induction into the way of life of a group is done in such a way that it minimizes our awareness of it and undercuts our ability to evaluate its assumptions against our own experience, it becomes indoctrination.

Our indoctrination would not so easily place us in bondage to it were we not so intent on gaining acceptance from our indoctrinators. We feel a need to be approved of, and this need becomes all the greater for being related to our economic well-being. "Our needs for external affirmation are so great that we are willing to subordinate our independently based pictures of reality to the prevailing view of the system. Because we would rather reject our own experience than risk being denied their acceptance, we are highly vulnerable to exploitation by the organization system."[5] In his influential book of the 1960s, *The Organization Man*, William Allen Whyte was arguing the dangers to the individual of accepting the organizational doctrine that what is good for the organization is necessarily good for him or her. We need to distinguish our needs from those of the organization, he maintained, and to learn how to fight for them, when they are important enough, in ways that are not self-destructive. Culbert is giving us the same message today.

Culbert argues that there are what he calls "mantraps" that are set for us both by the organizational system and by the education and conditioning we bring with us to the system. They are traps because "they limit the extent to which we manage our organizational lives, and subject us to excessive influence by the system."[6]

The traps set by the organization are assumptions with which we are indoctrinated. "Gaining more control begins by explicating these assumptions and questioning how they might be incomplete or even inaccurate."[7]

One of these traps is the assumption that being offered choices and alternatives increases our power and control. We need to bear in mind that these choices were established by someone else and may blind us to others that are not open to us. Or, as very often happens, we may not be given the information we need to reach a decision. In this way, our bosses maintain a kind of paternalistic control. The information we need is gradually leaked to us "in a form that accentuates their benevolence and our dependency."[8] Generally, Culbert believes, this form of control is not exercised consciously, although sometimes it is. He cites the example of the executive who said, "My plan is to offer Hugo our job in the East. . . . Then if he turns *us* down, we can mention the other options."[9]

Another trap is the assumption that if the organization holds us responsible it also provides the conditions that allow us truly to be responsible.

> Much of our organization life involves going along with precedents, without a good perspective of what we're doing or why we're doing it a certain way. Yet when something goes wrong we're expected to come forward and take the blame. . . .
>
> If we learn anything, we merely learn which situations to avoid or how to spread the blame. We don't learn how to shake loose from precedent and take command.[10]

In addition to traps of this sort that the organization creates through its indoctrination, there are traps, Culbert believes, in assumptions we bring to the organization. One such assumption is that self-determination is an ability somehow inherent in our very nature, so that we're not in danger of losing it. We act as though whatever compromises we make we can always unmake. "We believe that we can go for long periods of time focusing on goals that others hold up for us without losing track of those goals that have primary meaning for us. We also believe that we can immerse ourselves fully in organization life and not be unwittingly influenced in any significant way."[11] The result is we don't recognize how profoundly shaped and limited we are by so many of our experiences within the organization. Culbert quotes Paulo Freire's belief that "only beings who can reflect upon the fact that they are determined are capable of freeing themselves."

Another such dysfunctional assumption that we bring with us to the organization is that the world inevitably divides into *we* and *them* and that our overriding commitment should be to the team we work with.

> It is this assumption that can lead entire marketing groups to misrepresent their products, even though the consumers they thus mislead include members of their own organization and families. Similarly this assumption leads groups to withhold information from other groups in the same organization. . . .

> None of us can be counted on to remain conscious of the cause we're serving when our allegiance is to a particular work team. . . . If we could, then there would be no mantrap here.[12]

Not only do our pictures or maps of organizational life and of ourselves in it contain assumptions that unduly limit our control of our life in the organization, but the de-centered way that we hold these pictures does the same. Both our sense of the way things work and of what things are valuable are taken over from the organization. If Carl Rogers is right, this is simply an extension of the way we typically learn most of our values. We "introject" them from various groups or individuals because we believe this will result in our being accepted or esteemed. We regard them as our own, although "often there is a wide and unrecognized discrepancy between the evidence supplied by [our] experience, and these conceived values."[13] Since they are not grounded in our experience, Rogers contends, we cannot use our experience to test them or to resolve conflicts between them. "If [we] have taken in from the community the conception that money is the *summum bonum* and from the church the conception that love of one's neighbor is the highest value, [we] have no way of discovering which has more value for [us]."[14] Being unable to test our values by experience we become rigid about them.

In the case of the organization, Culbert maintains, the values we take over from the system "become implanted in our minds as if they constituted a moral code that we must observe. We worship competence, results and dedication to the job."[15] Rigidly held values make us judgmental. We become overly critical of ourselves and of others, unable to take into account the full range of circumstances involved, not to mention the other's point of view.

What, then, can be done to transform our experiential learning in the organization to something more functional for us? The key lies in the fact that there is far more to an experience than the process of our indoctrination and all the ways that we and others continually rein- force it. As Culbert puts it, "Our daily work experiences would reveal hidden perspectives of ourselves and the organization if we knew how to extract the tacit lessons they contain."[16]

Despite our indoctrination, we remain persons who also evaluate our own experience and, although we may have little awareness of the evaluations we are making, we do give ourselves warning signals. "We are seldom out of control for a long time," Culbert maintains, "without experiencing internal signals, however vague, that something's off. I call these signals *feelings of incoherence.*"[17] These feelings are produced by our experience of a discrepancy between our sense of who we are and what's important to us, on the one hand, and what the system expects of us or how it evaluates us, on the other. This is similar, of course, to what we discussed in Chapter 1 as the discrepancy between our organismic experience when we are growing up and messages we receive from our parents and others whose approval we seek.

Our feelings of incoherence, then, tell us where to look to find the lessons that will help us learn to function as autonomous persons within the organization. "But most of us, most of the time, need addi- tional skills and support to learn these lessons."[18] These needed skills are what Culbert terms "skills for divergent problem-solving."[19] In divergent problem-solving, the aim is to use inductive reasoning to generate alternative interpretations of a situation. "When we search for the meaning of an event rather than reacting concretely to the event itself, when we treat a problem-statement as if it were a symp- tom rather than a basic ill, when we inquire into the meaning of our difference with someone else, we use these thought processes."[20] What Culbert is driving at here becomes clearer when we contrast this approach with what he calls "convergent problem-solving," a pro- cedure at which most of us are far more skilled. "This is simply the process of accepting a particular problem more or less as presented and directing our own thoughts and actions toward affecting a solu- tion that makes sense in terms of the problem."[21]

Culbert provides the following example of the contrast between divergent and convergent problem-solving: Students in a new Profes- sional Masters Program in Management submitted a petition to the dean complaining of the quality of some of the teachers and the lack of sufficient access to their faculty outside of class. After an investiga- tion, the dean determined the students had good reason for their complaints and called a faculty meeting to discuss how the teaching and availability could be improved. Reasoning divergently, Culbert saw the problem differently:

> The students were reacting to discrepancies in our [i.e. the faculty's] relationship to the academic system. Facing these discrepancies could lead to fundamental change, but the way we were formulating the problem made this unlikely. Our formulation would lead us to make adaptional changes that would merely cover over the cracks in the present system. We were about to attack a symptom and miss a basic ill.

> When this type of problem-solving approach is recognized in industry, it's called fire-fighting, and results in solutions that rid people of a problem only to have the underlying issue come back to haunt them in another form.[22]

Part of improving our skills in divergent problem-solving is learning to ask the right question. "Each of the mantraps we've been discussing," Culbert maintains, "reflects our inability to understand something basic about what it means to have a choice, to have an alternative, and to take responsibility."[23] Choices differ from alternatives in being concerned with different routes to a given objective, while alternatives concern differing objectives. When we are presented with a choice, we need to ask whether this is really a disguised way of getting us to do what someone else wants us to do, whether the objective is one to which we can assent, and whether we are well-informed about the various means to it that are available. If it is a concealed form of what someone else wants, the alleged choice is actually a subtle manipulation and "the process of choosing becomes little more than our trying to guess what others will think and then performing in a way that insures they will get the right impression."[29]

Culbert gives the example of an engineer who was asked to take on a temporary three-month assignment in a city one hundred and fifty miles away. He agreed to do it, believing it would lead to a promotion. To avoid the expense to the company and the disruption to his family of a short term move, he further agreed to commute weekly to the new job. The sacrifices to himself and his family, however, turned out to be far greater than he imagined, as the assignment dragged on for twenty-two months. He ended up feeling angry, first at himself, and then at the company, although it seemed as though no one were really to blame. Culbert comments that "As long as he wanted the promotion and remained ignorant of other ways he might earn it, he had but a single option. . . . To have a real choice he should have known the probability of promotion following his sacrifice as well as any other options available to show his worth and be promoted."[25]

Alternatives are genuine when we are choosing between different objectives, each involving a different way of being related to the organization. To test whether we are really presented with alternatives, we need to ask whether the options are "based on different assumptions about our relationship with an organization, where one approximates our nature and/or ideals more closely than the relationship we're currently living."[26] The engineer in our previous example saw his relationship to the organization in terms of his desire for promotion. The question is whether the high priority he assigned this desire was consistent with his entire set of values. Generally, Culbert believes, the organization is far more likely to present us with choices than with alternatives. For the most part, it's up to us to formulate alternatives for ourselves. An example would be "a manager who realizes that he enjoys doing his own technical work more than supervising the technical work of others, and decides to return to his technical specialty."[27]

Finally, we need to be able to ask whether we are capable of taking responsibility for what we do in the organization. We have seen that our questions about choices and alternatives are aimed at situation learning. Do we really know what choices we have and what values are at stake in our work situation? The same is true concerning responsibility. How adequately do we understand both how things work in our situation and what forces are influencing us? At some point we may say "I wasn't promoted because I lacked initiative." But the question is whether we ever did "learn the areas where we fail to initiate and the reasons why we have such difficulty."[28] There are many things that influence us to act the way we do and, if we are to achieve significant freedom and the responsibility that goes with it, we need to understand our behavior and how it is being influenced. Only then can we act in ways that truly express our nature and values.

One of our needs, then, is for adequate skills in divergent problem-solving. In addition, Culbert maintains, we also need some form of support. This is because "learning the lessons of our experience means accepting insights that go counter to the prevailing organization culture. This can be a disorienting and lonely task when attempted individually,"[29] especially since "we're conditioned to think 'If something is off, it's off with me, not the system.' This is our continuing problem with self-acceptance."[30]

There are many forms that such support can take. It can be some sort of structure, such as tenure for university professors, or rights that are guaranteed by a new contract. It may also come from close interpersonal relationships, from people who share similar needs, or from more structured problem-solving groups similar to Weight Watchers. Whatever its form, some sort of support is essential for functional learning in the organization, Culbert insists. "One person alone cannot stand the anxiety of raised consciousness."[31]

One sort of learning, then, that is important for our organizational life is to understand those indoctrinations that undercut our autonomy, and to develop the skills and resources of support needed to become more self-directing. Another valuable sort of learning about the organization is to recognize, and to understand the costs of, what Culbert and McDonough call survival tactics, "the underground way people are forced to fight" in pursuing their self-interests.[32] This may help us to minimize the damage such tactics can do to us and to the organization. We turn now to consider three such tactics.

The first is called *framing*. The framer paints a complex picture of some aspect of the organization that serves his self-interest. This may be seen as analogous to what logic books call a "complex question." If someone asks, "Have you given up being so negative about this project?" whether we answer "yes" or "no" we admit to having been negative. The question frames a picture of our past attitude.

Framing, in organizational life, is described as having three components: the framer's commitment to something of considerable value to the organization, the practical outcomes of that commitment, and the justification—usually by established authority—of the framer's point of view.[33] One example given by the authors is that of Nancy, a new employee who, although capable and hard-working, lost her job because she failed to frame her position. Nancy's program director quit soon after she was hired and, in addition to her regular responsibilities, she voluntarily—but all too quietly—moved into a leadership role in attempting to save a national convention for which the director had been responsible. The result was that some of her own work suffered and the convention was of rather mixed success. A new program director had been hired shortly before the convention and immediately did some framing. He announced that things looked very bad for the convention but that it might be possible for him to salvage something. The executive committee subsequently credited him with the convention's successes and chalked up its failures to Nancy's lack of experience.

Nancy's fellow workers, and even the executive director, tried to come to her defense, but their statements ''were read as after-the-fact testimonies of her amiability, not of her bottom-line accomplishments,[34] [and her own] honest and humble self-presentation was interpreted as an admission of incompetence. . . .''[35] Nancy lost, the authors maintain,

> because board members lacked the categories for seeing her inputs, her accomplishments, and her commitments at the time she was delivering them. Why didn't they revise their perception when her story was told? Because . . . after the fact, people can justify anything. . . . Before she ever started pitching in she needed to market a reality that would allow others to value both her orientation and the contribution that orientation would produce.[36]

In Nancy's case, framing would have protected her interests without being a problem for anyone else. But one person's framing often works against the interests of another. When this happens, the second person may resort to the tactic of fragmenting.

Fragmenting is ''the tactic people use when they are on the receiving end of a reality that was constructed without their best interest in mind.''[37] One example presented of such a construction is a boss who criticizes the amount of overtime being put in by a subordinate's department, ignoring the fact that the subordinate is thinly staffed in an effort to save money and was trying to meet deadlines set by the boss. Another example is an employee who has been carried by his boss while he went through a divorce, but who sees that his boss is now going to ask more of him. He asks for a transfer, claiming he can't perform well under his boss's poor management.

The authors point out that it is often not very effective to try to respond by presenting the entire picture in all its complexity and perhaps even ambiguity. Consequently, one usually responds by parcelling out the full truth a little at a time. In such fragmenting,

> people tell different stories to different listeners; they define the responsibilities and obligations associated with their roles differently at different times; they promise one set of standards in selling what they are about to do and use a different set of standards in justifying what they just did; and they send out messages which are internally inconsistent. Moreover, much of this is done without conscious deception intended.[38]

In the examples cited, one would be fragmenting if he responded by saying to his boss, ''I assumed that your recent directive stressing preferential treatment for our big customers implied a variance in my overtime budget," or by saying, about his subordinate, "I'm not surprised Jim felt things were out of control, but I think if you were to examine the situation closely you'd find that his people have been looking to me for their primary guidance for months now."[39]

The third tactic, *playing-it-both-ways*, is described as a type of fragmenting, but in this case one simply pays lip service to the interests of others while continuing to pursue his own interests. This happens, the authors believe, largely because "we're finite people, capable of only so much, living in a system in which people with diverse interests expect us to say yes to their requests and to embrace their viewpoints, knowing that any honest attempt to please all will prove immobilizing, and any direct attempt to extricate ourselves from ill-conceived expectations will lead to conflict."[40] An example presented of playing-it-both-ways is that of the university president who says to his governing board or to the state legislature that the main focus of his university is on quality education, while to the faculty he continues to emphasize research.

Framing, fragmenting and playing-it-both-ways are the results of experiential learning under conditions "where one cannot . . . expect others to share or even respect the definitions of commitment and responsibility that give rise to what he or she thinks and does."[41] We may call such learning adjustment learning because, although it is not functional, it does enable one to cope with dysfunctional conditions. It is not functional because it leads to what Culbert and McDonough call *disorientation*. Disorientation occurs when our behavior is no longer guided by the commitments we are trying to pursue. "Form begins to replace function and careerism begins to squeeze out institutional responsiveness and vitality."[42] *Careerism* refers to "the person who 'successfully' produces products while cheating on his or her responsibility for producing the conditions that allow others to contribute to the overall organization effort."[43]

The survival tactics, then, that are learned under conditions typifying institutional life today, damage both individuals and the organization. The authors cite the following examples of institutional malfunctioning:

(1) the Catholic teaching order where Brothers take lifelong vows of poverty, chastity and obedience in the name of teaching the poor and wind up primarily running military academies for the rich in order to meet expenses;

(2) the Toll Bridge Authority that for years functioned with costs of operating toll booths exceeding toll booth collections;

(3) the San Francisco Water Department's appeal for users to

flush their toilets two extra times a day in the height of a severe drought because an earlier appeal for conservation reduced revenues to the point where income was not meeting fixed costs.[44]

Other examples of disorientation cited are students expressing values they do not really hold, a personnel manager appearing to succeed while failing to accomplish what he believed the organization really needed, professors failing to investigate what they most wanted to, and bureaucrats being "easily forced into competitive, careerist, back-stabbing antics" despite their desire to be otherwise.[45]

Must we, then, resign ourselves to learning for adjustment rather than for autonomy in our organizational life? Much expert commentary in the organizational field would make it seem so. Let's consider, as an example, the view of one noted authority.

Managers, as well as organizations, this expert points out, may be oriented toward power, achievement or affiliation—roughly what we have referred to in Chapter 1 as impersonal, personal and interpersonal[46] power, respectively. Psychological studies of managers regarded as successful show them typically as having a high need for power, in the sense of control over others. This, he believes, works well when combined with a commitment to use this power toward organizational goals. Need for achievement, he maintains, should be moderate in a manager because it tends to focus too much on his personal interests. Need for affiliation should be low in a manager because good guys make poor bosses.[47]

Such a view seems inadequate to meeting the problem of disorientation described by Culbert and McDonough. There are two reasons for this. First, managers are as much (and probably even more) driven to use framing, fragmenting and playing-it-both-ways as are their subordinates. Second, they cannot determine the best interests of their subordinates. Only the subordinates themselves can do that.

Culbert and McDonough argue for an affiliation-oriented alternative, but one that is far more complex than simply being a good guy. We may call this a person-centered approach, to reflect its Rogerian assumptions. This alternative begins by seeing "self-interest as the primary force that determines what goes on in organizations today."[48] Self-interests are pursued in terms of alignments, "the basic guidance systems that tell people how to navigate through organizational happenings . . . how to do their job, how to interpret each organization event, and how to responsibly fulfill their organizational duties without neglecting the personal reasons which brought them to their job in the first place."[49] When we operate solely in terms of our alignment, ignoring those of others involved—as is the case in framing, fragmenting and playing-it-both-ways—we tend to undercut the autonomy of others, and to erode our own because of the disorientation which inevitably results.

In a person-oriented approach, we seek to *understand* the alignments of the others we are involved with, to *communicate* to them that understanding, to *share* with them our own alignment and, generally, to act in ways that communicate a *respect* for their autonomy as well as for our own. These are the conditions, we may recall from Chapter 1 that Carl Rogers maintains result in functional learning. Interactions in the organization that embody these conditions open up the possibility of working together in ways that accommodate the interests of each person involved.

How realistic is such an alternative? Carl Rogers reports evidence that it is both realistic and conducive to maximum productivity. He cites, first, an experiment conducted by a very large industrial organization in which middle and upper level management of some of its plants were trained by a consultant to be person-centered, while those of other plants were not. In both cases, the plants involved were already considered to be well run. The results are as follows:

> During the past seven years the people in the experimental plants have become more and more deeply involved with a person-centered philosophy. Employees tend to be trusted by those in charge, rather than having their work closely supervised, inspected and scrutinized. Likewise, employees tend to trust each other. The degree of mutual regard among the employees is unusually high, as is their respect for each other's capabilities. The emphasis of the consultant and of the plant personnel has been upon building up good interpersonal relations, verticle and horizontal two-way communication, and a dispersion of. responsibility, choice and decision-making.
>
> Now the results are clearly apparent. In the experimental plants the average cost of a particular unit is about twenty-two cents. In the control plants [not operating in a person-centered way] the average cost of the same item is seventy cents. In the experimental plants there are now three to five managers. In the control units of comparable size, there are seventeen to twenty-three managers! . . .
>
> The profit gain to the company is so great that this is regarded as a trade secret. . . .[50]

Rogers also reports a study done by G.W. Cherry, in which very sophisticated methods were used to study the bearing on good management of those personal traits that make for a person-centered approach—traits that Rogers describes as those of the "fully functioning person." The study found that behavior scientists were in very large agreement about what those traits are, that a group of thirty-seven high level managers were equally in agreement about the managerial traits valued by the institutions they were part of, and that there was a considerable difference between these two sets of traits.

> He discovered that the cluster of traits having to do with warmth, capacity for close interpersonal relationships, compassion, and considerateness correlated very significantly with the qualities of productivity, creativity, cooperativeness and job satisfaction. . . .

> Finally, a cluster of characteristics often associated with management—power-oriented, aggressive, exploitative, achieving goals by manipulation and/or deceit—is not correlated with productivity, and has a negative correlation with creativity, cooperativeness and job satisfaction.[51]

It seems, then, that conditions which limit so much learning in the organization to adjustment and survival are not inevitable but can be altered to support truly functional learning. But what of the person caught in the typical organization which produces the dysfunctional kinds of learning Culbert and McDonough are describing?

Given an adequate understanding of organization traps and survival tactics, and given a good support system, Culbert and McDonough believe the individual may have some success in adopting a person-oriented style and in minimizing his need for survival tactics despite the lack of a person-oriented approach by his manager and most others in the organization.[52] But, they emphasize, we need to be realistic about the problems that will be faced in attempting this. Meaningful survival

> depends on knowing yourself well enough to stay self-oriented and on knowing how to get your contributions to the organization seen and valued. It also depends on knowing how to block others and hold them off when you sense that the interpretations they are pushing will make life more difficult for you.[53]

One business consultant reports asking five employees of a business firm to indicate what sport is most analogous to life in their organization. Responding independently of one another, all five answered "roller derby." This seems an apt image of the life in our organizations that many investigators, such as Culbert and McDonough, find to be typical. If we work in a large organization, it seems that we quite probably face conditions that lead to dysfunctional learning.

Under such conditions, we are very likely to be indoctrinated with beliefs that undercut our autonomy. This is especially true insofar as we act out of a need to be approved of. We are also apt to learn and to be confronted with survival tactics that result in a disorientation in which what we do actually works against the commitments that we most want to pursue.

By this account, for our organization learning to become more functional, we need to start by recognizing and understanding the sources of those indoctrinations and survival tactics. This is best done by combining a careful study of such books as *The Organization Trap* and *The Invisible War* with careful attention to the feelings of discrepancy—feelings that something is off—that we are likely to have in various parts of our organization life. As our next step, we need to work at developing skills in divergent thinking and in relating to others in a person-centered way that respects both their right to autonomy and our own. Finally, while taking these first two steps, we need to develop forms of psychological support that will see us through the tensions involved in such learning. As Carl Rogers contends, our learning becomes functional when we make contact with those who prize us, listen to us with empathic understanding, and respond to us with openness and honesty that is nonjudgmental and that *en*-courages us to relate to ourselves and others in the same way.

III

Some Strategies and Tools

CHAPTER EIGHT

Active and Passive Experiencing

Our experiential learning is often dysfunctional, always incomplete. We need to use present experience to test our beliefs, correcting the misinterpretations we've made, lifting the veils we've placed between ourselves and reality. We also need to see and hear and feel where we've been blind and deaf and unfeeling. Yet we often manipulate our experience to fit our beliefs. We see and hear and feel selectively, tending to experience what we expect to experience, wish to experience, or fear to experience. In this way, we may simply impose our maps upon our present perceptions, endlessly renewing the mistakes, the distractions, the partialities of our past learnings. If we are not to bind ourselves to portions of our past, we need to break these cycles of reindoctrination, using our experience to test what we have learned rather than merely to reembody it.

We test our beliefs when the way we experience is nonconformist rather than conformist. To be nonconformist in our experiencing we may ask new questions of our experience or seek to experience openly. Question asking is fundamental to effective problem solving and is at the heart of the various scientific methods. The scientist does not simply observe the world in whatever way it may happen to present itself to him but actively questions the world, manipulating it in ways designed to provide answers to his questions. Similarly when we ask questions about our everyday experience we notice things which otherwise would have escaped our attention. No matter how long we have been in a situation we can still learn from it by asking some new questions and so looking at it with a new angle of vision. We may think of this as an active or questioning way of experiencing.

On the other hand, there is a limitation to what we can learn by beginning with questions because we are apt to miss the things we are not asking about. Another way to learn from our experience, then, is to experience without imposing on it our usual assumptions and interpretations. We tend to experience what we expect to experience. By breaking out of our perceptual habits we may experience familiar things as though for the first time. The ability to do this opens the way for new ideas in every area of endeavor, including science. We may think of this as a passive or receptive or contemplative way of experiencing. When we experience passively we allow our world, or even some part of ourselves, to communicate itself to us in its own way rather than actively imposing our questions on the communication process. We come to our world with a sense of wonder. Questioning is especially useful to increase our control. An attitude of wonder is especially helpful to increase our enjoyment of or intimacy with the other.

ASKING THE RIGHT QUESTIONS

Let us examine first the asking of new questions. Perhaps the most important goal of higher education is to initiate us into new perspectives on our experience. As we read Freud or Marx or Tillich or Dostoevsky, or as we study Picasso or Schonberg, we begin to think about and see and hear things in new ways. One of the most fruitful preparations for learning from experience is gaining the questions that intensive work in an academic discipline can provide.

A major problem with this is that we often leave these questions and insights in the classroom. One of the ways we may be helped to activate some of these questions while we are engaged in our learning situation is to arrange to meet regularly with an instructor or seminar group to discuss our learning situation in light of these questions. Another of the ways we may be helped to do this is by reading a book that is relevant to our learning situation while we are involved in it. The closer in time our reading is to our experience the more likely we are to connect up the two.[67]

Another way of questioning our experience is by examining the maps by means of which we interpret experience. We tend to experience what we believe we will experience. Those beliefs by which we anticipate the future constitute our picture or map of ourselves and our world. We have diagrammed the relation between our map and our experience in this way (see Fig. 8).

Because our maps are so closely related to our experience, the way we locate our experience on our maps and perhaps change our maps in the process will have a lot to do with our ability to learn from experience.

We have said in an earlier chapter that our maps mislead us about our experience when we overgeneralize, delete, or distort. To see

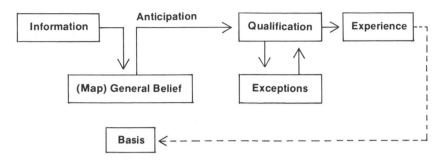

Figure 8

whether we are mapping in any of these ways, we may begin by writing down or tape recording some of our beliefs that are involved in our learning situation or perhaps in our life situation generally, paying special attention to problem areas (except where this might raise a high degree of anxiety and so sharply limit our freedom to learn). Are there ways in which we feel trapped, things we feel we just can't do anything about? Are there ways in which other people affect us that are a problem for us? Are there ways in which we affect others that are a problem for them? What things worry us considerably? What do other people think or feel about us that we find upsetting? Are there *shoulds* and *should nots* that we feel strongly about? Are there things that confuse us or seem terribly vague to us—things we don't seem to be able to get a handle on?

When we have written down or recorded a number of our beliefs, we may begin our examination of them by picking out the generalizations—beliefs referring to "everybody," "nobody," "always," "never," "completely," "entirely," and the like. We may then ask what we may call specifying questions, questions such as "Who specifically?" or "When specifically?" or "In what instances specifically?" Next we may consider whether we are overgeneralizing so that it will be more accurate to say "Some people" rather than "Everyone," and often more helpful to say "John and Mary" rather than just "Some people."

In terms of our diagram, in asking specifying questions we will be examining how well grounded our maps are in our experience. As Bandler and Grinder point out, the more specific our maps are the more choices we may feel we have. We may be able to make a response to the way John and Mary are treating us, for example, that would not be possible if everyone were treating us that way. Problems which seem insoluble when we see them in terms of "everyone" and "always" may appear quite manageable when we see them in terms of John and Mary at certain times.[2]

Related to overgeneralization is a vagueness that beliefs often have. Some beliefs may refer to persons, things, or events without making it clear just what persons, things or events are meant. We may call this kind of mapping "vague reference." For example, we may believe "One finds it hard not to fall back into old habits." But it is unclear to whom "one" refers and what habits are meant. Other beliefs may use verbs that are vague. Perhaps we believe "I don't use my time very well," yet this leaves it unclear what uses of our time we consider inadequate. It can sometimes be helpful to reformulate vague beliefs to make them more specific.

Another way in which our maps may fail to represent our experience adequately is deletion. In this case, our belief omits part of our experience. Perhaps we believe "I want to communicate better." But communication is always to someone and about something and neither of these parts of our experience of wanting is included in the way we've formulated our belief. Bandler and Grinder give the following examples of statements containing deletions (left column) and corresonding statements with these deletions filled in (right column).[3]

You always talk as though you're mad.	You always talk *to me* as though you're mad *at someone*.
My brother swears that my parents can't cope.	My brother swears *to me* that my parents can't cope *with him*.
Everybody knows that you can't win.	Everybody knows that you can't win *what you need*.
Communication is hard for me.	*My* communicating *to you my hopes about changing myself* is hard for me.
Running away doesn't help.	*My* running away *from my home* doesn't help *me*.

   ·   ·   ·   ·   ·   ·   ·   ·   ·   ·

I laughed at the irritating man.	I laughed at the man who irritated *me*.
You always present stupid examples.	You always present examples *to me* which are stupid *to me*.

Self-righteous people burn me up.	People who are self-righteous *about drugs* burn me up.
The unhappy letter surprised me.	The letter which made *me* unhappy surprised me.
The overwhelming price of food is disturbing.	The price of food which over-whelms *me* disturbs *me*.

Another kind of deletion to look for often occurs with expressions of necessity and of impossibility. Expressions of necessity include "have to," "should," "necessary," and "must." Perhaps we believe "It is necessary to put family interests over personal interests." In addition to the deletion concerning what specific interests are meant, we have deleted the *reason why* this is necessary. We can fill in the missing part by asking "What would happen if this were not done?"

Expressions of impossibility include "unable," "impossible," and "can't." We may believe "I can't tell the boss what I really think." In addition to the deletion concerning the specific thoughts meant, we have deleted the *reason why* we can't. We can fill in the missing part by asking "What prevents me from doing this?" We may call deletions involving necessity and impossibility "deletions of the consequence."

It may seem at first that, even though we express some of our beliefs vaguely or incompletely or too sweepingly or with an unexplained claim of necessity or impossibility, what we mean is obvious and so we are not likely to be misled by these formulations. But there is much evidence that the way we express things is closely related to how we see them and that we may be pretty fuzzy about things which become perfectly obvious once they are stated.

A third way in which our maps may become rather disconnected from our experience is distortion. In this case we reduce our control of our lives by misinterpreting the way things are related or their value or disvalue for us. One type of distortion we may look for in our beliefs concerns the relation between our emotions and someone else's behavior, or between our behavior and his emotions. We distort this relation when we maintain that one person's behavior causes another's emotions. We may call this form of distortion "false cause." If we see our emotions as caused by someone else, we locate the control of our emotions in that person rather than in ourselves. If we translate a belief such as "John makes me angry when he comes late to the meeting" into "I react when John comes late to the meeting by becoming angry because ――――" we can then fill in the reason we react this way—the belief which is implicit in this reaction—and go on to ask whether it is realistic and useful to react like this and whether some other sort of action would be more realistic and useful.

As we said in the chapter on "Changing Our Emotions," an emotion is about something and includes the way we look at—what we believe about—the thing in question. Perhaps we find that we react with anger when John comes late to the meeting "because I believe he is showing disdain for my leadership." If we now ask whether this by itself is the belief that constitutes the heart of our anger we see that it is not, because our anger is basically the way we evaluate this belief. This evaluation is itself a belief and, again, we may ask about the reasons for it. Perhaps we now say "because I believe he is showing disdain for my leadership, *and* that is pretty bad because it undermines my effectiveness in the following ways: ———." We get a much fuller picture of our emotional response when we express it in the form: "I react to (event) with (emotion) because (belief) and (evaluation) because (reasons for evaluation)." We are then able to ask how we know our belief is true and, if it is, whether our evaluation is realistic. Even if it is true that John is showing disdain for our leadership, is this really as bad as we are telling ourselves it is? Perhaps it is much less of a threat to us than we believe.

In taking this last step, we are checking our beliefs for what Albert Ellis terms "catastrophizing." We overreact to something because we tell ourselves that it is much worse or better than it really is. Aaron Beck points out that beliefs open to this sort of distortion are rules by which we evaluate the danger or safety of a situation or the pain or pleasure potential it has.[4] The question of danger concerns psychological as well as physical harm.

> Psychosocial harm covers the variety of hurt feelings, humiliations, embarrassments, and sadness that occur after a person has been insulted, criticized, or rejected. It should be noted that these feelings can occur when a person simply *thinks* he has been insulted, criticized or rejected—when indeed he has not been.[25]

If we exaggerate the risk involved we become unrealistically cautious. If we underestimate the risk we make ourselves needlessly vulnerable.

In evaluating for pleasure and pain we may exaggerate the extent to which our happiness depends on one source and so not only become overly concerned about that area of our lives but also fail to see or fully appreciate the potential of other areas. Consequently, we may drive ourselves unnecessarily hard to achieve the success on which we

think our happiness depends and become needlessly sad or depressed when things go badly. Beck lists the following rules which commonly make us needlessly vulnerable to becoming sad or depressed.

(1) In order to be happy, I have to be successful in whatever I
undertake.

(2) To be happy, I must be accepted (liked, admired) by all people
at all times.

(3) If I'm not on top, I'm a flop.

(4) It's wonderful to be popular, famous, wealthy; it's terrible to
be unpopular, mediocre.

(5) If I make a mistake, it means that I'm inept.

(6) My value as a person depends on what others think of me.

(7) I can't live without love. If my spouse (sweetheart, parent,
child) doesn't love me, I'm worthless.

(8) If somebody disagrees with me, it means he doesn't like me.

(9) If I don't take advantage of every opportunity to advance
myself, I will regret it later.[6]

It is not difficult to see the trouble we let ourselves in for by such
beliefs. If we set up unrealistic requirements for being happy we
create a no-win situation for ourselves.

Another of these misleading ways of mapping for which we may
check our beliefs is expressing what is really an ongoing process as
though it were something unchanging and completed. We may call
this "freezing the process." What is appropriately expressed by a
verb we express by a noun. When we look at what is happening as a
process we see that we have some control over it but when we look at
it as a finished event there seems to be nothing we can do about it.
Perhaps we believe "I regret my *decision* to keep the job." If we
replace the noun *decision* with the verb *deciding* we get "I regret that
I'm *deciding* to keep this job." We can then ask what prevents us from
changing our mind. As Bandler and Grinder point out, nouns which
stand for a process can be detected by asking whether it makes sense
to precede them with the term *ongoing*. "Ongoing desk" and "ongoing tree" do not make sense while "ongoing anger" and "ongoing
separation" do. Anger and separation are processes; desks and trees are
not.[7] In the following, the left column presents static formulations,
the right column presents the process version:

My divorce is painful.	My wife and I divorcing is painful.
Our terror is blocking us.	Our being terrified is blocking us.

My wife's laughter causes my anger.	My wife's laughing causes me to feel angry.
Your refusal to leave here forces my departure.	Your refusing to leave here forces me to depart.
Your perceptions are seriously wrong.	The way you are/What you are perceiving is seriously wrong.
My confusion has a tendency to give me no relief.	My being confused tends to stop me from feeling relieved.
I resent your question.	I resent what you are asking/the way you are asking me.
I'm afraid of both your rage and your help.	I'm afraid of both the way you rage at me and the way you help me.
His intuitions are remarkable.	The way he intuits things/What he intuits is remarkable.[8]

We may summarize what we have suggested about examining our beliefs as follows:

1(a). Overgeneralization:
    Everybody   Question: Who or when,
    Nobody   specifically?
    Always
    Never
    Completely

1(b). Vague reference:
    "One finds it hard not to fall   Questions: Hard for whom,
    back into old habits."   specifically? What habits, specifically?

2(a). Deletion:
    "I used to communicate better."   Questions: To Whom? About what? Better than what?

2(b). Deletion of the consequence:
    Should   Question: What would happen if
    Have to   this were not done?

    Impossible   Question: What prevents me from
    Can't   doing this?

3(a). False Cause
    "John makes me angry when he   Translation: I react when John

comes late to the meeting." comes late to the meeting by becoming angry because (belief) and (evaluation) because (reason for evaluation)
Questions: Is my reaction based on a realistic belief and evaluation? Are the consequences desirable for me? Would some other sort of reaction be more realistic and useful?

3(b). Catastrophizing:
"In order to be happy I have to be successful in whatever I I undertake."

Translation: "I won't like it if I don't always succeed."

Questions: Is the goal realistic? Why does the goal seem necessary to happiness? Is it for everyone? In what other way might it be possible for me to be happy?

3(c). Freezing the process:
"I regret my decision to keep this job."

Translation: "I regret that I'm deciding to keep this job."
Question: "What prevents me from changing my mind?"

To see more clearly the way we commonly map by overgeneralization, vague reference, deletion, deletion of the consequence, and false cause, the following transcript may be helpful. The session was a demonstration before a group of counseling trainees, one of whom volunteered to work with the trainer. *B* is a woman in her late twenties, divorced, and mother of two small children.

B: What should I do first?
T: Tell me what you are doing here; you said in the interview you wanted some help with something (*referring to a two-minute interview an hour before in which five people were chosen for this demonstration*).
B: Let's see, what am I doing here . . . I . . . I want help with . . . well, it's my roommates.
T: Roommates? . . .
B: (Interrupting) Karen and Sue, they share the house with me. We also have four children between us.
T: What kind of help would you like with these two people?
B: They don't seem to understand me.
T: How do you know they don't understand you?

B: I guess, it's that they're too busy . . . .

T: Too busy for what?

B: Well . . . too busy to see that I have needs.

T: What needs?

B: That I would like for them to do something for me once in a while.

T: Such as what?

B: They really have a lot of things to do, but sometimes I feel that they are insensitive.

T: Whom are they insensitive to?

B: Me. And . . . .

T: In what way are they insensitive to you?

B: You see, I do a lot of things for them, but they don't seem to do anything for me.

T: What don't they do for you? What needs don't they see that you have?

B: I'm a person, too, and they don't seem to recognize that.

T: How don't they recognize that you're a person?

B: They, both of them, never do anything for me.

T: They NEVER do ANYTHING for you?

B: No, not never, but I always do things for them whether they ask or not.

T: Let me see if I understand at this point. If someone recognizes that you are a person, then they will always do things for you whether you ask or not?

B: Well, maybe not always . . . .

T: I'm a bit confused at this point; could you tell me what those things are that they would do if they recognized that you're a person?

B: You know, like help with the dishes or babysitting, or just anything.

T: Could you also explain how your roommates are supposed to know what these things are that you want done?

B: If they were sensitive enough, they would know.

T: Sensitive enough to whom?

B: To me.

T: If they were sensitive enough to you, then they should be able to read your mind?

B: Read my mind?

T: Yes, how else could they know what you need and want? Do you tell them?

B: Well, not exactly . . . .

T: Not exactly how?

B: Well I kinda hint.

T: How do you kinda hint?

B: I do things for them.

T: Then, since you do things for them, they're supposed to know that you want them to do something in return?

B: It sounds sorta funny when you say it like that.

T: Sort of funny how?

B: Like I'm not being honest or something, but you just can't go around demanding things all the time or people will not want to give them to you.

T: Wait a second; who can't go around demanding things all the time from whom?

B: I can't go around demanding things from Sue and Karen or they won't want to give me anything.

T: I thought you said that they didn't give you anything anyway.

B: Well, they do sometimes, but not when I want it.

T: Do you ask them when you want something?

B: (pause) . . . (*Puts her hands in her lap and her face in her hands*). Mui . . . kannnt (mumbling).

T: (*Softly, but directly*) Beth, do you ask when you want something?

B: I can't.

T: What prevents you?

B: I just can't . . . I JUST CAN'T.

T: Beth, what would happen if you asked for something when you want it?

B: I can't because people will feel pushed around if I ask for things from them.

T: Do people ask for things from you?

B: Yes.

T: Do you always feel pushed around?

B: No, not always, but sometimes I do.

T: Beth, are you aware that thirty minutes ago you came to me and asked if I would work with you? You asked for something for yourself?

B: (pause) Yesssss.

T: Did I feel pushed around?

B: I don't think so.

T: Then, could you imagine asking for something for yourself from one of your roommates and their not feeling pushed around?

B: Yes, maybe.

T: Would you like to try?

B: Yes, I would.

T: And how will you know if your roommates feel pushed around?

B: Both of them would probably tell me.

T: Beth, do you tell people when you feel pushed around?

B: Not exactly, but I let them know.

T: How do you let them know?

B: I guess just by the way I act; they should be able to tell.

T: How? Are they supposed to be able to read your mind again?

B: Well, no.

T: What stops you from telling them directly that you don't want to do something or that you feel pushed around?

B: I couldn't hurt their feelings.

T: Does telling someone no, or that you feel pushed around, always hurt their feelings?

B: Yes, nobody likes to hear bad things.

T: Beth, can you imagine that you would like to know if your roommates feel pushed around by you so that you could be more sensitive to them?

B: Yes.

T: Then, could you also imagine your roommates wanting to know when you feel pushed around so that they could become more sensitive to you?

B: . . . ummmmmmmm . . . (pause) I guess you're right.

T: About what?

B: If I let them know when I feel pushed around or want something, then maybe they would be more sensitive.[9]

Once we have examined some of our beliefs we again face the problem we earlier discussed, namely, how to take the results of our reflections with us into our active engagement with our world. We rely largely on habit in our everyday transactions and we are likely to continue to act unthinkingly on the basis of long standing beliefs even though we have decided they are unrealistic or overly general or otherwise inadequate and have revised them accordingly. One way of learning to act on a newly formulated belief is to make a contract with ourselves either to ask a specific question or to tell ourselves something specific whenever a situation arises to which we wish to apply this belief. For example, in a situation in which we are accustomed to telling ourselves "I can't tell my boss what I really think" we may decide in advance to ask "What would happen if I did?"

By asking this question we bring to mind the results of our previous thinking about it. We also activate that side of ourselves which is relatively free of our childhood conditioning and is oriented around realistic assessment, the side that Eric Berne calls our adult self. This may be especially important in connection with those distortions we have called castrophizing, for these are often carryovers from childhood and have their effect on us only when our child self is in action—that side of us which embodies attitudes and behavior we first learned as children.

CLEANSING THE DOORS OF PERCEPTION

We have been examining ways in which we may learn by asking new questions of our experience. But we also noted that this has the limitation that we are apt to miss the things we are not asking about. A different way of learning is to set ourselves to experience more openly than we ordinarily do—to experience familiar things as though for the first time. In William Blake's phrase, it is a cleansing of the doors of perception. Let's examine this more closely in terms of our experience of other persons.

In the chapter on "Learning to Know Other Persons" we said that to see the other on his terms we must be willing and able to let him be as he is rather than wanting to evaluate and to change him. If we have the security in ourselves, we can take a Taoistic, receptive, noninterfering attitude toward him. We can keep our categories of interpretation, expectations, biases, fears, and needs out of the way so we can simply listen and wait openly, patiently, even wonderingly for the other to disclose himself in his own way. To repeat a quotation from Siddhartha, "When someone is seeking it happens quite easily that he only sees the thing that he is seeking; that he is unable to find anything, unable to absorb anything, because he is only thinking of the thing he is seeking. . . ." We are truly in touch with the other only when we see both him and his world from his point of view. We use our feelings and our own experience to enter into his experience, his way of being in the world.

Genuine openness in our experience of the other implies a respect for him and, so, tends to increase his sense of autonomy. Along with this it tends to increase his desire and ability to communicate himself. John Wallen has discussed ways of responding to the other which convey this openness and respect and ways of responding which communicate the opposite. The latter tend to increase his sense of being subordinate and to decrease his desire and ability for self-disclosure.

Wallen lists the following responses as tending to reduce the other's autonomy:

Changing the subject without explanation: For example, to avoid the other's feelings.

Explaining the other, interpreting his behavior: "You do that because your mother always. . . ." Binds him to past behavior or may be seen as an effort to get him to change.

Advice and persuasion: "What you should do is. . . ."

Vigorous agreement: Binds him to present position—limits his changing his mind.

Expectations: Binds to past, "You never did this before. What's wrong?" Clues him to future action, "I'm sure you will. . . ." "I know you can do it."

Denying his feelings: "You don't really mean that!" "You have no reason to feel that way!" Generalizations, "Everybody has problems like that."

Approval on personal grounds: Praising the other for thinking, feeling or acting in ways that you want him to; that is, for conforming to your standards.

Disapproval on personal grounds: Blaming or censuring the other for thinking, acting, and feeling in ways you do not want him to; imputing unworthy motives to him.

Command orders: Telling the other what to do, includes "Tell me what to do!"

Emotional obligations: Control through arousing feelings of shame and inferiority, "How can you do this to me when I have done so much for you?"[10]

To this list we may add R. D. Laing's account of autonomy-reducing responses that may lead the other to disbelieve his or her own experience. In the following account, Jack is trying to repress something but needs Jill's cooperation to succeed.

If Jack succeeds in forgetting something, this is of little use if Jill continues to remind him of it. He must induce her not to do so. The safest way would be not just to make her keep quiet about it, but to induce her to forget it also.

Jack may act upon Jill in many ways. He may make her feel guilty for keeping on "bringing it up." He may *invalidate* her experience. This can be done more or less radically. He can indicate merely that it is unimportant or trivial, whereas it is important and significant to her. Going further, he can shift the *modality* of her experience from memory to imagination: "It's all in your imagination." Further still, he can invalidate the *content*: "It never happened that way." Finally, he can invalidate not only the significance, modality and content, but her very capacity to remember at all, and make her feel guilty for doing so into the bargain.

This is not unusual. People are doing such things to each other all the time. In order for such transpersonal invalidation to work, however, it is advisable to overlay it with a thick patina of mystification. For instance, by denying that this is what one is doing, and further invalidating any perception that it is being done by ascriptions such as "How can you think such a thing?" "You must be paranoid." And so on. . . .[11]

Genuine openness to the other involves responses which tend to increase his autonomy and sense of equality or worth. Wallen presents the following as responses of this sort.

Active, attentive listening: Responsive listening, not just silence.

Paraphrasing: Testing to insure the message you received was the one he sent.

Perception check: Showing your desire to relate to and understand him as a person by checking your perception of his inner state; showing acceptance of feelings.

Seeking information to help you understand him: Questions directly relevant to what he has said, not ones that introduce new topics.

Offering information relevant to the other's concerns: He may or may not use it.

Sharing information that has influenced your feelings and viewpoints.

Directly reporting your own feelings.

Offering new alternatives: Action proposals offered as hypotheses to be tested.[12]

What is meant by "paraphrasing" is often misunderstood. The aim is to test our understanding of what the other is saying by reformulating it to introduce greater specificity or to supply deleted parts or to make the message more explicit in some other way. But we do not test our understanding if we simply repeat the other's words. If someone says to us "Communicating is hard for me" we won't learn anything if we simply reply "you find it hard to communicate." But if we reply "It's hard for you to tell me about your hopes for changing yourself" we are filling in deletions concerning whom it is hard to tell and what it is hard to tell about, so that the other can correct us if we've gotten one or both of these deletions wrong. Similarly if the other exclaims "Everyone misunderstands me" and if we think he has his family in mind we may test this by saying "you often feel misunderstood by your family."

It's important to keep in mind that our aim in paraphrasing is to understand what the other is saying and not to challenge or correct it. If someone says "I just can't do anything about it" and we reply "Surely you mean it would be hard to do something, rather than you can't," we may very well be denying his feelings, as Wallen put it. Instead we might respond "The obstacles to doing something just seem too great." This accepts the other's feeling of being hemmed in and seeks to clarify whether this feeling is based on believing the available alternatives to be unacceptable rather than being based on not seeing any alternatives. If this interpretation is correct, it may open up a discussion of the obstacles and so provide an opportunity for the other to discover whatever distortion there may be in his "I can't" formulation. The reader may find it helpful at this point to review overgeneralization, deletion and the other misleading ways of mapping we have discussed and to consider in each case what paraphrase might be helpful.

As we become more attentive and open to the communications of another we learn more effectively from our experience of him. The same is true of other areas of our experience. The trick is to give our full attention to what is so familiar it doesn't seem to need attention. Most of our experiencing, thinking and doing is a matter of habit. A glance tells us all we need to know and we can respond automatically. The other begins to speak and at once we think we know roughly what he is going to say and so we begin to rehearse our response. When we act out of habit, we conserve energy for things that are especially interesting or unfamiliar or threatening or that otherwise command our attention.

But when we only experience in ways that have become second nature for us we miss a lot and it may be worthwhile from time to time to do more than glance. If we put aside for the moment our concern with the future or absorption in the past or preoccupation with tasks in the present we can give our full attention to simply looking at what is in front of us, or to listening to what is being said and to the way it is being said, or to being in touch with what we are feeling. "Is she saying things I haven't been hearing? Am I feeling things I've been shoving aside?'' For the moment we can suspend any desire to change anything and simply experience the present out of curiosity or enjoyment.

In preparing to do this, we may find it helpful to consider ways in which we might be more open and times when this might best be attempted. We might also rehearse just how we plan to do this and make a contract with ourselves about just when we will do it.

We can also aim at greater openness to experience when we reflect on past experience. This is a key part of the approach to journal keeping which is discussed in the chapter on ''The Journal As a Tool in Experiential Learning.''

We have been considering two approaches to improving our ability to learn from experience. On the one hand, we may ask new questions of our experience. On the other, we may seek to experience more receptively. These approaches, however, are complimentary. Being open to experience is an important source of new ideas and new questions. Moreover, in experiencing passively or receptively we are, of course, using our ability to understand. We have this ability because we bring to our encounter with the world a complex set of meanings in terms of which we understand. In using these meanings we are, in a sense, already asking questions of our experience. As we learn new questions and new meanings we become more richly receptive of communications from our world.

CHAPTER NINE

Different Ways People Learn

No two of us learn in quite the same way. Learning is a complex process in which we employ a large variety of skills, some of which are far better developed and more frequently used than others. Some of us read well, others learn best by listening to someone. Some of us like to work within well developed patterns of thinking, others are good at coming up with new approaches and ideas. Our success in learning also varies with the situation. Some of us learn well by ourselves, others function better in various sorts of interactions with others.

A PROFILE OF LEARNING SKILLS

Let's look at some of the basic skills and situations involved in learning so that we can go on to ask which skills we have strength in, how well these match the skills required by one or another of the situations in which we are or may become involved, and which skills we might want to improve.[13] We can also then ask which skills are particularly important to the various kinds of learning discussed in the first chapter. We shall consider five different sorts of learning skills: those involved in symbolizing, thinking, judging, and remembering and those of a more general nature.

Symbolizing

The first set of learning skills are involved in *expressing and receiving information* and in mapping our experience. We humans are the symbol-using animals. By means of symbols we represent our world to ourselves (and to others) and so we can step back away from it, contemplate it, evaluate it, imagine it different than it is, and act to bring what we imagine into being. In the same way we also represent ourselves to ourselves and so can choose to be different than we are. We may learn, then, not only in receiving information but also in expressing it. In writing or talking about something we may grasp it more clearly or even get new ideas about it. In personal matters, especially, we may not understand something—perhaps one of our feelings—until we express it. Then, too, we need to test our beliefs by expressing them and obtaining feedback.

The first five skills in this set concern using languages to communicate. Notice that we may be highly skilled in one sort of language use, say talking, yet not at all good in another such as listening.

The next three skills concern sending and receiving information by means of our senses. Here, of course, is the foundation of our interaction with our world. Some of us may experience the world in very rich, visual terms, others may derive little meaning from what we see. In Chapter 2 we discussed mapping by our senses as well as by words.

The last five skills in this set concern our use of information in our face to face interactions with others. Often, for example, our success in relating to another depends on our ability to understand his or her point of view.

1. *Reading: Receiving meaning through written words.*
   Learns well from books, magazines, letters, written instructions, lecture notes.
2. *Writing: Expressing meaning through written words.*
   Succeeds in being understood through essays, letters, written explanations.
3. *Listening: Receiving meaning through spoken words.*
   Learns well from lectures, cassettes, discussions on radio, conversational responses of another.
4. *Talking: Expressing meaning through spoken words.*
   Succeeds in being understood in conversations, discussion groups, questioning a lecturer, giving a talk.
5. *Graphics: Expressing and receiving meaning through abstract visual presentations.*
   Learns and communicates well by means of graphs, tables, maps.

6. *Receiving, processing and expressing information in terms of visual experience.*
   Is sensitive to visual experience, thinks well by means of visual images, is at home with such expressions as "Do you *see* what I mean?" and "I get the *picture*."

7. *Auditory: Receiving, processing and expressing information in terms of auditory experience.*
Is sensitive to auditory experience, thinks well by means of inner conversations or melodies, is at home with such expressions as "That *sounds* right" and "Now I *hear* what you're saying."

8. *Kinesthetic: Receiving, processing and expressing information in terms of physical or bodily experience—touch, bodily movement, feelings.*
Is sensitive to touch, feeling, bodily movement, thinks things through in terms of feelings, is at home with such express as "That was a *moving* experience" and "That *feels* right to me."

9. *Empathy: Understanding things from another person's point of view.*
Is able to enter into another's feelings, beliefs, overall way of looking at things.

10. *Kinesic: Understanding and communicating well by body language.*
Is sensitive to the meaning of facial expression, bodily posture, tone and movement; can establish rapport and otherwise communicate well by physical expression.

11. *Proxemic: Judging the physical and social distance expected by another.*
Can determine well the role one is expected to play, the degree of familiarity one is expected to express toward another.

12. *Transactional: Influencing others through communication.*
Can communicate with another in a way that persuades, inspires confidence or otherwise influences him or her.

13. *Histrionic: Using a wide repertoire of behaviors to achieve a desired effect on another.*
Can play a role or "perform" in a way that helps another feel appreciated, facilitates his learning, evokes a particular feeling, and the like.

Thinking

The second set of learning skills are involved in *organizing and processing information*, two additional aspects of mapping our experience. We need to arrange information in forms that allow us to understand it. We also need to reformulate it, draw consequences from it and use it in other ways to solve problems. The first three skills in this set are concerned with organizing information, the next five with processing it.

14. *Structure: Understanding by classifying, defining, and making and applying rules.*
Can grasp information well by outlines and summaries. Seeks clear cut distinctions. Does well on true-false tests.

15. *Relation: Understanding by relating one thing, idea or experience to another.*
Can grasp meaning well by examples, anecdotes, analogies, and applying what is said to personal experience. Tends to see things as complex. Does well on essay tests.
16. *Comparison: Understanding by comparing or contrasting one thing, idea or experience with another.*
Can grasp meaning well by seeing similarities and differences between one thing and another.
17. *Analysis: Breaking a whole down into its unique parts.*
Successful at such tasks as determining how things work, how each individual action contributes to a group effort, the ingredients in a sauce or chemical compound.
18. *Synthesis: Combining separate elements to form a coherent whole.*
Successful at such tasks as working out compromises, uniting apparently different points of view in a wider perspective.
19. *Convergence: Utilizing a number of facts or clues to solve a problem (reasoning inductively).*
Successful at reasoning from the particular to the general, forming useful hypotheses, using clues to solve a mystery.
20. *Divergence: Creating a variety of alternatives for action or interpretation.*
Successful at brainstorming, finding new ways of looking at something or new uses for it.
21. *Deduction: Seeing implications, reasoning from premises to necessary conclusions.*
Successful at such things as geometrical proofs, drawing consequences from an hypothesis, following a debate.

Judging

The third set of learning skills are involved in judging or evaluating information, another aspect of mapping our experience. We need to select and use criteria and standards to determine the significance, quality, appropriateness, or priority of courses of action, goals, and, indeed, every aspect of ourselves and our world with which we must deal. Criteria concern the different respects in which a thing is judged, for example, the durability, efficiency, and prospective resale value of a car. Standards concern the degree to which something must posess a certain quality to be acceptable, for example, the car must get at least twenty-five miles per gallon.

22. *Evaluation: Selecting and using criteria and standards to determine quality, appropriateness or priority.*

Successful at determining whether a product is worth the price, what course of action is most likely to succeed, which player is most valuable to a team.

23. *Ethic: Selecting and using criteria to determine the moral rightness or wrongness of a course of action.*
Understands the principles which underlie moral decisions and can use these principles to think through difficult moral issues.

24. *Esthetic: Judging and appreciating qualities of beauty.*
Able to appreciate music, art, and other creations, to determine such things as how a room or house or yard can be made more attractive.

25. *Sense Integration: Giving a useful interpretation to sense data.*
Able to respond quickly and appropriately to immediate situations such as making a play in a sport, operating complicated equipment, responding to an emergency while driving a car.

26. *Self Knowledge: Judging personal strengths and weaknesses.*
Deciding appropriate goals and courses of action in light of one's abilities, needs and desires.

Remembering

The fourth set of learning skills are involved in storing and retrieving information. To say we have stored something is simply to say we are able to retrieve it, but the ways we store and retrieve often involve different factors. We shall consider one of these factors, namely, the role which an external stimulus may play in retrieval.

We shall also consider the kinds of things we are most likely to remember. These are the things we fear or like or find useful or are otherwise interested in. To avoid undue complexity, however, we shall not consider such important factors as the role played by images, sounds, feelings and words or the destinction between long and short term memory.

The first three skills in this set are concerned with storing information, the next three with the types of things we remember best, and the last three with retrieving information.

27. *Rote Memory: Storing verbal information by repeating it in sequence.*
Successful at memorizing travel directions, formulas, poems.

28. *Somatic Memory: Storing physical "information" by repeating muscular movements in sequence.*
Learning complex physical movements such as dance steps, gymnastics, bicycle riding.

29. *Association: Storing information by relating it to information already stored.*

Successful at remembering someone's name when you see him or her, movies an actor has played in, details of a trip, arguments for and against a position.

30. *Processes: Remembering the steps by which something is done or the stages in which something happened.*
Successful in retaining the steps for reassembling a bicycle or knitting a sweater, or in bringing to mind a chemical process or the stages in child development.

31. *Concepts: Remembering the meanings of and relations between abstract ideas such as justice, beauty, rectangle.*
Successful in retaining principles, theories, designs, types of argument.

32. *Entities: Remembering information about individual persons and things.*
Successful in retaining information about friends, musicians, football teams, historical monuments, ones own car.

33. *Recall: Remembering without the help of an external stimulus.*
Able to recite a poem, recall a melody, recount a conversation, remember a telephone number.

34. *Recognition: Identifying, in response to an external stimulus, concepts or information previously learned.*
Able to identify the composer of a musical score, the author of a quotation, the name of a car, or to determine the accuracy of a definition or the correct answer from a list.

35. *Utilization: Giving practical application to something previously learned.*
Using past learning to interpret a situation differently or to behave differently in a situation.

General Learning Skills

The fifth set of learning skills are not limited to such particular activities as processing or storing information but are involved in a wider range of learning activities.

36. *Internal Motivation: Stimulating and rewarding oneself for learning activities.*
Motivated by one's own goals and needs; successful in working independently of others.

37. *External Motivation: Responding well to the stimulation and reward from others for learning activities.*
Motivated by rewards from others such as approval, recognition, grades, money; helped by frequent support from others.

38. *Positive Self Concept: Learning is encouraged and supported by positive picture of oneself as a learner.*

Able to approach a given learning environment with confidence that one can learn well.

39. *Attention: Concentrating on a particular stimulus.*
Able to focus attention on something over a period of time, noting detail, interrelations and the like, as in following an argument, searching for a clue, clarifying a problem.

40. *Repression: Ignoring internal and external stimuli that are irrelevant to a learning task.*
Able to study effectively in spite of noise, mild physical discomfort, psychological pressure of one's problems and other responsibilities.

41. *Time Use: Managing one's time well in learning tasks.*
Able to budget and distribute one's time realistically, to meet deadlines.

Preferred Learning Situations

This final set of items concerns not learning skills but situations and relations in which we make most effective use of our skills.

42. *Independent: Learning by oneself.*
Has the internal motivation and abilities to learn without the help of others.

43. *Group: Learning through group interaction.*
Able to learn through group discussion, participation in team sports, and the like.

44. *Subordinate: Learning from someone with greater knowledge or skill.*
Able to learn from lectures, coaching instruction, or face to face discussion with someone more advanced.

45. *Peer: Learning through a one-to-one relationship with a peer.*
Able to learn by interaction with a co-learner of rather similar knowledge and skills.

BASIC SKILLS IN EXPERIENTIAL LEARNING

In looking at a learning situation in light of this inventory, we can ask how well our learning skills match those required by the situation. We can also ask what opportunity the situation provides for improving our learning skills. Perhaps our learning goal is coming to understand children of a different social class than our own.[14] Situations which provide this opportunity require such skills as empathy and kinesic, the abilities to see things from another's point of view and to understand his body language. If we have these and related skills sufficiently, we may gain considerable understanding of such children through our involvement in one of these situations. At the same time, in the successful exercise of these abilities we are likely to improve them.

But suppose that we have very little ability along these lines. If we throw ourselves into working with children, then, with the best intentions in the world, it is likely to be a bad experience for us, not to mention for the children. So much will depend, of course, on whether we are working with other adults and, if so, whether they have these abilities themselves and what their attitude is toward helping us with them. But we are far more likely to learn in situations that are basically rewarding than in those which give us pain. Bad experiences tend to block functional learning or to result in dysfunctional learning or both. We may come out of painful experience less able to empathize than ever.

In selecting a learning situation, then, it is important to distinguish between opportunities to *use* our learning skills and opportunities to *develop* these skills. The latter have the special significance of contributing to the life long process of learning from experience. But, if our goal is to develop one or more of these skills, we need to ask whether a situation allows for their development in a gradual, step by step way, whether resources will be available to help us in this learning such as the presence of someone who exemplifies these skills, and whether we will experience this development process as rewarding—whether, for example, others in the situation will be supportive of our efforts.

Some of the skills in this inventory are particularly important to one or another of the various kinds of learning we discussed in the second chapter. Suppose that some of our goals have to do with response learning, a change in the way we are prepared to respond in a certain situation. First of all, the new response may involve physical coordination; the inventory calls this *somatic memory*, the ability, for example, to learn a new dance step or new movements in a sport. The more time we give to complex physical tasks the more skilled we become in learning new physical movements which involve complex coordination.

Secondly, we may want to respond to something differently but not know what sort of new response would be helpful. One of the abilities which is useful here is that of applying to our present situation something we have seen someone else do or something we've read about or something we've discussed in class—*utilization*. We're more apt to use the emergency brake in our car if we occasionally rehearse in our mind the movements we will make if we need emergency braking. We're more likely to utilize something we've learned in class if one of the things we do in learning it is to think through its possible implications for our own ways of responding.

Thirdly, we become better able to come up with new behavior as we increase our control over our behavior generally, becoming more able to act a part, to tailor our response to fit another's feelings or needs, to remain composed when threatened. The inventory labelled this ability *histrionic*. When we experience our behavior as self-chosen we can be more receptive and imaginative concerning new ways of responding.

A fourth consideration about skills in response learning is our need to see our possible new behavior from the point of view of another. The appropriateness of our behavior often depends in some degree on how others will respond to it. Perhaps we want to be more helpful to them, to work more effectively with them, to enjoy them more. The skills of empathy, kinesic and proxemic, then, are often important in response learning. Our ability to take another's point of view, recognize his nonverbal communications and to judge the physical and social distance he desires is important to our efforts to determine the appropriateness of our responses insofar as they involve him. Our ability to empathize tends to improve from novels, plays, motion pictures, and the like when they sensitively portray a variety of persons, especially persons quite different from ourselves. Our responsiveness to the body language of others is likely to increase if we occasionally give our complete attention to the gestures, facial tone, and other physical expressions of someone nearby, perhaps in a restaurant or on a bus or on television, especially with the sound turned off.

Empathy, kinesic, and proxemic are important skills in much response learning because we use them in interpreting the meaning of situations in which other persons are involved, and response learning depends on how we interpret a situation. As we interpret a situation differently, what we seek in that situation changes. Situation learning and response learning are closely interrelated. As we *develop* our skills in empathy, kinesic or other aspects of situation learning we are engaged in transsituation learning—a change in our ability to interpret situations.

Somatic memory, utilization, and histrionic are basically skills not in interpreting but in doing. But response learning and situation learning are so closely interrelated that as we use these skills to develop new ways of moving and acting we are really also engaged in a form of situation learning. The reasons for this are, first, that we understand our world basically in terms of the possibilities for our own actions and for being acted on by others and, second, that we map our world not only by natural language but also by our senses as well. As we discover new ways of moving and acting in a situation we discover new meanings in it. We know our world as possibilities for seeing and being seen, hearing and being heard, touching and being touched, responding in terms of feelings and being responded to in the same way. As our ways of seeing, hearing, or feeling change, our world changes. As we learn to dance, music takes on new meaning. As we learn to drive we experience distance differently. As we learn to make love, intimacy gains new dimension.

Because using such skills as somatic memory, histrionic, and utilization to explore new action-meanings of a situation is really a form of situation learning, *development* of these skills is a form of transsituation learning—a change in our capacity to explore new meanings. As we develop our capacity for graceful movement, for example, we increase our ability to explore the potential of a situation for different forms of such movement—as a child discovers what he can do in a swimming pool.

Our discussion of skills basic to response learning has inevitably involved situation learning as well. As we have seen, empathy, kinesic, and proxemic are three skills basic to much situation learning. Still others are relation, comparison, analysis, and synthesis, skills in seeing interrelations between things. Particularly important here is synthesis, fitting the various experiences and bits of information we have into a pattern that constitutes something as a whole. We see a chair from many angles and we relate these experiences to one another as seeing the front, side, top, and bottom of the same object. We engage in a group discussion and see the various comments that are made as developments of an overall theme. We walk into a room and all of the things we see go together to give us a general impression of it. Just as our skill in solving detective mysteries or in determining the way the cards are probably distributed in a game improves as we do these things, so the more we give attention to interrelations in our job situation or in a project we're involved in the more easily we grasp these patterns.

Yet another skill basic to situation learning is evaluation, using criteria to judge the quality or adequacy of something. In choosing a career we will ask about such things as the preparation and personal characteristics it requires, the kinds of rewards it offers, the opportunities for employment it provides. Nothing is more central to the meaning of a situation for us than our judgment of the values it involves. Although it contributes to the development of many skills, the example of others often plays an especially important role in developing our ability to evaluate. We may learn a lot about what to look for in a motion picture or in a novel by reading the work of a good critic. A competently conducted art appreciation course may enhance our enjoyment considerably.

Development of these skills in situation learning is what we have called transsituation learning. Any change in our ability to interpret a situation is learning of this sort, but its generally most important form is the development of our capacity to examine an interpretation—especially one of our own—and to develop alternatives to it. The key to transsituation learning, in other words, is contrast. The more we learn to think in terms of contrasts, to direct our attention to them as they occur and to generate them for ourselves, the more creative we can be in working with the meaning of a situation.

One of the skills basic to creating alternative interpretations is that just discussed—evaluation. Our ability to evaluate involves not only the application of criteria but also the determination of what criteria to apply. Contact with those who use criteria different from our own is often helpful in learning to consider more than one way to evaluate something.

Another skill which contributes to our capacity to develop alternative interpretations is *divergence*, the ability to find alternatives in a given situation—new ways to use things, new questions to ask, new ways to see the situation itself. We have seen the emphasis which Samuel Culbert gives to divergence in working clear of the traps of organization life:

> However, using discrepancies to begin a new stage of
> consciousness-raising and reflection goes against our natural in-
> clinations to reduce conflict and solve problems. But just as
> new skills and support helped us to resist inclinations to avoid
> feelings of incoherence, so new skills and support can help us
> counteract our inclinations to solve problems.
>
> These skills are called skills for divergent problem solving, in
> contrast to skills for convergent problem solving. . . .
>
> When we search for the meaning of an event rather than
> reacting concretely to the event itself, when we treat a
> problem-statement as if it were a symptom rather than a basic
> ill, when we inquire into the meaning of our differences with
> someone else, we use these thought processes.[15]

The natural tendency to reduce conflict may work against divergent thinking but may also provide impetus toward it. When we hold conflicting ideas side by side without dismissing one because it is unfamiliar or goes against conventional wisdom, our mind begins to search for meaningful connections between the two. Our original idea may be enriched or a significantly new idea may emerge. In traditional terms, thesis and antithesis drive toward a synthesis of the two. Not only is the antithesis a divergence from the thesis but the synthesis is as well.

Skill in divergence tends to improve as we open ourselves up to the ideas of others, especially to those who see things from quite a different angle of vision than we do. Talking with or reading the work of those in an academic discipline or other field of activity different from our own can be a fruitful source of contrasting ideas. Contact with a different culture can be another. Even contrasting ideas that occur accidentally or are generated in a completely random way and which seem irrelevant to the situation may turn out to create a productive tension with the original idea. We might simply reach for the first red-covered book we come to on the shelf, open it in the middle, take the first sentence our vision falls on, and do a kind of brainstorming for what it may suggest about new ways of approaching our situation. The chances are much against any one of these random ideas turning out to be useful and most will not merit more than a few minutes of our time; but they have the great advantage of enabling us to escape from long-standing assumptions and habits of thought.

In seeking to develop our capacity for divergent thinking it may be helpful to remind ourselves of our discussion of contrast in the section on "Four Kinds of Learning." Although we tend to reduce conflict, we also cannot think without contrast. As we noted, "My little dog has fleas" conveys meaning because in place of each word at least one with a contrasting meaning could be used—*your* in place of *my* for example. Consequently, any meaningful interpretation of a situation contains the seeds of one or more contrasting interpretations. We need only to imagine some of our relationships reversed to enter a divergent point of view. Perhaps we see a situation primarily in terms of being loved, respected, empowered by another. Taking the role of the other, we can try on the use of our powers to do the loving, the validating, as well. Or we may approach our situation as a playwright does a weak scene, imagining how this part or that might be revised, a new part introduced—ways of interpeting that scene differently. Practice in taking the perspective of another—whether actual or invented—may enhance our skill in divergence considerably. A summary of our discussion of learning skills that have special importance for response, situation, and transsituation learning is presented in Table 2.

Our discussion of skills basic to transsituation learning has included a consideration of the development of these skills, and such development is what we have called transcendent learning. In transcendent learning, we change the concepts we use to interpret a situation. At

Table 2. Skills For Three Types of Learning

Skills Basic to Response Learning

Skill	Use in Response Learning
13. Histrionic	Performing or role playing in new ways
28. Somatic Memory	Responding with new physical movement and sensation
35. Utilization	Giving new application to previous response learning
9. Empathy	
10. Kinesic	Evaluating alternative behavior from the point of
11. Proxemic	view of another

Skills Basic to Situation Learning

Skill	Use in Situation Learning
15. Relation	
16. Comparison	Seeing new interrelations between things
17. Analysis	
18. Synthesis	
13. Histrionic	Discovering new meanings in a situation through
28. Somatic Memory	
35. Utilization	new ways of moving and acting
22. Evaluation	Using new criteria to judge aspects of a situation

Skills Basic to Transsituation Learning

Skill	Use in Transsituation Learning
20. Divergence	Developing new perspectives on a situation
22. Evaluation	Developing new criteria for assessing situations

its fullest development, this change is not simply a better ability to adopt other concepts already available in our culture but an increased facility in creating new concepts. As we have noted, the ability to welcome contrasting ideas and to hold them in tension with familiar ones is a key factor in the creative person.

Finally, what can we say about the place of learning skills in the three areas of life we have considered, namely, our emotions, our more intimate interpersonal relations, and our participation in large organizations? Because interpretation is basic to all three, the skills used in situation learning are of first importance. In the case of learning to understand another, the interpretations we learn are hers, and may or may not seem viable for us. Concerning our emotions, the skill of evaluation is fundamental because cognitive evaluation is their core element.

Skills in transsituation learning also have a key role in each of these areas insofar as our emotional, interpersonal and organizational learning involve taking on *new* interpretations. We gain control of our emotional life only as we become able to evaluate the evaluations we are making and to create viable alternatives. In our personal interactions, coming to know each new person requires us to enter into a new set of interpretations. The awareness that we ourselves could be a different person with a different set of interpretations of our life-situations is indispensible to coming to know another. Concerning our organizational life, Culbert has emphasized the need to replace many of the interpretations with which we have been indoctrinated. He has also stressed the ability to be person-centered in our organizational interactions and so we see here, too, the significance of skills that enable us to enter into the interpretations—the alignments, as Culbert and McDonough called them—of our fellow workers. In each of these central areas of our life, then, skills in divergent thinking and evaluation—the abilities to try on new interpretations and new criteria of evaluation—have valuable roles to play.

Some additional skills are needed for learning to understand others. Visual, auditory, and kinesthetic skills are necessary if we are to understand those who receive, process and express information in terms of what they see, hear or feel. Also helpful are kinesic and attention, the abilities to understand another's body language and to focus attention on her over a period of time, taking in as much detail as possible, seeing interrelations, and the like. Many therapists, such as Carl Rogers, report that when they are listening to a client it is very often as though they were in a kind of tunnel, cut off from the rest of the world. For that time, their attention is given solely to the other. Then, too, histrionic has a valuable role to play, the ability to act in a way that helps the other feel prized and understood. As Rogers emphasizes, to help another understand and share her unique stance toward life, we need not only to listen to her empathically and to accept her but also effectively to communicate to her what we are learning and feeling.

CREATING A PROFILE OF YOUR SKILLS

The following "Learning Skills Profile" questionnaire can be used by you to create a picture of your sense of your learning skills. To do this, answer each question (see Fig. 9) with a number between 1 and 5. An answer of 1 means you see yourself as rather poor at what is being asked, 5 as very good, 3 as just fair, and so on. It might be well to keep in mind that this is not some sort of test of your merits and demerits but simply a way of giving yourself an overall picture of what skills you feel you've developed and what skills you haven't. There are many different ways of functioning well as a person, and not having developed a particular skill is important only if you wish to function well in an area that requires that skill. What creating your profile will do for you is give you a clearer sense of your strengths and enable you to determine whether, in light of your involvements and goals, you would benefit from developing some of the skills you've neglected.

A LEARNING SKILLS PROFILE

1. I learn well from books.
2. I feel I can communicate well by writing a letter.
3. When listening to someone I have a good sense not just of what he or she is saying but of how he or she is saying it.
4. I'm good at making myself understood orally.
5. I'm good at reading maps.
6. I find it natural to use visual expressions such as "That plan *looks* good to me," "I *see* what you're saying" and "Do you get the *picture*?"
7. I rely a lot in communication on the way voices sound.
8. I react to things a lot in terms of my feelings.
9. I'm good at understanding someone else's point of view.
10. I generally know how to use nonverbal communication to establish rapport with another.
11. I can usually sense the role others expect me to play.
12. I'm good at persuading others about something.
13. I'm good at role playing.
14. In learning something I often find it helpful to make outlines.
15. To understand something I usually try to apply it to my personal experience if its possible to do so.
16. I'm good at comparing and contrasting different positions on an issue.
17. I can do well at determining the various causes that explain a complex event or reasons that resulted in a personal decision.
18. I'm good at working out compromises.
19. I'm good at using several bits of information to determine why someone is late or angry or playing his or her cards in a certain way.

1 _____	46 _____	91 _____	136 _____	_____
2 _____	47 _____	92 _____	137 _____	_____
3 _____	48 _____	93 _____	138 _____	_____
4 _____	49 _____	94 _____	139 _____	_____
5 _____	50 _____	95 _____	140 _____	_____
6 _____	51 _____	96 _____	141 _____	_____
7 _____	52 _____	97 _____	142 _____	_____
8 _____	53 _____	98 _____	143 _____	_____
9 _____	54 _____	99 _____	144 _____	_____
10 _____	55 _____	100 _____	145 _____	_____
11 _____	56 _____	101 _____	146 _____	_____
12 _____	57 _____	102 _____	147 _____	_____
13 _____	58 _____	103 _____	148 _____	_____
14 _____	59 _____	104 _____	149 _____	_____
15 _____	60 _____	105 _____	150 _____	_____
16 _____	61 _____	106 _____	151 _____	_____
17 _____	62 _____	107 _____	152 _____	_____
18 _____	63 _____	108 _____	153 _____	_____
19 _____	64 _____	109 _____	154 _____	_____
20 _____	65 _____	110 _____	155 _____	_____
21 _____	66 _____	111 _____	156 _____	_____
22 _____	67 _____	112 _____	157 _____	_____
23 _____	68 _____	113 _____	158 _____	_____
24 _____	69 _____	114 _____	159 _____	_____
25 _____	70 _____	115 _____	160 _____	_____
26 _____	71 _____	116 _____	161 _____	_____
27 _____	72 _____	117 _____	162 _____	_____
28 _____	73 _____	118 _____	163 _____	_____
29 _____	74 _____	119 _____	164 _____	_____
30 _____	75 _____	120 _____	165 _____	_____
31 _____	76 _____	121 _____	166 _____	_____
32 _____	77 _____	122 _____	167 _____	_____
33 _____	78 _____	123 _____	168 _____	_____
34 _____	79 _____	124 _____	169 _____	_____
35 _____	80 _____	125 _____	170 _____	_____
36 _____	81 _____	126 _____	171 _____	_____
37 _____	82 _____	127 _____	172 _____	_____
38 _____	83 _____	128 _____	173 _____	_____
39 _____	84 _____	129 _____	174 _____	_____
40 _____	85 _____	130 _____	175 _____	_____
41 _____	86 _____	131 _____	176 _____	_____
42 _____	87 _____	132 _____	177 _____	_____
43 _____	88 _____	133 _____	178 _____	_____
44 _____	89 _____	134 _____	179 _____	_____
45 _____	90 _____	135 _____	180 _____	_____

20. I can do well at thinking up new ways to use something such as a shoebox or scrap of leather or pieces of metal.
21. If I study a complex system of beliefs, such as in a religion, I'm good at seeing whether each belief is consistent with the others.
22. I'm good at determining which player is most valuable to a team or which worker to an organization.
23. In a complex and unusual moral situation in which the moral rules I ordinarily follow don't enable me to see the right thing to do I can do well at judging it on my own (e.g., whether to tell a "white lie").
24. I can do well at determining how such things as a room or yard can be made more attractive.
25. In an emergency situation while riding a bicycle or driving a car I'm good at seeing the right thing to do with the vehicle.
26. I have a good sense of my strengths and weaknesses.
27. I can do well at memorizing words in a new language.
28. I can learn new dance steps quickly.
29. Give me the name of an author (actor, composer) who I've read (seen, heard) and I'll remember the names of a number of his books (movies, compositions).
30. I like to understand the way movements evolve or ideas develop or life moves through stages.
31. I have a good memory for theories, principles, arguments.
32. I like to think about things in very concrete and specific terms, focusing on individual persons, groups, objects and the like.
33. I'm good at memorizing poems and speeches.
34. When I see things I'm interested in, such as cars or flowers or birds, I'm good at remembering their names.
35. I'm good at applying what I learn in school to my life.
36. I'm good at taking responsibility for getting things done.
37. The way other people see me plays an important part in much that I do.
38. I feel good about myself as a student.
39. I can maintain concentration for quite a while.
40. Even when I'm upset about something I can generally put it to one side when I need to study.
41. I'm good at budgeting my time to get things done.
42. I find working alone an effective way to study.
43. I'm good at blending my talents in with other members of a team.
44. I can learn well from lectures.
45. I find a friend can often be helpful with a problem.
46. I can make good use of lecture notes.
47. I'm good at giving written instructions on how to do something.
48. I'm good at following an oral debate.
49. I can express myself well in talking with a friend.
50. I can work well with diagrams.
51. I rely a lot in communication on eye contact, seeing the other person's face, gestures, posture.

52. I find it natural to use auditory expressions such as "That *sounds* right," "I *hear* what you're saying," "I want you to *listen* carefully to what I'm going to say."
53. Apart from being pleasant or needed, I find touching is an important way of communicating.
54. I can easily imagine what it would be like to be all sorts of other people.
55. I can sense another's feelings by his or her body language.
56. I usually know the degree of informality that is appropriate in my face to face or group interactions.
57. In things that matter I often have an influence on others.
58. I have the skills to act a part successfully.
59. I can do well at making and applying rules, for example, rules governing my own behavior (e.g. moral rules), rules to facilitate interaction in groups and organizations.
60. In learning something I especially like to have examples.
61. When planning an expensive purchase of such things as a house, car, set of golf clubs, or set of china, I can do well at shopping around and comparing what's available.
62. I'm good at seeing the play of a team or workings of a group in terms of the actions of each individual member.
63. I can do well at combining the best parts of two different points of view.
64. I'm good at using my past experience to anticipate the future such as knowing the best place to buy certain articles or the best person to ask about something or the best person to accomplish a certain task.
65. I'm good at brainstorming for new ideas.
66. I can do well at following a closely reasoned debate.
67. In making an important purchase or vocational decision I can do well in determining what criteria I need to use and then using them.
68. I can do well at determining the sorts of situations to which a given moral rule applies and the sorts to which it does not apply.
69. I can really appreciate at least some kinds of good music or art.
70. I can do well at such things as operating complicated equipment.
71. I can do well at setting my goals in terms of my needs, wants, and abilities.
72. I'm good at memorizing a speech.
73. I can easily learn things like riding a bicycle or skiing.
74. It's easy for me to memorize the pros and cons of an argument.
75. I'm interested in the processes by which things are made.
76. I like to work with ideas.
77. In reading a novel, whether or not I pay attention to the symbols or ideas expressed, I do usually have considerable interest in the characters involved.
78. I'm good at remembering telephone numbers and addresses.
79. I can do well at true-false, or matching, or multiple choice tests.
80. I'm good at things like changing my buying behavior when I learn things about products.

81. I do a lot of things simply because of what they mean to me.
82. It's often helpful to me in getting my work done to have a little prodding or encouragement from others.
83. Learning is usually a good experience for me.
84. I can get a lot done when I have to.
85. I can generally ignore noise when I'm studying.
86. I generally keep appointments on time.
87. I have the skills to learn on my own.
88. I often learn well from group discussion.
89. I feel ok about working with someone who is an authority.
90. I'm good at giving a friend constructive suggestions and in making use of his or her suggestions in turn.
91. I'm good at following written instructions.
92. I can get my ideas down on paper pretty clearly.
93. I'm good at really listening to what another is saying.
94. Talking about my thoughts is often helpful to me.
95. I find it helpful to put information on a chart where I can get the whole picture at once.
96. Visual experiences of things like scenery, floral arrangements, paintings, or sunsets can be really vivid for me.
97. I often find it helpful to carry on an inner conversation or, in trying to remember something, to think about the way it was said.
98. I find it natural to use kinesthetic expressions such as "That really *moved* me," "I can't get a *handle* on it," "What you say *feels* right to me."
99. People often find it easy to talk to me about their problems.
100. I'm good at communicating without words.
101. I'm good at judging how familiar I can be with someone.
102. People usually give serious consideration to what I have to say.
103. I can either hide or reveal my feelings quite effectively.
104. When working on a difficult subject I often feel a special need for clear cut definitions.
105. I can do well at thinking of a lot of things to say on an essay test.
106. I can do well at comparing the relative strengths and weaknesses of teams, political candidates, performers, teachers, and the like.
107. I'm good at determining how things are put together.
108. After hearing the ideas of a number of people in a reasonably harmonious group I can do well at creating a plan which at least most of them will find acceptable in light of their point of view.
109. When I'm not sure why something is going wrong I can do well at thinking up plausible explanations.
110. I can do well at coming up with alternative plans, methods, solutions to a problem.
111. I'm good at drawing consequences from an hypothesis, reasoning in an "if . . . then . . ." form.
112. I'm good at arranging things in their order of importance.
113. I am able to determine right and wrong based on my own understanding rather than simply on rules I've been taught.

114. I can really enjoy things like sunsets, waterfalls, snowfalls.
115. In rapid group interactions, such as in team sports or games at a party, I can do well at quickly sizing up what move to make.
116. I have a good sense of what my basic values and beliefs are.
117. I can do well at memorizing instructions on how to get someplace.
118. I easily pick up things like roller skating or walking on stilts.
119. It helps me to remember someone's ideas or beliefs by comparing or contrasting them with the ideas or beliefs of others.
120. I'm good at following the instructions for building or assembling something.
121. I like to get at the basic principles underlying a point of view.
122. In reading history, one of the things I'm most likely to give attention to is the role played by individual persons or groups.
123. I'm good at remembering the cards played in a game or exactly what was said in a conversation.
124. When I hear a familiar musical score or quotation I'm good at remembering the name of the composer or author.
125. I'm good at changing the way I see people who are very different than I am as I get more information about them.
126. I don't need much prodding or support from other people to get my work done.
127. If it wasn't for the grade involved I would be less concerned with doing well in school.
128. I generally feel ok about the results when I really make an effort in my school work.
129. I can take in a lot of the detail of something when I want to.
130. I'm not easily distracted when I study.
131. I'm good at judging how long it's going to take me to run some errands or do some chores.
132. I'm good at setting my own goals and making my own decisions.
133. I usually have a good sense of what's happening in a group I'm part of.
134. I feel it often saves time to learn from someone who is an authority.
135. I'm good at helping friends with problems.
136. I'm good at reading between the lines of a letter.
137. Putting my thoughts down on paper is often helpful to me.
138. I'm good at following instructions given orally.
139. I'm good at expressing myself in a group discussion.
140. I can learn well by means of graphs.
141. I find it helpful to picture things in my mind.
142. Listening to things like music, a voice, the ocean, wind in the trees or familiar footsteps can be a vivid experience for me.
143. The feeling of wind in my face, sun on my skin, of running across a field, of the texture of clothing can be a vivid experience for me.
144. I can usually sense what the other is feeling.
145. I can sense how well I'm communicating with someone by his or her body language.
146. I have a good sense of how close I can sit to another.

147. I have the skills to make an effective salesperson.
148. I can convey just about any emotion I wish to in a given situation.
149. It's easy for me to decide what category I think something belongs in (e.g., whether an action is right or wrong, a sweater is attractive or unattractive, a plan is good or bad).
150. I tend to see the complexities of things like issues, motivations, vocational decisions.
151. In considering alternative possibilities for a job, or a vacation, or a schedule of courses I can do well at determining the relative pluses and minuses of each.
152. I'm good at breaking an argument down into its component parts or an overall point of view down into its component beliefs.
153. If I were involved in politics I would be good at creating a platform around which a number of different interest groups could unite.
154. When I'm part way through a well written novel or play or movie I can usually form at least a vague sense of some of the additional things that might happen in it.
155. I can usually think of alternative reasons why someone has done something or why a project failed.
156. I can do well at constructing a logical proof such as proving a theorum in geometry or demonstrating why the butler must be the guilty one.
157. I can do well in determining which of several courses of action is most likely to succeed.
158. I have a good sense of the general ideas that underly Western morality.
159. I can do well at determining which clothes or pieces of furniture or types of buildings go well together.
160. I can usually do well at sizing up a situation when I first walk into a room.
161. I can usually judge how well I'll be able to do something.
162. I'm good at memorizing telephone numbers.
163. I can make rapid progress in learning a sport.
164. Once I understand the basic ideas of a theory it's easy for me to retain other information connected with it.
165. I have a good memory for complicated procedures in cooking or knitting or assembling things.
166. I can work well with abstractions such as designs, plans, or basic mathematical ideas.
167. I like to deal with my world in concrete ways, knowing important differences between cars, knowing about the leading actors, musicians or athletes, knowing how to care for my house, garden or equipment.
168. I'm good at remembering melodies or the names of movies I've seen.
169. When I see well-known persons I'm interested in, such as actors or sports figures or political leaders, I'm good at remembering their names.
170. I'm good at changing the way I look at a social problem as I learn more about it.
171. Being my own person is important to me.
172. I often do things for the sake of approval or recognition by others.

173. I feel I have good learning skills.
174. I can really get absorbed in things I'm doing.
175. My mind doesn't wander very often when I'm working on something.
176. I generally have a good sense of just how well I'm keeping up with my studies or other long term projects.
177. I'm able to discipline myself to work effectively alone.
178. I find working in a group a good way to learn.
179. I'm good at taking instruction from a coach.
180. I find it's often helpful to study with a peer.

To score your Learning Skills Profile below, add your scores by rows (e.g., *1, 46, 91* and *136* are row 1; *2, 47, 92* and *137* are row 2) and enter these totals on the score sheets which follow. A score of 4 is the lowest rating you could give yourself, *20* the highest. A score of *12* means that you see yourself as being only fair at that skill.

ROW	TOTAL		LEARNING SKILL
		I.	*Symbolizing*
1	_____		Reading
2	_____		Writing
3	_____		Listening
4	_____		Talking
5	_____		Graphics
6	_____		Visual
7	_____		Auditory
8	_____		Kinesthetic
9	_____		Empathy
10	_____		Kinesic
11	_____		Proxemic
12	_____		Transactional
13	_____		Histrionic
		II.	*Thinking*
14	_____		Structure
15	_____		Relation
16	_____		Comparison
17	_____		Analysis
18	_____		Synthesis
19	_____		Convergence
20	_____		Divergence

| 21 | _____ | | Deduction |

III.   *Judging*

22	_____		Evaluation
23	_____		Ethic
24	_____		Esthetic
25	_____		Sense Integration
26	_____		Self-Knowledge

IV.   *Remembering*

27	_____		Rote Memory
28	_____		Somatic Memory
29	_____		Association

30	_____		Processes
31	_____		Concepts
32	_____		Entities

33	_____		Recall
34	_____		Recognition
35	_____		Utilization

V.   *General Learning Skills*

36	_____		Internal Motivation
37	_____		External Motivation
38	_____		Positive Self-Concept
39	_____		Attention
40	_____		Repression
41	_____		Time Use

VI.   *Preferred Learning Situations*

42	_____		Independent
43	_____		Group
44	_____		Subordinate
45	_____		Peer

CHAPTER TEN

The Journal as a Tool in Experiential Learning

In discussing the dimensions of learning involved in experiential learning, we have emphasized that learning is change. We have also stressed that change in our behavior is inseparable from change in our understanding of the situation within which that behavior takes place. As we see the meaning of a situation differently, we open up a need for new forms of behavior. Conversely, as we come to behave differently, we experience our situation differently.

Whatever situation we choose, then, for our experiential learning, this learning will involve us as persons. Some learning situations will be less personal than others, but in every case learning will be changing both our behavior and our way of seeing that situation. This means that our method of learning must help us become clear about and explore alternatives to the meaning our learning situation has for us. One such method we have considered is the creation of what Culbert refers to as "support groups." Keeping a journal can be another effective way of doing this. These two taken together might be especially productive.

Whether the journal becomes an effective tool will depend especially on our attitude toward the situation in question. Even though we are part of each of our situations and each is a part of us, there is a tendency in our culture to treat certain situations as though this were not true. We try to see parts of our world as simply "out there," largely removed from our lives as persons. Out there, we say, are some realities that exist quite externally to who we are; we can deal with them without really involving ourselves. But everything in our world has a meaning for us, and it has this meaning because of the place it has in our lives. Some of these meanings are shared by a large group of people, but they will vary somewhat from member to member. The meaning that something has for us is the way we see its relation to us.

We may, for example, try to separate ourselves from our job. We withhold commitment and interest; our work is largely a means to something quite removed from it, namely, our financial needs. In the process, we ourselves, become a means to an end. One part of our life becomes a means to another part. We fail to integrate our working life into our life as a whole. Our work situation has meaning only as something alien to us.

If we experience our learning situation as largely unrelated to who we are as persons, we sharply limit what we can learn in it. We are largely out of touch with what we really experience in that area; we find there only a reflection of the beliefs we bring to it. We see in it only what we expect to see; very often what we expect to see is what we think we are supposed to see. We look at the present pretty much as we have looked at the past. Learning is change, and the less involved we are, the less change is possible.

For those who wish to be relatively detached from their learning situation, only a version of journal-keeping which focuses on external events will be appropriate. Others will want to extend the journal method to include the interior (or nonalienated) meanings of their situation and even the place of that situation in their life as a whole. In what follows, we shall discuss these three uses of the journal.

Since we are all involved in various organizations—family, school, church, business, government, and so on—let us begin by considering the following account by Culbert.

> Often in our organization life we think that we're on top of things while actually we have little idea of what's happening to us or what we're doing to others. We fail to see where our practice is less than ideal, and where our actual working conditions are different from what we've been led to expect. If we could identify such discrepancies, we'd have the beginnings of the perspective we need to put our relationship with the system on a more realistic basis. Let me illustrate with an example.
>
> *Example*
>
> In the academic system at UCLA, where I work, people are constantly being caught in the discrepancy between their belief that the publish-or-perish meat grinder has been done away with and the reality of what is actually going on. Some time ago, our administration formally acknowledged that a variety of professorial duties went into building a quality university and

that different people might have different types of excellence to contribute; that is, that some might be outstanding teachers and administrators who do not necessarily excel at research, while others might be excellent researchers who do not necessarily make outstanding teachers or administrators. The administration further acknowledged that people go through different phases during which teaching, administration, or research may be more central to their careers.

In this way, university administrators hoped to convince the students that the quality of teaching was evaluated and rewarded, and the professors that committee work and other administrative assignments counted. This was necessary because if the students stopped believing that teaching mattered, or if the faculty realized that teaching and administration had only a marginal influence on their promotions, the system might temporarily break down. But only temporarily, because if such a discrepancy arose, the students would demand some way of insuring teaching excellence, and the faculty would refuse to spend extra hours doing quality committee work until they were duly rewarded. But had the publish-or-perish ethic really changed?

Recently, a colleague named Tom was denied tenure because his research wasn't up to par. Usually, refusal of tenure is tantamount to being fired. But, in this instance, Tom had an outstanding record of teaching and committee service, and firing him would have created an obvious discrepancy between the administration's professed and actual criteria in making promotion decisions. It would have led the students to realize that their participation in course evaluations didn't really count and the faculty to realize that the long hours they spend pitching in on administrative work wasn't going to do much for their careers. At another level, Tom's dismissal would have caused university administrators to feel guilty as they came to realize that in the process of trying to make their ideal system work, they had misled Tom.

University administrators are like the rest of us, consciously we want to be equal to our ideals, but unconsciously we want it both ways if we can get it. In order to maintain the illusion that other activities besides research truly mattered, while at the same time keeping other professors focused on doing research, an illusionary mechanism needed to be found. They found one. The administration decided to release Tom from all duties other than research and to consider him for promotion again the following year.

On the surface, it seemed as if Tom was getting the opportunity he needed to prove himself. The administrators, the students, the faculty, even Tom himself, were all delighted that Tom was getting this chance. However, at the unconscious level, this decision helped the members of the system to avoid seeing what kind of productivity truly counts.

Thus, the administration's solution was subversive, no matter from whose perspective it is viewed. For Tom, it was subversive because it had the effect of systematically stripping him of all those tasks in which he had succeeded, locking him up in his office to come eyeball to eyeball wth his failures. Tom's research area is close to my own, and it requires time in the field to see what's going on before sitting down and writing theoretically. But the pressure was on him to write.

Firing Tom, on the other hand, would have allowed him to leave feeling good about his teaching and administrative skills, although perhaps bitter about being misled by the system. But if he were to fail to get promoted the following year, he'd be likely to leave without feeling good about his areas of established excellence.

The action was also subversive for the faculty because they could see that Tom's dedication was being rewarded with extra privileges and could thus continue to believe that teaching and committee work really counted. It was subversive for the students because they could continue to believe that their anonymous end-of-term evaluations of faculty mattered. Finally, the action had a subversive effect on the administrators because the year's delay in their probable firing of Tom gave them a way to avoid facing up to how their system actually operated. They would probably feel okay about firing him the next year when they could think, "We gave him every chance, and there's no reason for us to feel guilty."

Feelings of Incoherence and Discrepancies

We are seldom out of control for a long time without experiencing internal signals, however vague, that something is off. I call these signals feelings of incoherence. Basically, there are two kinds of conflicts, or discrepancies, that produce such feelings of incoherence. The first is produced when the system expects something unnatural to us or inconsistent with our best interests. For Tom, these feelings would be produced if he were to accept the system's assumption that the only factor stopping him from publishing enough research to be promoted was insufficient time to write. The second type of discrepancy is produced when we do what seems to come naturally only to discover afterward that what we did was disapproved of, inappropriate, or wrong. For Tom, such feelings might come were he to undervalue his accomplishments in teaching and school service because they weren't sufficient to get him promoted.

By and large, feelings of incoherence tend to be ignored. This is not because they are so very uncomfortable. They're not. But acknowledging their presence sends us on a search for discrepancies in our relationship with the system. Facing up to such discrepancies is unpleasant, even painful, because we're conditioned to think, "If something is off, it's off with me, not the system." This is our continuing problem with self-acceptance. If we were capable of more self-regard and were less dependent on personal regard from others, we wouldn't resist facing up to discrepancies nearly as much as we do.[1]

As we talk about using a journal, one of the things we can keep in mind is how it can help us learn from such "feelings of incoherence" when they occur. As we shall see, the last section of the journal we discuss, titled the "Period Image", can be especially useful in doing this.

Perhaps the best way to understand and make effective use of a journal is to think of it in terms of the idea that, as one philosopher-psychologist has put it, "To be a person is to have a story to tell."[2] Each of our lives moves in its own unique direction. The many events that make them up, sometimes dramatic, more often routine, are woven together in a complex pattern. The meaning of each event is its place in this pattern.

Much of this process of giving shape and significance to our myriad transactions with ourselves and with our world is carried forward at subterranean levels. But the ways in which we respond to this process consciously may damage or enhance it. We may deny expression to important motifs, block the growth of vital powers, sing with only a few notes of the scale. Or we may consciously support our impulses to fuller life, increasing the intensity and depth of our life movement.

We become aware of bits and snatches of this movement in a number of ways. To some extent, we sense some meaning in each event as we live it. Much of the time, our response is so routine that the event adds little or nothing to our sense of our lives. Some events, though, carry a feeling of special meaning. Later we reflect on them in moments of aloneness, talk about them with friends, write about them in poems or letters, dream of them. Keeping a journal is another way in which we may grasp a fuller meaning in these events and in the situations in which we undergo them.

Writing a journal does a number of things to facilitate this learning. First, it provides a regular occasion for making these explorations. Second, it represents events and situations in a new form. Each form of expression, such as memory, conversation, or dream, opens up new possibilities of awareness. We experience the meaning of an event or a concern differently depending on whether we talk about it, describe it in writing, or read aloud what we have written. Third, it brings many events together in one place, helping us to see their interrelations. In other words, it helps us grasp a larger pattern or meaning in what is happening. Fourth, it provides a means for getting in touch with the deeper meaning that these events have for us at our subconscious level. Finally, it enables us to return to our activities with a fuller awareness of the questions, values and alternative possibilities which they involve.

The use of the journal to help us see a pattern in our experience is such a basic part of its potential as a means of learning from our experience that it may be helpful to discuss more fully the relation between pattern and meaning. We have said that the meaning of any event for us is the place we give it in the complex pattern we discern, at some level of consciousness, in all the things we experience. Consider the different meanings an exam in biology may have for those involved. One student is planning to go to medical school and doing well on the exam is important to that goal. Another is planning to work in the family business after graduation and is only concerned to pass the exam as a step toward getting his degree. A third orients much of her life around a deeply felt need to excel, to demonstrate her worth as a person. A fourth sees his life as a series of failures, especially in school, and believes that others tend to see him as incompetent. Yet another has always loved the world of nature and is delighted with the insights she is finding in her course work. The instructor is under a number of heavy demands on his time and reading the exam is going to add to the strain. He also sees the exam as a way of giving students the rewards or punishments they deserve according to the effort they are making. These brief descriptions, of course, only suggest the complex orientations that give the exam such varied meanings. But they are at least suggestive of how the meaning of the exam is related not only to the past but also to the anticipated future experiences of each person involved.

In the short story we have read by Dorothy Canfield we have another example of the way in which the meaning of one experience depends on the way we relate it to other experiences. When Aunt Minnie lost her way in the cornfield at sixteen she "could hear Cousin Ella saying, 'There are plenty of men in this town that wouldn't like anything better than . . .'" and could see the way she looked when she said it. Later, the meaning of this experience changes for her as she relates it to some of her experiences with her son, Jake.

The more meaningfully interrelated our experiences are the richer and more valuable they are. This interrelatedness gives them that quality we refer to by the term *esthetic*. One of the ways we judge a work of art, for example, is how organically related each of its parts is to each other part. If a dollar bill were pasted on Van Gogh's painting, "Starry Night," it would be easy to see it did not belong there. We quickly lose interest in a story that is filled with digressions and incidental occurrences that have little bearing on the basic theme. Conversations in which neither is really listening to or responding to what the other is saying are dull and pointless. We might call them *an*esthetic. Just as an anesthetic deadens, so esthetic quality enlivens and gives vitality. It is natural for us, then, to give esthetic form to our activities. By becoming conscious of the pattern we are giving to our lives, we can further our success in this shaping and live more fully and vividly the meaning which this pattern gives to our experience. Keeping a journal can be of considerable help in getting more in touch with and strengthening or altering the pattern in what we do.

Those who wish to work intensively with their experiential learning will do well to take a look at Ira Progoff's book, *At a Journal Workshop*.[3] Drawing on long experience and with much originality, Progoff has gone far beyond anyone I know of in developing the journal as a tool for learning, for integrating the elements of one's life and for intensifying one's overall growth process. Chapters I and V will give a pretty good picture of what he has to offer. His method requires a considerable investment of time. But it can have a profound effect on the quality of our learning experience, and it may pay to spend less time in an active involvement and more time in drawing from it its full meaning. In what follows, we shall consider less demanding uses of the journal, uses suggested in part by Progoff's work.

T. S. Eliot has suggested that experience is like a partially developed role of film. As we later reflect on it, and especially as we look back from a new perspective, we may develop it further, bringing out more of its meaning. "I know now," we heard Aunt Minnie say, "that I had been, all along, kind of interested in him. . . ." Journal keeping is a means of grasping more fully what it is we experience.

THE LEARNING SITUATION LOG

The meaning an event has for us will depend on the context in which we experience it. Begin your journal, then, by creating a log in which you describe the situation you have selected for your project in experiential learning. To grasp this situation as creatively as possible, it will help if you come at it in the frame of mind you have when you are looking for new ideas, alternative possibilities, new ways of looking at things. This seems to mean, for everyone, moving away from a serious, critical orientation to a relaxed, even playful, one. When we evaluate, we impose on our experience our old way of looking at things. The more you can move away from evaluating and simply get in touch with what you have experienced, the more your experience will affect you and, so, the more you will learn. If you choose to stay somewhat detached from your learning situation, you close yourself off from some of the more significant levels of experience in this area and must simply accept this as a limitation to what you can learn.

The situation on which you are focusing may be new to you or it may already have a history in your life, perhaps a long one. In any case, begin by focusing on that situation as it is for you in the present, for this will be the immediate context in which you will undergo your learning experiences and in relation to which they will take on their meaning.

The present may be a short period or a long one. It may have begun a few days ago or a few years ago. If your learning situation is a vocational one, its present meaning for you may have begun with a promotion to new responsibilities, the emergence of a major problem, a growing sense of being in a dead end, or entrance into an educational program at the University. Begin your "Learning Situation Log" with a one or two sentence description of whatever marks the beginning of the present period.

Next, ask what events have been especially significant during this period. Largely, these will be events which evoked fairly strong feelings and emotions in you. They captured your attention to such an extent that you later spent time thinking about them, discussing them or returning to them in some other way. First, note them on scratch paper as they occur to you, and then record them in your Situation Log in chronological order. It doesn't matter whether they seem negative or positive, and it will be helpful if you can disregard any such evaluation. It may be useful to give each event a name, such as "New Idea," "Cash Flow Problem," or "Encounter With Boss." Follow each name with a one sentence description.

If you are working within an organization, it will also be important to pay attention to any events which evoked what Culbert described as "feelings of incoherence . . . internal signals, however vague, that something is off." These are likely to occur "when the system expects something unnatural to us or inconsistent with our best interests" or "when we do what seems to come naturally only to discover afterward that what we did was disapproved of, inappropriate, or wrong." For the present, simply record these events from which such vague feelings of incoherence arose, without any attempt to evaluate them.

The importance of not evaluating may be seen in Culbert's emphasis on our tendency to be self-critical. Insofar as we share this tendency, we will interpret discrepancies in our transactions with the organization in the way we've been conditioned to think: "If something is off, it's off with me, not the system."[3] Or we may fall into the trap that Culbert maintains is generally true of minority groups: "Too often consciousness-raising results in their blaming the system for all their conflicts. Many cannot get beyond their anger to a point where they can take constructive action."[4] In either case, we impose a past judgment on our experience. In the method of journal keeping we are discussing the aim is, rather, to look afresh at our experience so we may learn from it.

Keep the descriptions short and limit the number of events you describe so that you can see them as a set and get a sense of the pattern they form.[5] Now read them over, thinking about their interrelations and making a brief note of anything that occurs to you, but attending simply to what is rather than to judgments about its value or disvalue. Especially helpful will be any way that comes to you of characterizing the situation as a whole. This may come to you as a thought or a feeling or an image. You may sense its overall meaning as "dead end," "being used," "stepping stone," "personal growth," "performing a worthwhile service," "good compensation," "exciting challenge," "sacrifice of family time." Images can be an important way in which the message underlying a feeling of incoherence can make itself clearer to us. Ignore any thought about whether the meaning which comes through is good or bad. Simply record the situation's meaning for you. The meaning will come through to you much more fully if you do not judge it by thinking, "it's not good that it's like that," "I'm fortunate it's working out so well," and similar things.

In thinking about the interrelations between the events you have recorded, it is important to maintain an open, receptive attitude, simply recording anything that presents itself. If you start to press hard to uncover such interrelations you are in danger of imposing your expectations on the events rather than letting them speak for themselves. The meaningful patterns in our experience may be either so complex or so unfamiliar that for a time we can only sense them. Or we may only pick them up subconsciously. It is over a period of time, as we relate each section of our journal to the others and as our record of significant events grows, that we gradually become more conscious of the way we are connecting things.

DIRECTIONS AND STEPS

Using the journal to reflect on your experience can help you not only to see the meaning of your situation more clearly but also to prepare yourself to benefit more from your future experience. Your journal, then, will look both backward and forward. Every event in which we are involved both reflects the past which led up to it and points to possibilities for the future which develop from it. Its meaning for you is its relation both to your past and to your future. The "Directions and Steps" section has the aim of sharpening and enlarging your sense of the potentialities for the future that are embedded in your learning situation. You open up new possibilities for learning when you bring to your situation a definite sense of changes to which you are committed and actively seek opportunities to bring those changes about.

Our minds subconsciously continue to work on material to which we have given a period of conscious attention and effort. It may be helpful, then, to put your "Learning Situation Log" aside for a day or two. When you return to it, let yourself once again enter into a relaxed state so that you will be receptive to anything that may come to mind. Read through the Log and add a description of any events or of thoughts about connections between events or of thoughts about the overall meaning of the situation that may present themselves.

Now let yourself move ahead through the next few weeks of involvement in your learning situation. Make some brief notes in your journal of the experiences and outcomes you anticipate as likely. Now ask what possibilities these next few weeks hold which are other than what you expect. Just jot them down on some scratch paper as they come to mind without judging whether they are desirable or realistic or important to you. New ways of seeing a situation usually have their beginning for us in our subconscious mind and, when they have gained enough strength, we may become aware of them by getting in touch with that situation in a relaxed, nonjudgmental way. If you wish, you may be able to add to your list of possibilities by thinking of two or three people who have made a special impression on you and imagine a conversation with each of them in which you discuss the situation with them. You may sense them suggesting something you hadn't thought of or raising a question that leads you to something new.

Even if, for the time being, no new possibilities come to mind, you will have given this question added force in your mind, and this may lead to new perceptions in the future. If some new potentialities have presented themselves, let yourself try them on. Imagine yourself acting on them. How do you feel about them? What sort of change in you would each involve? Is it mainly a change in behavior or do you also begin to think and feel somewhat differently? Enter a brief description in your journal of your response to each possibility.

For those which now seem worth investing in, if any, ask what step you could take to begin achieving those changes. Imagine yourself taking that step: What happens? Do you see anything else you might do? Make a note in your journal of whatever comes to mind here.

THE PROCESS LOG

The first two sections of your journal have had the aim of drawing out more fully the meaning your learning situation has for you, and especially your sense of its future possibilities; for it is this context which will give your learning experiences their immediate meaning.[6] As events of special importance occur, then, go back over these sections with these events in mind. Even when you learn nothing from this consciously, it will add to the perspective from which you work with things subconsciously.

In the "Process Log" section of your journal, you focus on events that unfold as you participate in your learning situation. As soon as possible after each day's involvement in that situation, take a few minutes to get into a receptive frame of mind, and then on the left side of the page in your journal write down a name for and brief description of those events which evoked the strongest feelings in you, events that you are most likely to return to as you reflect on or talk about the day. Next ask whether you experienced any of the "feelings of incoherence" that Culbert refers to, feelings that may occur in connection with the expectations that an organization has of you. Often such expectations are expressed in an assignment that you are given or in negative reactions that you experience after handling something in a way you felt quite good about. If any of these vague feelings of uneasiness come to mind, simply write down a name for and brief description of the event or events from which these feelings arose. Try to keep the number of events you select small enough so that you don't lose sight of the whole picture because of too much detail.

Now go back over each event and ask what its significance is for you. Record very briefly whatever comes to mind on the right side of the page opposite your earlier description of that event. Was some new behavior begun? Some old behavior modified? Did you come to see the situation in a way that is slightly, or perhaps even considerably, different? Was a new question raised, a new problem posed, a new opportunity presented?

You will now have before you the key pieces that make up your picture of your day as a whole in your learning situation. Let your mind wander across the page and get a feeling for or image of the whole. What thought or image captures what it means to you? What possibilities come to mind? Use the same process in working with these as you did with possibilities in the "Directions and Steps" section. Record your results.

Meanings will emerge more fully as you see connections between one day and another and between the materials in all three sections of your journal. As you have time, then, it will be helpful after working in your "Process Log" to go back over earlier entries and also to return to the "Directions and Steps" and "Learning Situation Log" sections. Record any new thoughts in the appropriate place. Your sense of your learning situation may have been changing, for example, and some further entries in the "Learning Situation Log" will bring it up to date. Or you may get new insight into the meaning of an event for you and wish to add that to the "Process Log."

In keeping your "Process Log" it may not always be possible to record events very soon after they happen. Progoff recommends a way of handling this that seems to be helpful for most people. Let your mind go back over the days which have not been recorded and write a short paragraph summarizing the overall significance of what has been happening. Then begin to make notes on some scratch paper of events of special significance that you recall. As you begin to note these events, they will probably remind you of still others and before long you will have noted several for each day. These may then be recorded chronologically in your journal, following the same process described above.

THE LIFE SITUATION LOG

The "Learning Situation Log," "Directions and Steps" and "Process Log" sections, taken together, form a unit. You may wish to limit your journal keeping to these three sections. The events of your learning situation, however, take their meaning not only from this situation but also from their place in your life situation as a whole. If you wish to relate them also to this wider context, you can add a "Life Situation Log" section to your journal. The procedure for this is the same as that for your "Learning Situation Log" except that you are dealing with the events of the present situation of your life as a whole.

This larger perspective may add a great deal to your learning possibilities, especially in the case of a work situation which has lost any significant challenge or become downright monotonous. While there may not seem to be much to learn in terms of the immediate goals of that learning situation itself, there is likely to be much you can learn in terms of your life as a whole. Does the disappointing situation have something to say to you about the best choice of a vocation for you? Do you have feelings of incoherence that suggest that you are trying to do something that runs against beliefs and values that are important to you? Does this experience have implications for other areas of your life? Is there something to be learned about how you cope with negative experience and about your orientation to the situation that causes you to miss some of its positive aspects? In his long experience as a therapist, Ira Progoff has found that more often than not our most significant growth processes take place subconsciously precisely at those times of boredom, frustration, depression, and the like when it seems to us on the surface that nothing worthwhile is happening at all. Getting in touch with the growth that we are working on subconsciously can turn the whole situation around for us into one with significant meaning and potential.

It is a commonplace to note that our subconscious plays a fundamental role in our creativity. We tap this creative source not only in our dreams but also in the images and symbols that occur to us while awake. Images express meanings in our lives far more fully than propositions do. In discussing the various sections of the journal we have included suggestions for being receptive to images that may occur in our minds at various points. But the focus in those sections was on the conscious activity of our minds in remembering and recording events or anticipating the future. If you wish to shift your focus to the subconscious dimensions of meaning you can add what Progoff calls the "Period Image" section of the journal. Among other things, this may be helpful in getting in touch with the message behind any feelings of incoherence. We tend to ignore these feelings at the conscious level, but the "discrepancies in our relationship with the system"[7] that they signal continue to involve us subconsciously. If we become more receptive to these feelings and to related images, the message behind them can come through more clearly. In preparing to work in this section of the journal it may be especially helpful to read Chapter 6 of Progoff's *At a Journal Workshop*. The main procedure, however, can be given in a few excerpts.

In the "Period Image" section we receive and record "Twilight Imaging" which "takes place in the twilight state between working and sleeping."[8] Concerning these images Progoff emphasizes that

we do not consciously or deliberately put these perceptions there. We ourselves do not determine what they shall be.

> Rather, being in a quiet and passive position, we *behold* them.
> We turn our attention inward and we wait in stillness, and let
> ourselves observe. . . . We observe them as though they were
> dreams. We follow the direction of their movement without
> directing or altering their contents.[9]

In preparation for this we go back over the "Period Log." We then
sit quietly with our eyes closed and give our attention to this period.

> We are not thinking of it but letting it present itself to us in the
> form of images, impressions, emotions, and especially through
> symbolic awarenesses that come to us in many sensory forms.
> We may see them, hear them, smell them, intuit them. . . . It
> may come at first as stirrings in our body, as joyous surges or
> as stomach knots.[9]

As they come, in whatever form, we record them in the journal.

When this has been completed there is another, important step to
take, namely, to consider the "Period Log" and "Period Image" side
by side. The "Period Image" may confirm or contradict or comple-
ment the "Period Log."

> It may be, for example, that while we have been living through
> a period when our projects and relationships have been going
> well, we have a visual image in which we see a glass fall off
> the table. . . . [Or] a nonvisual image may come to us that is
> nothing more definite than a vague feeling of uneasiness or dif-
> ficulties or dangers lying ahead.[11]

When there are conflicts between these two accounts there is no
need to analyze them or choose between them. We are simply
perceiving

> the wholeness of the situation of our lives. . . . We see that
> each moment contains its opposites inherently within itself.
> Growth and decay, conflict and harmony, all the opposites are
> part of the movement of time. . . . All circumstances will even-
> tually be transformed in their time and in accordance with their
> inner nature. The indications of that change in their next im-
> mediate stage . . . are often shown to us ahead of time on the
> symbolic level by means of twilight imagery.[12]

There is a passage by Rainer Maria Rilke which relates to this and
also to Progoff's belief that more often than not our most significant

growth processes take place subconsciously precisely at those times when it seems to us on the surface that nothing is happening at all.

Consider whether these great sadnesses have not rather gone right through the center of yourself? Whether much in you has not altered, whether you have not somewhere, at some point of your being, undergone a change while you were sad? Only those sadnesses are dangerous and bad which one carries about among people in order to drown them out; like sicknesses that are superfically and foolishly treated they simply withdraw and after a little pause break out again and more dreadfully; and accumulate within one and are life, are unlived, spurned, lost life of which one may die. Were it possible for us to see further than our knowledge reaches, and yet a little way beyond the outworks of our divining, perhaps we would endure our sadnesses with greater confidence than our joys. For they are the moments when something new has entered into us, something unknown; our feelings grow mute in shy perplexity, everything in us withdraws, a stillness comes, and the new, which no one knows, stands in the midst of it and is silent.

I believe that almost all our sadnesses are moments of tension that we find paralyzing because we no longer hear our surprised feelings living. Because we are alone with the alien thing that has entered into our self; because everything intimate and accustomed is for an instant taken away; because we stand in the middle of a transition where we cannot remain standing. For this reason the sadness too passes: the new thing in us, the added thing, has entered into our heart, has gone into its inmost chamber and is not even there anymore—is already in our blood. And we do not learn what it was. We could easily be made to believe that nothing has happened, and yet we have changed, as a house changes into which a guest has entered. We cannot say who has come, pehaps we shall never know, but many signs indicate that the future enters into us in this way in order to transform itself in us long before it happens. And this is why it is so important to be lonely and attentive when one is sad: because the apparently uneventful and stark moment at which our future sets foot in us is so much closer to life than that other noisy and fortuitous point of time at which it happens to us as if from outside. The more still, more patient and more open we are when we are sad, so much the deeper and so much the more unswervingly does the new go into us, so much the better do we make it ours, so much the more will it be our destiny, and when on some later day it "happens" (that is, steps forth out of us to others), we shall feel in our inmost selves akin and near to it. And that is necessary. It is necessary—and toward this our development will move gradually—that nothing strange should befall us, but only that which has long belonged to us. We have already had to rethink so many of our concepts of motion, we will also gradually learn to realize that that which we call destiny goes forth from within people, not from without into them. Only because so many have not absorbed their destinies and transmuted them within themselves while they were living in them, have they not recognized what has gone forth out of them; it was so strange to them that, in their bewildered fright, they thought it must only just then have entered into them, for they swear never before to have found anything like it in themselves. As people were long mistaken about the motion of the sun, so they are even yet mistaken about the motion of that which is to come.[13]

Whether you choose to do the longer or shorter versions of the journal we have described it will be helpful to look for relations between each section as you proceed. In this way your journal will work toward a unified expression of your learning experiences.

Notes

PREFACE

1. "Editor's Notes: The Boom in Experiential Learning," in Morris T. Keeton and Pamela J. Tate, eds., *Learning by Experience—What, Why and How* (San Francisco: Jossey-Bass Inc., 1978), p. 2.

2. "Experiential Learning Theory and Learning Experience in Liberal Arts Education," in Steven E. Brooks and James E. Althof, eds., *Enriching the Liberal Arts Through Experiential Learning* (San Francisco: Jossey-Bass Inc., 1979), pp. 79–80. The authors present data indicating that the "concrete-reflective" learning style distinctive of the typical liberal arts student majoring in one of the humanities is especially well-suited to experiential learning (pp. 84–90).

3. "Practical Experience and the Liberal Arts: A Philosophical Perspective," in Brooks and Althof, p. 12.

4. Ibid., p. 11.

5. "Toward a Modern Approach to Values: The Valuing Process in the Mature Person," in *The Journal of Abnormal and Social Psychology* (No. 68, 1964), p. 164.

6. Ibid., p. 162.

CHAPTER ONE: LEARNING AND THE STRUGGLE TO BE

1. *Reason and Emotion in Psychotherapy* (Secaucus, NJ: The Citadel Press, 1979), pp. 61, 63.

2. *Man's Search for Meaning* (NY: Simon & Schuster, 1970).

3. N.Y.: Norton, 1975.

4. *Helplessness* (San Francisco: W.H. Freeman, 1975).

5. *The Courage To Be* (New Haven: Yale University Press, 1952), p. 53.

6. *The Broken Connection* (New York: Simon & Schuster, A Touchstone Book, 1979).

7. "Toward a Modern Approach . . ." p. 165.

8. Ibid., p. 161.

9. Ibid., p. 165.

10. Ibid.

11. Ibid., p. 164.

12. See, for example, Carl Rogers, *On Becoming a Person* (Boston: Houghton Mifflin Co., 1961), pp. 50–57.

13. "Toward a Modern Approach . . ." p. 164.

14. *The Anatomy of Human Destructiveness* (Greenwich, Conn.: Fawcett Publications, Inc., 1973).

15. "Toward a Modern Approach . . .," p. 162.

16. Ibid.

17. *Reason and Emotion in Psychotherapy*, p. 60.

18. Sixty-eight percent of the wealth in the United States, for example, is owned by five percent of the population.

19. This need not imply a conscious conspiracy on the part of a power elite. Social systems of reward and punishment are easily rationalized and are shaped by a great many factors of which the economic seems generally to be the most powerful.

CHAPTER TWO: THE FOUR KINDS OF EXPERIENTIAL LEARNING

1. By Dorthy Canfield. Reprinted from *The Yale Review* (Copyright 1945 by Yale University Press), by permission of *The Yale Review* and the executors of the literary estate of the author.

2. We often understand a lot more than we are able to talk about clearly. But by reflecting on these things we may be able to improve our understanding and to act on them more effectively.

3. *Steps to an Ecology of Mind* (N.Y.: Ballantine Books, 1972), pp. 279–308.

4. From this point on, I shall use "response learning" in this restricted sense to mean operant conditioning.

5. *The One Quest* (New York: Viking Press, 1972), p. 221. (Italics are added.)

6. I use the term "reinterpretation" to emphasize that situation learning is a change in interpretation. In a new situation, though, the change is the addition of an interpretation to our total view of things, rather than a change in one.

7. Ibid., p. 302.

8. There are, of course, many ways in which we quite properly depend on one another and so have nothing to do with dependency in the sense of asking another to do for us what we should do for ourselves.

9. "How People Change," *Commentary* (May, 1969).

10. On the other hand, the sense that our structures of meaning are relative to the particular culture and age in which we live may be experienced as more threatening than liberating. Many respond with the feeling of nausea, the sense of vertigo, that Jean Paul Sartre portrays so vividly. And the more we are motivated by fear and anxiety, the more we cling rigidly to our categories, insisting that they are necessary and final. In every culture, certain interpretations of common situations are dominant ones and their modification often meets considerable resistance. It is when we are able to trust and to delight in

ourselves and our world and our ability to create the forms and orders by which we live, and out of this trust and delight to generate the courage to face the dark side of things, that we may gain from the relativity of our values and meanings a sense of liberation.

11. In Chapter 10 we shall examine some of the skills basic to each type of learning and how these skills may be developed.

12. See *Childhood and Society* (New York: Norton Press, 1950); *Identity and the Life Cycle* (Psychological Issues, Vol. I, No. 1; N.Y.: International Universities Press, 1959); *Identity: Youth & Crisis* (N.Y.: Norton Press, 1968).

13. *Identity and the Life Cycle*, p. 52.

14. Ibid., p. 89.

15. Ibid, p. 97.

16. Ibid, p. 98.

17. A helpful introduction may also be found in *Born to Win* by Muriel James and Dorothy Jongeward (Reading, Mass.: Addison-Wesley, 1971).

18. We shall explore these questions more fully in Chapter 9.

19. *Existence and the World of Freedom* (Englewood Cliffs, New Jersey: Prentice-Hall, 1963).

CHAPTER THREE: MAPPING EXPERIENCE

1. Since "picture," "image," and "map" are visual terms, they will be meaningful to you only insofar as you deal with your world in terms of what you see. If you are oriented primarily in terms of what you feel or what you hear, you may find it helpful to translate this sentence into "We bring these beliefs together in a way that gives us an overall sense or feeling for the situation" or "that sounds right to us about the situation."

2. In *The Uses of Argument* (Cambridge: The University Press, 1958), Stephen Toulmin uses a somewhat similar diagram to analyze the structure of argument. See pp. 97–125.

3. Similarly we may be looking for information about the past which will explain some other part of the past. What, if it had happened, we may then ask, would have led us to anticipate the past event we are seeking to explain?

4. *Cognitive Therapy and the Emotional Disorders* (N.Y.: International Universities Press, Inc., 1976), pp. 246ff.

5. Ibid., pp. 247–48.

6. Qualitative as well as quantitative considerations are involved here.

7. Beck lists nine such rules on pp. 255–56. A related set of rules is presented by Albert Ellis in Chapter 3 of his *Reason and Emotion in Psychotherapy*.

8. Pragmatic adequacy also applies to our beliefs, however, as does correspondence to our evaluations. We ask, for example, whether we actually experience the happiness we anticipate on the basis of our evaluations and our rules for acting on them.

9. Yet rules may be related to beliefs. A rule emphasizing the value of being liked and admired by everyone on all occasions implies the beliefs that this is possible and that it is essential to being happy or to having a sense of worth.

10. *The Structure of Magic* (Vol. II; Palo Alto, CA: Science and Behavior Books, 1976) pp. 3–25.

11. Ibid., pp. 16–18.
12. Ibid., p. 17.
13. Ibid., p. 15.

CHAPTER FOUR: RESISTANCE TO LEARNING

1. *The Organization Trap* (New York: Basic Books, 1974), p. 73.
2. I am specially indebted to a discussion of this by Richard Bandler and John Grinder, although I differ from them a bit in language and conception. See *The Structure of Magic*, Vol. 1, especially, Chapters 3 and 4.
3. Cited by Richard Bandler and John Grinder, *The Structure of Magic*, Vol. I.
4. Ibid., p. 15.
5. Ibid., p. 16.
6. Muriel James and Dorothy Jongeward, *Born To Win* (Reading, Mass.: Addison-Wesley, 1971), pp. 31–32.
7. Cited by James and Jongeward, p. 79.

CHAPTER FIVE: CHANGING OUR EMOTIONS

1. Psychologists R.S. Lazarus and colleagues maintain that "the traditional distinction between the emotional and the rational . . . is to a large extent arbitrary and has probably been as much a hindrance as a help when it comes to theorizing about emotion." ["Towards a Cognitive Theory of Emotion," in Magda Arnold, ed., *Feelings and Emotions* (NY: Academic Press, 1970), p. 231.] They note the continuing tendency in brain research, for example, to associate cognition with the cortex and emotion with the older, more primitive subcortex, and they point out that both levels of brain activity now appear to underly both cognitive and emotional processes, (*Ibid.*, p. 214. See also Robert Leeper, "Motivational and Perceptual Properties of Emotions," in Magda Arnold, ed., *Feelings and Emotions*, p. 156).
2. *The Emotions* (Baltimore: Williams and Wilkens, 1922).
3. Stanley Schachter, *Emotion, Obesity and Crime* (NY: Academic Press, 1971), p. 1. See Canon, "The James-Lange Theory of Emotions," *American Journal of Psychology*, 1927, 39, 106–24.
4. "Contribution a l'Étude de l'Action emotive de l'Adreoline," *Revue Franc d' Endocrin*, 21, 301–25.
5. "Some Effects of Spinal Cord Lesions in Experienced Emotional Feelings," *Psycophysics*, 3, 143–56.
6. "The Generation of Emotion: A Psychological Theory," in Robert Plutchik and Henry Kellerman, eds., *Theories of Emotion* (NY: Academic Press, 1980), p. 227.
7. *The Passions* (Garden City, NY: Anchor Press/Doubleday, 1977), p. 162.
8. Schachter, S. and Singer, J.E., "Cognitive, Social and Physiological Determinants of Emotional State," *Psychological Review*, 69, 378–99.
9. For a succinct account of this research, see Woodworth, R.S. and Schlosberg, H., *Experimental Psychology* (NY: Holt, 1954).
10. "Emotion and Feeling" in Paul Edwards, ed., *The Encyclopedia of Philosophy* (NY: MacMillan and Free Press, 1967), Vol. II, p. 485.

11. "Emotion," in *Mind* (74, N.S., 1965), p. 335. Such terms, then, as *judgment, appraisal,* or *evaluation* are not entirely satisfactory because they can be taken to mean a conscious act. In this respect, William Alston concludes that:

> terms like *apprehension* or *recognition* are preferable. Perhaps the most judicious choice would be "perceive *x* as . . ." or "take *x* to be . . .," with the understanding that *perceive* is being used in a wide sense in which it can evoke memory, belief and intellectual realization. . . . ("Emotion and Feeling," p. 481).

Robert Leeper defines emotions as "perceptions of situations." They are, he maintains, "perceptual processes . . . in the full sense of processes that have definite cognitive content." ("Motivational and Perceptual Properties of Emotions," p. 156.)

There are shortcomings, then, in the use of either *appraisal* or *perception* to describe the relation of an emotion to its object. The one may suggest a necessarily conscious act, the other a passive relation lacking any cognitive dimension. We see here an instance of what leads Amélie Rorty to the philosophical conclusion that "a proper account of the emotions requires a revision of the whole map of psychological processes and activities, and of their complex interrelations." ["Introduction," in Rorty, ed., *Explaining Emotions* (Berkeley: University of California Press, 1980), p. 3.]

On balance, it seems best to emphasize the cognitive aspect of emotion by speaking of appraisal or evaluation. Alston's instincts seem sound when, having considered the advantages of using *apprehend* or *perceive*, he adopts *perceptual evaluation* or, if we wish to be concise, simply *evaluation* ("Emotion and Feeling," p. 481).

12. Ronald de Sousa puts it that emotions "are in part patterns of attention," and illustrates this by Othello:

> Consider how Iago proceeds to make Othello jealous. His task is essentially to direct Othello's attention, to suggest questions, to ask: "did Michael Cassio, when you woo'd my lady—know of your love?" and then to insinuate that there are inferences to be drawn. . . . "Look to your wife." Once attention is thus directed, inferences which on the same evidence would not even have been thought of are experienced as compelling: "Farewell, the tranquil mind. . . ."

("The Rationality of Emotions," in Amélie Rorty, ed., *Explaining Emotions*, pp. 141, 136-37).

13. Feelings and actions that are customarily a part of our emotional 'experience need not follow from our judgments but may rather contribute to them, as when we are irritable from overwork, or illness, or overstimulation and consequently become angry where ordinarily we would not. Or such behavior as slamming doors, singing, or curling up in a fetal position may significantly influence our judgment.

14. Emphasis on thought or judgment as of fundamental importance in emotion dates back to Aristotle, and was given an important development by

Benedict Spinoza in his *Ethics*. Among its many current formulations, I find that of Robert Solomon in *The Passions* especially suggestive and in certain ways persuasive.

15. Some bodily reactions and behaviors, of course, may be typical of fear but not of anger. Our facial muscles, for example, usually will respond differently in the case of fear.

16. In its authoritarian form.

17. To simplify our discussion, we are considering only the de-centered form of dysfunctional emotions. Emotions based on infantile narcissism are also dysfunctional, failing to involve genuine relations with others.

18. NY: Grove Press, 1964. See also Eric Berne, "Transactional Analysis," in *Active Psychotherapy*, Harold Greenwald, ed., (NY: Atherton Press, 1967).

19. "Still making that judgment" means here still responding to the person or persons involved in terms of the judgment we made about them in the past; e.g., this is the one who wronged me last summer.

CHAPTER SIX: LEARNING TO KNOW OTHER PERSONS

1. "Dialogue," in *Between Man and Man*, trans. Ronald Gregor Smith (Boston: Beacon Press, 1955), pp. 13–14.

2. *The Anatomy of Human Destructiveness* (Greenwich, Conn.: Fawcett Publications, Inc. 1975), p. 5.

3. Ibid., p. 51.

4. "Toward a Modern Approach . . ." p. 166. (Italics added.)

5. We also transcend these relations when we step back from them to look at them, evaluate them, and imagine them changed. We both create our relations and are created by them.

6. "Self-Conceptions: Configurations of Content," in Chad Gordon and Kenneth J. Gergen, eds., *The Self in Social Interaction* (New York: John Wiley, 1968), p. 116. I take this definition to mean the self is both process and structure.

7. *Principles of Group Treatment* (NY: Oxford University Press, 1964), p. 364.

8. Muriel James and Dorothy Jongeward, *Born to Win*, p. 44.

9. Ibid., p. 45.

10. Ibid., p. 44.

11. *The Anatomy of Human Destructiveness*, p. 191.

12. "Thought Reform of The Chinese Intellectual: A Psychiatric Evaluation," *Journal of Social Issues* (13, No. 3, 1957).

13. "Toward a Modern Approach to Values," p. 164.

14. There are, of course, approaches to therapy that are designed to minimize any intrusion of the past into the therapeutic process.

15. *The Passions*, p. 361.

16. Ibid., pp. 361–62.

17. Ibid, p. 362.

18. Ibid.

19. Included here are the processes of the many organisms with which we share our bodies. Biologists see our cells as "ecosystems more complex than Jamaica Bay" because of the many little animals that inhabit them and are

essential to them. One sort are the mitochondria which spend their entire lives within our cells supplying them with "oxidative energy." They replicate themselves and have their own DNA and RNA. "Without them, we would not move a muscle, drum a finger, think a thought." Lewis Thomas, *The Lives of a Cell* (N.Y.: Bantam Books, 1975).

20. Cited by Allen Wheelis in *How People Change* (Harper Colophon Books; N.Y.: Harper & Row, 1973), p. 77.

21. *How People Change*, p. 73.

22. Reflecting on this, it may even occur to us that when father looked at us in a certain way he may have been seeing himself through the eyes of his father and so, in a sense, we also know ourselves from grandfather's point of view. Of course, just as we see ourselves the way we *think* our father saw us so we are only in touch with the way our father *thought* his father saw him.

23. See *The Tacit Dimension* (Garden City, N.Y.: Doubleday, 1966).

24. The opposite may also be true. Just as we may behave purposefully without consciously intending to, so we may plan or intend to do something and then be unable to do it or simply change our mind.

25. See, for example, A.C. MacIntyre, *The Unconscious* (New York: Humanities Press, 1958), pp. 60–62.

26. Traumatic childhood experiences can be used to explain or partially explain certain neurotic behavior without any reference to the picture of the unconscious we have been discussing. We should bear in mind, too, that the problem in using *unconscious* as a noun to refer to an inner room in which unconscious thoughts and experiences take place is not that it then refers to something in principle outside of experience. Scientific theory often uses pictures of entities not open to direct experience, such as genes, magnetic fields, electrons, and radio waves. In these and other ways we often use pictures from some areas of our experience to help us deal with other areas. Freud pictures the unconscious the way we in the West have tended, under the influence of Descartes, to picture the conscious mind, namely, as a *separate* kind of thing or process or room. Later we shall question the usefulness of this Cartesian picture itself. For now, we wish only to be clear that there is no objection to be raised against Freud's borrowing a picture from an area of our experience to postulate a realm not accessible to experience. The objection is that this picture, like the notion of ether which former scientists attempted to use, or that of an invisible elf, appears to be useless in providing explanations.

27. *A Treatise of Human Nature*, Vol. 1, Book 1, Part IV.

28. (NY: The Viking Press, 1961), pp. 52–53, 58–59.

29. In these chapters, I have used *person* and *self* interchangeably. A distinction can be drawn, but for our purposes, that is not necessary.

CHAPTER EIGHT: LEARNING AND LIFE IN THE ORGANIZATION

1. *The Organization Trap and How to Get Out of It* (NY: Basic Books, 1974), pp. 3–4.

2. Ibid., p. 5.

3. Ibid.

4. Ibid., p. 4.

5. Ibid., p. 5.
5. Ibid., p. 54.
6. Ibid., p. 20.
7. Ibid., p. 12.
8. Ibid., p. 60.
9. Ibid., p. 14.
10. Ibid., p. 17.
11. Ibid., pp. 20–21.
12. Ibid., pp. 27–28.
13. "Toward a Modern Approcah to Values: The Valuing Process in the Mature Person," p. 161.
14. Ibid.
15. *The Organization Trap*, p. 54.
16. Ibid., p. 87.
17. Ibid., p. 72.
18. Ibid., p. 87.
19. Ibid., p. 88.
20. Ibid.
21. Ibid.
22. Ibid., p. 89.
23. Ibid., p. 33.
24. Ibid., pp. 33–34.
25. Ibid., p. 35.
26. Ibid., p. 37.
27. Ibid., p. 38.
28. Ibid., p. 39.
29. Ibid., p. 10.
30. Ibid., p. 73.
31. Ibid., p. 74.
32. Samuel Culbert and John McDonough, *The Invisible War: Pursuing Self-Interests at Work* (NY: John Wiley & Sons, 1980), p. 75.
33. Ibid., p. 80. The authors give, as a masterful example of such framing, Senator Barry Goldwater's presentation of his position on a strong defense budget: "*First,* he described the security that comes from a nation's ability to actively wage war. *Second,* he talked about deterrents and the role a strong defense system plays in the United States' ability to position its interests on the world political stage. *Third,* he described the technological payoffs associated with defense research and the contribution defense spending makes to economic health. *Last,* he characterized military service as a leveling force for our country, contributing greatly to advances in civil rights, maturation of youths and the development of leaders." (P. 81) The overall picture is positive. Then, when he spoke against welfare, he presented a complex picture of something negative.
34. Ibid., p. 79.
35. Ibid.
36. Ibid., pp. 79–80.
37. Ibid., p. 88.
38. Ibid., p. 91.

39. Ibid., p. 92.

40. Ibid., p. 102.

41. Ibid., p. 109.

42. Ibid., p. 111.

43. Ibid., p. 178.

44. Ibid., pp. 111–12.

45. Ibid., p. 121.

46. Affiliation, of course, refers to the cooperative rather than the competitive forms of interpersonal power.

47. McClelland, David C. and David Burnham, "Power is the Great Motivator," in the *Harvard Business Review*, Vol. 54, No. 2, pp. 100–110.

48. Ibid., p. 177.

49. Ibid., p. 131.

50. Carl Rogers, *On Personal Power* (NY: Dell Publishing Co., A Delta Book, 1977), pp. 101–2.

51. Ibid., pp. 98–100.

52. *The Invisible War*, pp. 201, 207–8.

53. Ibid., p. 196.

CHAPTER EIGHT: ACTIVE AND PASSIVE EXPERIENCING

1. A number of books are directly oriented to learning from experience. Especially well known is *Born to Win* [Muriel James and Dorothy Jongeward (Reading, Mass.: Addison-Wesley, 1971)] applying the perspectives of transactional analysis and gestalt psychology to personal communication and related topics. *Telling Your Story* [Sam Keen and Anne Valley Fox (Garden City, N.Y.: Doubleday, 1973)] may be helpful to those who want to get a clearer picture of their lives as a whole. *The Organization Trap* [Samuel Culbert (N.Y.: Basic Books, 1974)] presents a number of questions about how organizations work, utilizing the psychological perspective of Carl Rogers and techniques of consciousness raising.

2. *The Structure of Magic*, Vol. 1, p. 80.

3. Ibid., pp. 63–63.

4. *Cognitive Therapy and the Emotional Disorders*, p. 246.

5. Ibid., pp. 247–48.

6. Ibid., pp. 255–56.

7. This is true, at least, of what we ordinarily think of as a process.

8. *The Structure of Magic*, Vol. 1, pp. 76–77.

9. Bandler & Grinder, *Ibid.*, 134–53, with omission of their commentary.

10. Taken from Parnes, Sidney J., *Creative Behavior Workbook and Creative Behavior Guidebook* (N.Y.: Charles Scribner's Sons, 1967), pp. 195–96.

11. *The Politics of Experience* (NY: Ballantine Books, 1967), pp. 36–37.

12. Parnes, *Creative Behavior Workbook*, p. 195.

13. In the account that follows, I am indebted to Robert Schnucker *et al. Learning to Learn Better* (c Learning Instruction Facilitators, Kirksville, Mo., 1977), although I differ from them in a number of ways.

14. I am not advocating, of course, that we ever relate to anyone simply as a means to learning or to anything else, for that matter.

15. *The Organization Trap*, p. 80.

CHAPTER TEN: THE JOURNAL AS A TOOL IN EXPERIENTIAL LEARNING

1. *The Organization Trap*, pp. 70–73.
2. Sam Keen and Anne Valley Fox, *Telling Your Story*, p. 2.
3. N.Y.: Dialogue House Library, 1975.
4. Culbert, *The Organization Trap*, p. 73.
5. Ibid., p. 83. Another reason for keeping your descriptions short is the point that Progoff argues that when we start to elaborate we begin to impose our past interpretations on the experience rather than being open to the meaning it has in the context of the present.
6. I use the term "immediate" here because your experiences have a wider range of meaning through their place in the context of your life process as a whole.
7. Culbert, *The Organization Trap*, p. 73.
8. *At a Journal Workshop*, p. 77.
9. Ibid., p. 79.
10. Ibid., pp. 81–82.
11. Ibid., p. 83.
12. Ibid., p. 84.
13. *Letters To a Young Poet* (Rev. ed., trans. M.D.H. Norton; N.Y.: Norton, 1963), pp. 63–66.

Index